公共关系学

王艳辉 田睿 著

广东旅游出版社

中国·广州

图书在版编目（CIP）数据

公共关系学 / 王艳辉，田睿著. -- 广州：广东旅游出版社，2018.9

ISBN 978-7-5570-1480-3

Ⅰ．①公… Ⅱ．①王… ②田… Ⅲ．①公共关系学 Ⅳ．① C912.31

中国版本图书馆 CIP 数据核字（2018）第 199936 号

公共关系学
GONGGONG GUANXIXUE

广东旅游出版社出版发行
（广州市越秀区环市东路 338 号银政大厦西座 12 层　邮编：510180）
廊坊市国彩印刷有限公司印刷
（廊坊市广阳区曙光道 12 号）
广东旅游出版社图书网
www.tourpress.cn
联系电话：020-87347732
710 毫米 ×1000 毫米　16 开　17 印张　150 千字
2019 年 1 月第 1 版第 1 次印刷
定价：68.00 元

[版权所有　侵权必究]

本书如有错页倒装等质量问题，请直接与印刷厂联系换书。

以创新思维开展新闻传播教学与研究

——"新闻传播教学与研究书系"总序

杨中举

传播改变世界。人类每一次传播技术的发明都会引发人类社会文化的历史性变革，口语传播、文字传播、印刷传播、电子传播、网络传播等各个发展阶段，无不为人类积累了丰富的文化财富，掀起社会文化变革的无数次浪潮，比如对于印刷术的发明，法国浪漫主义文化生产者雨果曾充满豪情地写道："书籍将要消灭建筑，印刷术的发明是重大的历史事件，它是革命之母，它是人类全新的表现方式……在印刷的形式下，思想比任何时候都更易于流传，它是飞翔的、逮不住的、不能毁灭的，它和空气融合在一起……它是人类的第二座巴别塔。"（雨果：《巴黎圣母院》，陈敬容译，人民文学出版社，1994年，第211-218页）可以说，技术能够不断地拓展人类发展的新领域，展开更加富有魅力的文明画卷，也会翻开旧账簿，使古久的文化信息再次飞扬；同时传播也在过滤着一切，使不定型的东西定型，使虚伪的东西、无生命力的东西烟消云散。历史地看，人类传播是一个不断叠加的过程，从原初单一化的传播方式，到现代异彩纷呈的传播手段，传播已经滚雪球般成为一座文化星球，大放光芒。特别是互联网技术、微传播技术的高智能化发展，极大地解放了传播生产力，如电脑、手机等新传播工具的微型化、小型化、可视化、便携化，使得传统媒介与新兴传播媒介都插上了崭新翅膀，飞翔的姿态为之一新。在此背景下新闻传播学的教学与研究也被赋予了新的视角、新的阐释维度，由此进一步深化人们对传播领域的新认识、新探索。但是这种新探索，从逻辑上看，不能是单一的新技术手段与传播现象的简单相加，比如"互联网+"不能被简单地理解为"+互联网"（即互联网与不同行业的简单相加），而是一种新的思维方式、存在方式、生活方式，是一种对社会文化发展具有重要作用的新技术、新业态。因此，活在当下的人们无法回避它的影响与塑造，必须去学会、掌握、使用、批判它，以新思维、新视角研究和解决问题。

因之，新闻传播学的教学与研究日新，有关新媒体教学与研究的成果不断涌现，如网络文化研究、博客研究、微电影研究、微博研究、新媒体传播下的公共关系研究、手机（移动终端）传播研究等方面成果丰富，特别是青年学子们在硕、博士论文选题中更青睐新媒体研究，引入了新理论、新方法，为传播研究注入了新血液，增添了新活力。中国传播学研究中心城市北京、上海、武汉、南京、广州、成都、重庆等地的高校成为新媒体、新传播研究的学术重镇，成为学界、业界的领航员，为新传播研究培养了大批人才；同时，各地方高校、地方媒体相关专业学人也参与到这一时代的大合唱中，各自发挥自己的优势，进行相关研究，从"边缘"呼应着"中心"。

基于此，新闻传播学重点学科支持的"新闻传播教学与研究书系"也尝试以开放的姿态，以新传播技术为基础，一方面对传统的传播现象、传播文化进行再讨论，以期发现在新技术背景下传统的传播文化大大小小的变化，梳理其特征，探寻其规律，为业界、学界提供参考；另一方面，更多地关注传播新现象、新问题，对当下因传播新技术、新媒介的运用而产生的新变化、新领域进行研究，为人们更好地认识、理解、应用这些新媒介服务。这决定了"新传播教学与研究书系"的选题范围广、角度多，从传统传播研究到新兴传媒文化现象讨论均可以涉及，研究书系小组只论证大的框架结构，把握传播思想、立场、方向，严肃学术规范与知识产权问题，而把题目选择权、写作权、研究权交给作者，充分尊重作者的意见；研究方法也是开放的，量化、质化研究不限，自由思辨、逻辑论证交融，事实分析、科学论证与自主创意并存，传统与现代并用，中西方结合，跨学科交叉，从而彻底解放论者手脚，实现百家争鸣。

当然这种百家争鸣是建立在尊重传播规律，遵守科学范式，弘扬社会主义核心价值观基础之上，体现在制度自信、道路自信、理论自信、文化自信基础之上，每一位学人、从业者都应当担负国家民族责任、承担社会义务、明确教育职责和新闻传播职业操守、不辱学术使命、不失学人品格，要高境界、宽眼界、有边界，传播正能量。

本研究书系的作者，大都来自教育一线、传媒业界，来自不同的学科专业，摆脱了单纯的专业限制，这符合当下传播学跨学科、跨文化发展的实际。他们大都是青年教师、业界青年新闻传播工作者，有的还是在读研究生和相关专业本科学生，知识新、思维活跃，对新兴传媒有着浓厚兴趣，更是使用和实践新传播技术的主力军，从事相关思考与研究，有一点儿发言权；从这些作者的学术背景看，他们来自传媒理论、传媒技术、传媒艺术三个领域，同时学历背景文理兼容，能够满足新闻传播研究对人文社科知识和相关理工科技知识的要求。

当然，年轻人也有年轻的劣势，研究基础不牢，学术经验不丰富，深度不够，做事比较急躁，研究中一定会存在各种各样的问题。我们应当正视这些问题，加以提醒、解决，同时也要允许问题的存在，只要不是大方向走错，青年人的蹒跚学步也是其成长道路上无法回避的问题。这就需要传播学界前辈、专家学者关心年轻人，对他们给予指导、批评、纠正、引领。我们相信有学界前辈们的指点，有年轻人自身的奋发努力，有所在单位学术组织的督促，新传播环境下的新传播研究一定会不断涌现出新成果。

本册为双语对照式的公共关系学教程，是传播学研究的重要分支，是人际传播的重要体现，对新闻传播专业学生的学习与进行有效传播实践具有重要的指导作用。

序言

在以竞争为典型特征的市场经济中，国家之间、企业之间，以及个人之间的竞争越来越强烈，其中，公共关系作为现代社会组织中极具创造力的一种资源，越来越受到企事业单位乃至社会各界的广泛重视。纵观世界知名大企业、成功集团，无一不是因为其拥有先进的组织文化和有效的公共关系机制而在激烈的市场竞争中胜出。公共公共关系可以帮助一个组织建立并保持与公众之间的交流、理解、认可与合作，它越来越被看作是组织发展战略的一个重要组成部分，关系着组织的兴衰成败。作为一门学科，公共关系逐渐成为政府与企业关注的焦点、相关领域工作人员与专家、学者研究与实践的热点。

本教材是两位编者根据公共关系学学科特点、结合高等院校教学要求和自己常年双语教学经验，为使学生全面系统地掌握公共关系知识、理论和实务而编写的一本以理论为基础、关注公共关系实务内容的一本教材。在编写过程中，本书突出了以下特点：第一，双语讲述，促进学生对两种语言能力及其所代表文化的学习和成长。本书八章内容均以汉、英种语言进行讲述，旨在培养学生用英语学习、了解和掌握公共关系相关概念、理论和知识，进而增强其国际公共关系知识和意识，提高其国际公共关系能力。第一，理论性强，框架清晰。本书以公共关系原理为基础，结合案例分析对公共关系进行了总共八章的讲述，结构合理，讲述深入浅出，广大读者容易学习和掌握。第二，内容精炼，知识性强。本书用八章篇幅讲述的内容有：公共关系概述、公共关系从业人员、公共关系的工作程序、组织形象塑造、公共关系礼仪、大学生公共关系形象塑造、公共关系危机管理和政府公共关系。第三，视野宽阔、采纳国内外经典案例。公共关系学是一门实践性很强的学科，本书摒弃了以往陈旧的案例，采纳一些富有代表性和现实性的国外案例。例如，在第三章 公共关系的工作程序 第三节 公共关系实施中，就引用了美国农业部为了把杂交水稻推广开来，采用线性的步骤，让农民一步一步接受并推广此水稻，起到了非常好的效果。极具代表性、现实性的针对性，说服力强，而且看后印象深刻。

本书作为国内罕见的以双语形式介绍公共关系理论与实务的一本新书，可供大专院校相关专业的专科、本科、研究生、MBA、MPA、MPH等各个层次的师生教学使用，也可作为企事业单位、尤其是涉外企事业单位管理者和员工进行公共关系培训的教材，以及那些有意提高个人公共关系能力与技巧人士的参考书。

本书由临沂大学王艳辉和抚顺职业技术学院（抚顺师专）田睿执笔撰写、翻译与编排，在此过程中由于受到编者的视野和视角所限，难免有不妥之处，恳请读者和广大同人批评指正。公共关系是一门博大精深的学科，还有待我们进一步深入研究、不断实践，以期此本教材的日臻完善。

编者

2017,11

目录

Chapter 1 Overview of Public Relations

Part one Brief History of Public Relations 1

Part Two Definition of Public Relations（PR） 5

Part Three Features, Characteristics and Principles of Public Relations 10

Part Four Elements of Public Relations 13

Chapter Two Public Relations Practitioners

Part One Essential Qualities and Abilities of PR Practitioners 18

Part Two The PR Practitioner's Work Ethic and Personnel Training 26

Chapter Three Working Procedure of Public Relations

Part One Public Relations Investigation 32

Part Two Public Relations Planning 44

Part Three Implementation of Public Relations 54

Part Four Evaluation of Public Relations 59

Chapter Four Image-Building of the Organization

Part One Summarization of the Organization Image 63

Part Two Organization Images Building 68

Chapter Five Public Relations Etiquette

Part One The Outline of Public Relations Etiquette 79

Part Two Social Skills in Public Relations 88

Chapter Six Graduates' Public Relations Image Building

Part One Graduates' Public Relations Image Building 93

Part Two Relationships between the Graduates' Job-Hunting and Public Relations Image Building 98

Part Three Skills for Graduates' Job-Hunting 102

Chapter Seven Management of Public Relations Crises

Part One Summary of Public Relations Crisis 108

Part Two Prevention of the Public Relations Crises 111

Part Three Dealing with Public Relations Crises 117

Chapter Eight Government Public Relations

Part One Connotation and Characteristics of Government Public Relations 123

Part Two Significance and Functions of the Government Public Relations 126

Part Three Principles of Government Public Relations 131

Part Four Integral Principle 133

第一章 公共关系概述

第一节 公共关系发展史 138

第二节 公共关系定义 141

第三节 公共关系的特征、特点与原则 144

第四节 公共关系的要素 147

第二章 公共关系从业人员

第一节 公共关系从业人员的基本素质与基本能力 151

第二节 公共关系从业人员的职业道德及公共关系人员的培养 158

第三章 公共关系的工作程序

第一节 公共关系调查 162

第二节 公共关系策划 172

第三节 公共关系实施 184

第四节 公共关系评估 192

第四章 组织形象塑造

第一节 组织形象概述 196

第二节 组织形象塑造 200

第五章 公共关系礼仪

第一节 公共关系礼仪概论 211

第二节 公共关系中的社交技巧 218

第六章　大学生公共关系形象塑造与求职艺术

第一节　大学生公共关系形象塑造 222

第二节　大学生求职应聘与公共关系形象塑造 227

第三节　大学生就业技能 232

第七章　公共关系危机的管理

第一节　公共关系危机概论 237

第二节　公共关系危机的预防 240

第三节　处理公共关系危机 244

第八章　政府公共关系

第一节　政府公共关系的内涵和特征 249

第二节　政府公共关系的意义和作用 251

第三节　政府公共关系的原则 254

第四节　政府公共关系的模式 256

参考书目 259

Chapter1

Overview of Public Relations

Part one Brief History of Public Relations

I. Embryo of Public Relations

Public Relations originated from America in its modern sense. Public Relations developed from the press propaganda campaigns when they were popular for a while in the middle period of the 19th century. There appeared a kind of cheap newspaper, in which printed and published a large amount of popularized contents targeted at the ordinary public. It was so cheap that it cost only one penny, so it was also called Penny Paper. This kind of Penny Paper became popular soon and appealed to many readers, because of its emphasis on independence, enjoyment and excitement, as well as it low price. At that time, many companies and financial groups saw the opportunity and began to process seditious news to publicize themselves in overstated and false words. The press was glad to publish the news in order to cater to the resident readers. Under such circumstances, the press propaganda campaigns appeared. Known for his fabricating the sensational news, Fierce Barnum was a representative of the press agents in the period. Such kind press propaganda campaign is characterized by publicizing oneself, simply seeking sensational effect, at the cost of the public benefits by deceiving and cheating them. So it was called a dishonorable begging in the history of public relations.

II. Professionalization of Public Relations

America developed into its monopolization period at the end of the 19th century. The class contradictions between the labor and the capital were becoming increasingly serious because of the monopolizing capitalists' unscrupulous and greedy exploitation of the workers, which led to strong dissatisfaction in the society. Under these circumstances, the American press launched the Muckraking Movement aimed to uncover the capitalists' shameless conducts. Many articles disclosing and attacking the capitalists and their disgraceful behaviors were published in the American press, which became powerful offensive in the public opinion and resulted in extreme notoriety of many large-scale enterprises and capitalists. The monopolizing financial groups first took high-pressured measures, then they tried to take bribing as their tricks in order to quiet down the public opinion. These measures didn't work well. On the contrary, they aroused the public indignation. It was proposed that enterprises should tell the truth to gain the public trust, with which agreed by enlightened persons in the industrial and commercial circles. Ivy Lee was a representative of the trend of thought. Ivy Lee was a journalist. Considering the situation, he drew lessons from Barnum styled press propaganda campaign and proposed a brand-new thought of Tell the Truth---If an organization is willing to develop a reputation, it should expose the truth to the public and tell the public all the situations relevant to their interest rather than cheating the public by locking any news or deceit. Only in this way can it develop the public trust to the organization; The organization should adjust its image and behaviors rather than try its best to cover the truth if negative effect on the organization is produced from disclosure of the truth. Ivy Lee took Tell the Truth and the Public Must Be Informed as the basic principle of Public Relations. He founded the first formal office of public relations, opening its service to the society. From then on, professionalized public relations came into being, and Ivy Lee was praised as Father of Public Relations. Although Ivy Lee was the founder of modern public relations, his work related to public relations was on the basis of intuition, experience and imagination rather than scientific research method, and without the guidance of systematical theory of public relations. So his practical activities of public relations were considered as Only Art, Not Science.

III. Making Scientific of Public Relations

It was Edward L.Benays, a scholar of public relations, who laid the foundation of the theory of public relations and made scientific of the modern public relations. Benays published Public Opinion, a theory work on public relations, and Public Relations, a text book in 1923. He first set the Public Relations courses in New York University in 1923. It was Benays who completed the system of the theory and methods on public relations, and led public relations into its scientific stage. Benays first put forward the concept of Public Relations Consultation, and made it certain that one of the important responsibilities of public relations is to provide policy consultation for organizations, and that the whole activity procedure should include 8 steps, namely plan, practice, feedback, to assessment, the last step. He especially emphasized the pertinence of the public relations work, attached importance to public values and attitudes, and demanded that the public relations practitioners must launch organizational propaganda campaigns according to the public attitude, interests, and their expectations and demands to the organizations. Benays put the study result of social science into the practice of public relations. He suggested that the advising activities of public relations could work well only when guided by certain scientific theories. In the late 50's of the 20th century, many experts and masters on public relations, such as Cutlip, Sant and Jefkins carried on Benays'scientization of public relations. They published a series of important works on public relations, and put forward Bidirectional Symmetry, an important model of public relations. Master's degree and doctor's degree major in Public Relations were set up. Incorporated the knowledge of emerging disciplines and advanced measures of science and technology, Public Relations gradually became an independent discipline with rich contents, and the public relations practice developed further. In the modern world, acting as dissemination, and functioning as administration, public relations not only play an important role in economic field, but also become an indispensable part of jobs in noneconomic organizations, such as political, cultural, educational, sci-technological, hygienic, physical and military organizations. After China carried out reform and open policy in the 80's of the 20th century ,public relations began to play an important role in our socialist country.

Ⅳ. Development of Public Relations in China

Public relations developed well in China. Guangzhou Baiyunshan Pharmaceutical Factory took the lead in establishing public relations department in 1984, and began public relations activities; Shanghai Public Relations Association , the first public relations association at provincial level was founded in Nov. 1986; China Public Relations Association was founded in Beijing on Jun 22nd ; China International Public Relations Association （CIPRA） was founded in Beijing on Apr 26th, 1991. From generation and development of public relations in western countries and our country, we can draw the conclusion that public relations are affected and pushed forward by the basic social conditions as following

（1） Development of commodity economy and formation of market competition. （2） Association development of modern society. （3） Objective requirement of production socialization. （4） Development of political democratization. （5） Development of contemporary administrative science. （6） Educational popularization and improvement of public civilization level. （7） Development of industrial technology and public media.

Public relations has been widely used in many social economic fields since it developed in China many years ago. Both organizations, such as government and enterprises, and individuals have realized the necessity and importance of public relations. Steady progress in modern informatization and fast development in information technology provide a sound environment for public relations development. With development of the socialist market economy of China , public relations are stepping into its more professionalized and specialized stage marked by the vigorous development of public relations career on the mainland of China, the increasing public relations departments within social organizations, various professional public relations organizations' status established in public relations market.

Chapter 1 Overview of Public Relations

Part Two Definition of Public Relations (PR)

I. What is public relations?

Many try to define public relations strictly in terms of these kinds of high—profile images. However, publicity and public relations are not synonymous. publicity is just one of many tactics used by public relations practitioners. Perhaps it is best to think of public relations as a tapestry, with many parts intricately woven into one whole cloth.

II. The Search for a Definition

The research for a Definition of public relations

So what is public relations? To borrow a phrase from a popular 1950s television game show, that is the $64,000 question. Unfortunately, there is no definitive answer. The modern practice of public relations first came under serious study in the early 1900s, and educators and practitioners have struggled ever since with its definition. At the beginning of the 21st century, defining public relations remains we promise to give you our own definition of public relations; we think it's a good one. But first, we want to ask you a question: What do you think public relations is? We will not be surprised if you say "I don't know" or if your answer is vague. It is a hard question--so hard, in fact, that even people who practice public relations on a daily basis have yet to arrive at a single definition to describe what they do.

This confusion was illustrated in a survey of accountants, attorneys, and public relations practitioners. The three groups were selected because they had something in common--a counselor relationship with their clients. Each group was asked about its profession and its place within organizational structures. Although the accountants and attorneys clearly understood their roles, the public relations practitioners did not. This caused the study's authors to raise a pertinent question: If public relations practitioners are unclear about who they are and what they do, why should they expect anyone else to understand?

There isn't even any consensus on what to call the profession. Because of the supposedly negative connotations carried by the term public relations, many organizations use euphemisms such as "public affairs" "public information" "corporate Communications" or "community out reach" to describe the function.Burson—Marsteller, one of the world's largest public relations agencies, describes itself in its web site as a"global perception management firm."

Other organizations, especially government agencies, try to hide their public relations practitioners from the eyes of jealous rivals and zealous budget—cutters by giving them seemingly innocuous titles. Such as "special assistant" or "information manager" One state agency had its listing removed from the North Carolina state government telephone directory in an effort to avoid detection. Instead of answering the telephone by saying "public information office" the staff was instructed to answer by repeating the office's extension number.

III. Public Relations Defined

In 1976,Rex Harlow, a pioneer public relations educator who found what eventually became the Public Relations Society of America (PRSA), once complied more than 500 definitions from almost as many sources. After mulling them over and talking with leaders in the field, Harlow in the field, Harlow came up with this definition:

Public relations is a distinctive management function which helps establish and maintain mutual lines of communication, understanding, acceptance, and cooperation between an organization and its publics; involves the management of problems or issues, helps management keep informed on and responsive to public opinion; defines and emphasizes the responsibility of management to serve the public interest; helps management keep abreast of and effective utilize change, serving as an early warning system to help anticipate trends; and uses research and sound ethical communication techniques as its principal tools.

Others have sought to define public relations in fewer words. In Managing Public Relations, educators Todd Hunt and lames E. Grunig opt for a 1 0—word definite: "the management of communication between an organization and its publics. "

One area of agreement among public relations practitioners is the definition of the term public: any group of people who share common interests or values in a particular situation--especially interests or values they might be willing to act upon.

There are so many definitions of Public relations, here we just choose some of them One early definition that gained wide acceptance was formulated by the newsletter PR news: "Public relations is the management function which evaluates public attitudes Identifies the polices and procedures of an individual or an organization with the public interest, and plans and executes a program of action to earn public understanding and patience"

More succinct definitions are provided by theorists and textbook authors. Scott M. Cutlip, Allen H. Center and Glen M. Broom state in Effective Public Relations that "Public relations is the management function that identifies, establishes, and maintains mutually beneficial relationships between an organization and the various public on whom its success or failure depends"

The institute of Public Relations of England defines sustained effort to establish and maintain mutual understanding between an organization and its public.

Edward Bernays was the self-appointed FatherofPublic Relations. He saw public relations as an "applied social science" that uses insights from psychology, sociology, and other disciplines to scientifically manage and manipulate the thinking and behavior of an irrational and "herdlike" public.

Princeton university professor H. L. Chils said: "is what we are engaged in public relations activities, the relationships of known, these activities and relationship are public, and its social significance.

Chinese scholars such as Zhao Jianhua thinks: "public relations is communication activity and the code of conduct through which a social organization make themselves and the public know each other, and take mutual cooperation . "

Scholar Fan Quanyuan thinks that the public relations is a series of planned efforts and activities through which a social organization can promote the relevant public to understand, cooperate and support it.

Some scholars believe that "public relations is the constant work through which the enterprise review and improve their own methods and attitude and then open them to the society in order to obtain the good opinion and understanding of customers, employees and society ", "public relations is seeking unity within and development outside ", "public relations is to get useful friends for yourself" and so on.

Mr Wang Lefu says: public relations is a kind of seeking unity within and outside the operation and management of the development of art. Reasonable use of its principles and methods, through the plan and persistent efforts, to coordinate and improve the organization of internal and external relations, make this the policies of the organization and activities in accordance with the requirements of the public, set up a good image in the public, to seek the public know about this organization, trust, goodwill and cooperation, and mutual interests.

Although the definition of public relations is multifarious, but the book that overall, still can make all kinds of claim due to from the static and dynamic two angles to understand what is public relations.

When a public has a relationship with your organization, the public is called a stakeholder, meaning that it has a stake in your organization or in an issue potentially involving your organization. The fact is that as long as people are people, they will continue to view the world with differing perspectives. That's why it may be best to avoid the debate over the exact wording of a public relations definition and, instead, to concentrate on the various elements of the profession itself. Here is where one finds consensus. Common to any comprehensive definition of public relations are the following elements:

----Public relations is a management function. The relationship between an organization and the publics important to its Success must be a top concern of the organization's leadership . The public relations practitioner provides counsel on the timing, manner, and form important communications should take. In other words, practitioners aren't just soldiers who follow orders; they're also generals who help shape policy. And like all managers ,they must be able to measure the degree of their success in their various projects.

----Public relations involves two—way communication. Communication is not just telling people about an organization's needs. It also involves listening to those same people speak of their concerns.This willingness to listen is an essential part of the relationship—building process.

-----Public relations is a planned activity. Public relations is "planned activity". Actions taken on behalf of an organization must be carefully planned and consistent with the organization's values and goals.And since the relationship between an organization and the publics important to its success is a top concern, these actions must also be consistent with the publics' values and goals.

-----Public relations is a research—based social science. Formal and informal research is conducted to allow an organization to communicate effectively, possessing a full understanding of the environment in which it operates and the issues it confronts. Public relations practitioners and educators also share their knowledge with others in the industry through various professional and academic publications.

-----Public relations is socially responsible. A practitioner's responsibilities extend beyond organizational goals. Practitioners and the people they represent are expected to play a constructive role in society.

You may have noticed a common theme running throughout this list: the concept of relationship management. Far—sighted, well—managed organizations know they must have good relationships with publics important to their success. A 1 992 study that sought to define excellence in public relations noted that having good relationships with these publics can save an organization money by reducing the likely hood such as litigation, regulation, boycotts, or lost revenue that result from falling out of favor with these groups. At the same time, the study said that an organization makes more money by cultivating good relationships with consumers, donors, shareholders, and legislators. Therefore, nurturing these relationships is one of the most important roles public relations practitioners can play.

Public relations plays a critical role in effective communications. Through Public relations, individuals and organizations enter the great marketplace of ideas. And through the proper application of public relations, practitioners participate in the search for consensus.

Part Three Features, Characteristics and Principles of Public Relations

I. Six Basic Features of Public Relations

(1) Targeted at the Public

Public Relations refers to the mutual relations between certain social organizations and their relevant social public.

Taking the organization as a pivot, public relations aims to establish sound relations between the organization and the public. Only when the organization adheres to the principle targeted at the public and establishes good relationships with them, can it develop smoothly.

(2) Targeted at Good Reputation

Good image building is the core problem and goal pursuit of public relations. But good reputation should be accepted and assessed by the public instead of identified by the organization. Only when the organization establishes good relationships with the public through public relations activities, and secure the public understanding and support, can it build good images.

(3) Based on Mutual-Benefit Principle

Public relations emerged on the basis of commodity economy. It is backed by certain relations of benefit. It should benefit the public, as well as accomplish the organizational objectives. Only in this way can the organization and the public cooperate for long.

(4) Persistent in long-term development

Good public relations and organizational images can't be built in one day. Even built up, they need to be maintained, adjusted and developed. Public relations practitioners need to make efforts continuously. If they are anxious to achieve quick success, they will get just the opposite and make serious mistakes.

(5) By means of dissemination and communication

It is via various media and communication methods that public relations can establish and maintain exchanges between the organization and the public, that it can learn and affect the public opinions, attitudes and behaviors. This is a striking feature of public relations different from other jobs.

(6) Under the belief of sincerity

Social organizations must disseminate genuine information when they communicate with the public. Their attitudes to the public should be sincere. Only when the organizations are sincere, can they be trusted by the public, and cooperate with the public. So, sincerity is the basic belief of public relations.

II. Main Characteristics of Public Relations

Public relations aim to establish good images in the social public and surpass the competitors while establishing reputations. The target research of public relations is to research different kinds of relationships of relevant internal and external organizations.

Public relations focus on long-term effects rather than short-term ones. Enterprises will occupy markets, boost sales and establish good images by means of different public relations strategies.

Public relations lay stress on truth and equality to the public. They oppose making profits by fair means of foul. Only in this way can the organizations establish good public images and boost their sales. To some extent, public relations are indirect sales promotions

The basic method adopted by public relations is to coordinate relations, namely to connect the interior with the exterior and to communicate with the two parities. If its internal relations are coordinated, the enterprise will exist and develop well under a favorable environment. An enterprise must disclose its business information, as well as communicate well with the public, collect information for its further development, and understand the public demands

III. Activity Principles of Public Relations

Public relations should adhere to the following basic principles in their activities:

(1) Mater-of-Fact Principle

Mater-of fact principle demands public relations should be practical and realistic in their communicating activities. Here are the main points:

First, public relations scheme is drawn up according to the practical and realistic investigations of the market.

Second, the information disseminated both inwards and outwards must be practical and realistic.

Third, assessment must be objective and impartial.

Fourth, the will of the people should be respected in public relations activities.

Public relations will lose their base of existence and conditions of success if they are not practical and realistic in their activities; Public relations won't realize mutual understanding with the publics if they don't deliver information authentically and assess information impartially. Public relations job is of great application and practice. It must be practical and realistic. Prestige of organizations will be lost and their survival will be greatly influenced if avoidance is adopted.

(2) Innovation Principle

Public relations are an art of administrations. Only when they make innovations continuously can they keep the greater vitality. Promotion planning, advertisement planning, propagation planning and other planning of public relations won't be striking and impressive if they are not unique and distinctive. The public relations activities will go with the tide and copy mechanically, and thus will waste human resources, financial resources and material resources if they don't make innovations. Public relations advocate, "to think whatever others have never dreamed of, to try whatever others have never experimented."

(3) Public Interest Priority Principle

Public benefit priority is an important principle of public relations activities. It is also professional ethics which should be adhered to by the public relations practitioners. Only when the organizations keep to the principle, and think of the public interests anytime and anywhere, can they have a favorable reception of the public, and get greater and far-reaching benefits. Public interest priority principle doesn't mean to sacrifice the organizational benefits completely. It means to put public interests first while organizational benefits and public interests are taken into consideration.

(4) Mutual-Benefit Principle

Public relations are based on certain benefit relationships. They emphasize the view that the two parties should make profits and develop together in the course of association and cooperation. All the affairs that are bad for the organization relations will be bad for the organizations themselves eventually. So, to maintain the interests of organization public relations is to maintain the interests of the organizations. The mutual-benefit principle lays stress on balance and coordination between the organizations and the public, and "to develop with their public."

At he same time, only mutual benefits can help establish the most steady and reliable relationships. There won't be quality foundation, regular, equal and mutual-benefit social relations without mutual benefits in the commodity society.

Part Four Elements of Public Relations

Public relations activity is a kind of bidirectional communicating activity. The whole public process is actually the propagating process of public relations with the help of which the organizations and the public can understand each other better. Thus it can be seen that public relations consists of three elements, namely social organizations, the public and propagation of public relations. The organization is the subject of public relations, the public are the object of public relations, and propagation of public relations is the link and bridge between the organization and the public. Public relations activities can work well with interaction of the three elements. So, we should study the three elements first.

Ⅰ. Social Organization. It is a structure or body organized according to certain principles and approaches by people sharing common interests, such as enterprises, schools, hospitals, etc. There are a variety of social organizations. In terms of business, there are economic and noneconomic organizations. The typical economic organizations are enterprises which are characterized by the pursuit with economic-benefit-centered objectives. The noneconomic organizations are characterized by the pursuit with social-benefit-centered objectives, such as welfare organizations, schools, etc. In terms of scale, there are large, medium-sized and small-sized organizations according to the scales of human resources, material resources and financial resources. In addition, there are different social organizations classified according to their regions and ownerships. Social organizations are the subjects of public relations, so there should be as many types of public relations as types of social organizations. This book is to study the public relations of enterprises. `

Ⅱ. The Public. The public are the object and target of public relations, and the collection of individuals, groups and organizations relevant to social organizations. As the target of public relations, the public must have the following three requirements and attributes: First, relativity. It means that the public must have certain relations or connections with particular organizations. The public will be meaningful when they are connected with organizations, the subject of the public relations. Otherwise, the public will be meaningless.

In addition, the Connection here is of specified meaning. It means that the public opinions, attitudes and behaviors will have actual or potential influence or restricts, and that the policies, decisions, and behaviors of the organizations will have actual or potential influence on the public benefits. So, there is no the Public in the broad sense, but the Public in the narrow sense. Different organizations will have different public targets accordingly.

Second, integrity. As organizations should be associated with many aspects, and the relevant aspects will be the public of the organizations. So the public of the organization is a comprehensive whole. Let's take an enterprise as an example. Its public includes its internal employees, customers, suppliers of materials, communities, government, banks, etc. ,which take shape of the whole. Of course, we don't mean that all the targets will be involved in each public relations activity when we talk about the public integrity. In fact, onlyone or several parts will become the public concerning one public relations activity. As for the entire public activities,we must coordinate the relationships between the organizations and the whole public comprehensively and systematically.

Third, homogeneity. As mentioned above, the public integrity should be taken into consideration in the entire public relations activities. While the public homogeneity should be taken into consideration in each public relations activity.

So called Homogeneity means some targets with similar or the same benefits, attitudes, opinions, requirements, etc. . Only when the different targets share homogeneity can they be aggregated into a collective, and impose pressure on organizations. The public homogeneity should be taken into consideration in the particular public relations activities, as these targets are faced with the same problems. Take environment pollution as an example, as the public in the same community have suffered a lot from the pollution, they should be the targets of public relations activities of the enterprise as a homogenous collective. Thus it can be seen than even different public relations activities in the same enterprise have different public targets. In summary, the public, as the public relations targets, must have relativity, integrity and homogeneity. What's more, different organizations have different public, different public relations activities in the same organization have different public. However, although there are diversities of the public in organizations or publicrelations activities, most organizations or public relations activities still have some common public targets. Jeffjens thinks there are mainly seven kinds of basic public as the following, people in the same community, employees, material suppliers, distributors, financial public, consumers or subscribers, and influential public figures. Organizations must analyze their public carefully when they conduct public relations activities. They reasons are as following:

First, they analyze the public in an effort to identify their public and get to know all the individuals, groups and organizations who will get involved in their public relations activities. Then the organizations can work out pertinent public relations scheme and enhance the public relations effects. Second, the organizations will make priority principle and choice principle according to their public relations budgets and resources by analyzing the public and sort by their importance,as different public will play different roles to public relations activities of the organizations. Third, the organizations won't work out the pertinent results or meet the expected objects if they don't analyze the public. They would have lost their potential public because of dispersed energy and funds. Thus it is an indispensible process to analyze and identify the public in making public relations scheme.

Ⅲ. Public Relations Propagation

Public relations propagation is medium to connect the organization and the public. It conducts communications and exchanges between the organization and the public by means of certain media according to certain principles. Public relations propagation is the central part of all the public relations work, and will be illustrated in detail in the subsequent chapter of the book. Although public relations has administrative function, it isn't the whole of the function, it is not omnipotent. It functions as the following: One hand, it works as a counselor of the management. On the other hand, it informs the public of actions and decisions of the organization or the management. Public relations plays the role of a policy counselor to be involved in working out operation scheme of public relations, persuading the highest management to accept the scheme. coordinating the middle management and employees to obtain their cooperation. It also plays the role to deliver speech, draft speech text for others, and select the lecture for meetings.

Here is a case of "little swallow": there is a Japanese Hotel suburbs of Nara City, the external environment is very beautiful and the waiters are enthusiastic which attract customers a lot. But every spring, many swallows are nesting under the eaves to settle the manure ,the excrement stained the glass window and the corridor, and though the waitress was erasing, it is still making the passengers a little unpleasant. The hotel owner loves the swallows, but it is difficult to get rid of the swallows' feces timely, completely, it was very distressed. One day, the hotel manager came up with a coup. He notes: Ladies and gentlemen: we are just here from the southern spring swallow, without the owner's consent, making home here, and also to procreate. Our little baby is young and ignorant, our habits are not good, often dirty your glass and the corridor, making you unhappy. We are very sorry, ladies and gentlemen, please forgive me! There is one more thing to tell ladies and gentlemen, please do not complain about the waitress, they often clean up, but they are wiping. It's entirely our fault. Please wait a moment and they'll be here. Your friend: the little swallow.

This is obviously a letter written in the name of the little swallow to explain and apologize to the passengers. The hotel manager posted it to a prominent place. The guests were amused to see the open letter, not only to say no more, but also to be more affectionate to the hotel and to make a good impression.

This case fully demonstrates that the main body and object can eliminate misunderstanding through proper communication, win public understanding and support, and set up a good image of the organization.

Social organization, the public and propagation and communication are the basic three concepts of public relations, for they convey the relationships in the basic three elements of public relations.

Chapter Two
Public Relations Practitioners

The Public Relations Practitioner is a widespread and common address to the professional staff member who is engaged in public relations. The English for the public relations practitioners is PR Practitioner. There are many forms of address to the public relations professional in western countries, such as PR Practitioner, PR Man, PR Officer, etc. As an occupation, Public Relations has special requirements to its practitioners. Essential qualities and abilities of PR Practitioners could be conveyed in the normalized regulations.

Part One Essential Qualities and Abilities of PR Practitioners

Public Relations involves many layers, such as administration plan,
public relations analysis, news dissemination and even image appreciation, etc. . There is no doubt that PR Practitioners should have knowledge and abilities of administration, psychology, news dissemination, image design and appreciation of beauty.

I. Essential Qualities of PR Practitioners

The PR Practitioner is the main body of public relations. The PR Practitioner is required to do the job if the public relations activity is regarded as a task to build the image of an organization. To illustrate it more specifically, the PR Practitioner is required to get involved in operations on disseminating media to build the image of an organization. All the public relations activities are organized by people, and the PR Practitioners are the best professional choice for the activities. Any good public relations plan will be the castle in the air without the PR Practitioners' efforts. To a great extent, success or failure, effect and creativity of all the public relations activities lie on the qualities of PR Practitioners.

The qualities of PR Practitioners include the qualities of social culture, psychology and nature.

ⅰ. Social Culture Quality

Social culture quality includes ideological and political concepts, moral behavior regulations and cultural and scientific knowledge, etc. As a PR Practitioner, his or her social culture quality should have the following connotations:

1. Ideological & Political Quality and Ethical & Moral Quality。 Ideological & political quality and ethical & moral quality are prerequisites for the PR Practitioner to carry out public relations work. They embody a concentrated reflection of noble profession ethics, refining work style, earnest steadfast work attitude, self-sacrifice spirit and highly-developed sense of responsibility, etc. Public relations work has its strong purpose. Basically, any organization carries out public relations work in an effort to acquire higher popularity and reputation. Normally, PR Practitioners will represent organizations directly and communicate with outside world. They should be honest and upright in behavior, rigorous in conduct, excellent in quality, noble in morality, and seek no personal gain and be not swayed by personal considerations before they coordinate and deal with various public relations. High-level ideological and political quality and ethical and moral quality can help model both the practitioner's and his or her represented organization's images among social publics, even can make up for the defects in other qualities of the PR Practitioner. Public relations work will lose its prerequisite without good ideological and political quality or ethical and moral quality of the PR Practitioner. In result, public relations work won't be carried out smoothly, and social image of the organization will be damaged as well. In conclusion, the most essential part of the PR Practitioner's qualities are high-level ideological and political quality and ethical and moral quality

2. Cultural and Scientific Quality. Cultural and scientific quality is the base of the PR Practitioner to carry out public relations work. With the progress of the time, constant change of the world, intense competition among the organizations, cultural and scientific qualities of the PR Practitioners are faced with increasing challenges. The PR Practitioners should examine the structure of their cultural and scientific knowledge, enrich, improve and update the system of their cultural and scientific knowledge, and then advance their cultural and scientific level.

PR Practitioners should grasp the following knowledge:

(1) Professional Knowledge of Public Relations. Public Relations

is a theoretic summarization of public relations practices, which has summed up basic laws and procedures of public relations, introduced basic techniques and methods of specific public relations activities, which is a theory guide to the public relations activities of the PR Practitioners. Only when the PR Practitioners grasp the basic theory and method of public relations, follow the basic laws of public relations, and flexibly apply the techniques and methods of public relations can they reach the goals of public relations work effectively.

(2) Knowledge Closely Relevant to Public Relations. In a sense, public relations is an administrative activity which has drawn lessons from many theories of behavioral science of administration; By means of dissemination, public relations needs a great amount of interpersonal disseminations and public disseminating skills; Public relations work needs to be directly faced with society and people, to study people's psychology, attitude and behavior. Thus it can be seen that Public Relations is an interdisciplinary subject of comprehensive application involved in Administration, Marketing, Communication Science, Sociology, Psychology, etc. PR Practitioners should understand the closely relevant knowledge of these disciplines.

(3) Necessary Professional Knowledge to Carry out Specific Public Relations Work. PR Practitioners must understand the basic knowledge of circulation domain and the laws in commercial competition if they want to carry out public relations work for commercial enterprises; They should understand the knowledge of the counterparts' politics, economy, culture, customs, etc, as well as International Public Relations,

International Marketing and the basic situation of competition in the international market. Only in this way can the PR Practitioners have a well-thought-out plan, a definite object in the view and a good effect of public relations.

ii. Psychological Quality

Psychological quality, the quality of individual psychology, is key to success of the PR Practitioner. Generally speaking, the requirements for the PR Practitioner's psychology are as the following three aspects.

1.Self-Confidence

Self-confidence is an essential requirement for the PR Practitioner's professional psychology. Only when a person is self-confident, can he or she believe himself or herself, and then will be brave and powerful, finally create miracles.

As an old saying goes, "He who knows himself is wise; He who is self-confident is strong. " Self-confident PR Practitioners will face the challenges bravely, strive for excellence bravely. They believe themselves to outdo and beat others, thus constantly strive to become stronger.

The organization image built by such kind of PR Practitioners must be favorable. On the contrary, the organization image built by lowly and menial PR Practitioners may be mediocre. Public relations work is not simply mechanical operation. Although the PR Practitioners can forecast, to some extent, the result of their operation, they still need to take a risk, so self-confidence is necessary. Of course, self-confidence is not blind confidence. It's built on the basis of thorough investigation and research, and full understanding of the situation. An unconfident PR Practitioner will lose his or her head and be panicked when the organization comes across crises. It is difficult for him or her to hold the chance even if the situation turns for better, while a confident PR Practitioner will take a turn for the better in such situation. Just as Rousseau, a French philosopher observed, "Self-confidence is virtually a miracle for your career, with which your intelligence will be abundant and inexhaustible, and without which, you won't have the chance to succeed no matter how intelligent you are. "

2.Enthusiasm

The PR Practitioner should be enthusiastic. Public relations work is hard work requiring people to contribute their both mental and physical labor, rather than a relaxing work at which people just eat, drink, and have fun. Many PR Practitioners have no the concept of 8-hour working system in mind. What they have in mind is just overtime and overload work. So a person can't work well if he or she has no enthusiasm and doesn't devote himself or herself to the work. With enthusiasm, the PR Practitioner will have broad interests, be sensitive to the changes of surroundings and be full of imagination and creativity. A person who is interested in nothing and indifferent to anything isn't qualified to be a PR Practitioner. Such kind of person is even engaged in public relations work, his or her working style is passive rather than active, and the work effect is limited. The PR Practitioner should depend on enthusiasm to make contact with different people, make numerous friends and expand working channels. The person short of enthusiasm could neither accept others nor be accepted by others.

3.Openness

Public relations work should be open to the outside world, so the PR Practitioner should be open-minded. Public relations work is of great creativity, which requires people to be open-minded, take in new things, new knowledge and new ideas, be brave and creative and make outstanding contributions. Open-minded people are tolerant enough to accept people of different characteristics and styles from their own, seek common points while reserving difference, and build sound relationships with different people, which is requisite to the public relations work. The open-minded PR Practitioner will show high profiles in many aspects, calmly handle difficulties and setbacks during work, and won't haggle over every ounce of anything.

iii. Natural Quality

Natural quality, namely inborn psychological quality, including both psychological features of anatomy and functional features of psychology. Psychological features of anatomy includes weight, body and mind, skeleton, nervous system, etc; Functional features of psychology includes movement quality, reaction speed, burden limit, adaptive capacity, resist capacity, etc. The natural quality of the PR Practitioner should be "natural beauty", such as physical health, regular features, standard height accord with modern appreciation of the beauty, quick reaction, strong resistance, burden and adaptive capacity.

Meanwhile, the PR Practitioner should have the following consciousness

1. Conscious of Shaping the Image

The consciousness of image shaping is the core of public relations consciousness. Cherishing prestige and valuing image are the most important of public relations thoughts. Modern enterprises value highly the image. Sound image is an intangible and invaluable asset of an enterprise. The image of an organization should be true rather than false; Good corporate image must be built on the basis of good operation, high-quality products or services of the organization, rather than compiled. The PR Practitioner must be strongly conscious of image shaping, defending the corporate image just like protecting the eyeballs at every moment.

2. Conscious of Serving for the Public

The corporate image is built for specific targets which have certain relationships with the organization, and are the public of the organization. An isolated corporate image without the public is meaningless; the survival of the organization will be threatened if the public are ignored, not even to mention the organization development. Any public relations work of the organization should focus on the public. The public interests should be placed first when conflicts between the interests of the organization and the public occurred. Edward Berners, the pioneer of modern public relations education, the noted scholar of public relations, observed in 1923 that the public relations work aims to "gain the favor of the public", " The public relations work should serve for the public interests first. " The PR Practitioner must be conscious of serving for the public, take the public interests into consideration anytime anywhere, take advantage of or create conditions to serve for the public and make efforts to meet the public demands in every aspect.

3. Conscious of Honest Mutual Benefit

The consciousness of honest mutual benefit is a utilitarian consciousness of public relations. It is self deception to deny utilitarianism of the public relations work. An organization in the competitive society should be aware of competition, but it should be both competition and cooperation, mutual development and progress rather than "a life-or-death struggle" or "the strong bullying the weak" in our socialist country. Any organization pursues its own economic benefit and social benefit by means of public relations work, but the pursuit must be based on mutual respect, equal cooperation and mutual benefit instead of on deceiving others or doing any harm to the public. The PR Practitioner must be conscious of honest mutual benefit at work.

4. Conscious of Communicating

Communication consciousness is also a kind of information consciousness. In order to shape the good image, serve for the public and achieve the goal, the organization must make a communication network to know the changes of surroundings, protect the organization and stimulate the development. To some extent, the consciousness of communication is a kind of democratic consciousness in modern society. The public relations activity is a kind of democratic operation and administration activity. The organization must listen to the public suggestions and comments in order to shape the good image to be accepted by the public and get the support from the public; the organization must use communicating skills to publicize what it has done in an effort to popularize its good image and heighten its reputation. All this must rely on democratic spirit and consciousness.

5. Conscious of Making Innovations and Appreciation of the Beauty

Shaping the good image of an organization is a process to make innovations and appreciate the beauty. Once the good image has been shaped, it should be steady comparatively. However, comparative steady doesn't mean unchanging. It should be an actively steady state, in which breeding and containing development. Only on the basis of development can the true stability be realized, and similarly, only in the case of stability there will be true development. Now that the good image of an organization needs developing, the organization must need innovating, breaking through and surpassing, surpassing itself and other organizations. As for each public relations activity in the process of shaping the good image of an organization, its plan and design also needs innovating. Public relations is a creative art, and it must be of the value of appreciation. It is really hard to imagine that the good image of an organization is ugly rather than beautiful. Only a beautiful image can be appreciate and accepted by people; only a beautiful activity can be taken part in and devoted by people.

6. Conscious of the Long-Term Strategy

Shaping a good image of an organization can't get effect instantly, which can be achieved through long-term efforts and constant accumulation. The public relations activity is different from advertisement and sales promotion. The later focus more on short term, the direct benefits; while the former, fundamentally focuses more on long term and pursues the long-term benefits. Any organization anxious to achieve quick success won't develop sustainably.

II. Basic Abilities of the Public Relations Practitioners

Public relations job needs the practitioners to have good operation capacity. The Ministry of Labor and Social Security of China put forward in 1999 the professional capacities of the PR Practitioners are better expressive capacity in both oral and written language, coordinating and communicating capacity between the public inside and outside the organization, investigating, consulting, planning capacities and organizing capacity of public relations activities. The basic capacities of the PR Practitioners can be generalized as the following five aspects:

1. Expressive Abilities

Expressive abilities include written and oral abilities. The "ability to speak and write fairly well" is the basic ability of the PR Practitioner. The PR Practitioner shoulders the task to propagate both inward and outward. They have to write news reports, speech scripts and counseling plans, draft activity plans, and edit journals, which require the practitioners to have literal skills. Oral expression is the most convenient means of communication. The PR Practitioners need to communicate with the public, which requires them to spread information clearly and correctly.

2. Social Skill

Social skill means the ability to spread information, increase understanding and deepen the affection by social communication. The person who is not skillful in social communication will be faced with lots of thorny issues at work and in life. Working as the spokesmen of social organizations and the representative of organization images, the PR Practitioners shoulder the tasks to communicate with the public and build up images, which need certain social skills to achieve success. Social skill is a complex of different abilities, involving the abilities to market the organization, get along with others, attract, change and influence others and the ability to know well and comply with the etiquetteand norms of the social occasion.

3. Organizing Ability

Organizing ability means the ability to arrange and complete a particular activity in a planned and orderly way on purpose. An activity involves in many links, investigation, planning, organizing human resources and materials, process controlling, to name just a few, which is to examine the organizing ability of the PR Practitioner. Normally, public relations activities can't be separated from organizing activities, such as celebrations, press conferences, launch of new products, etc. The PR Practitioners are required to plan as a whole and arrange reasonably, and carry out the task successfully.

4. Flexibility

Flexibility means the ability to address the emergency. Anything in the world is ever- changing, no exception for the public relations. The PR Practitioners often encounter some emergencies in which they have to stay calm and handle urgently, which require them to be capable of controlling and handling the circumstances calmly.

5. Innovation Ability

Innovation ability means that the PR Practitioners should have innovative thinking at work, covering innovating job contents and working measures. The PR Practitioners are required to bring their thinking innovation ability into full play and design innovative public relations activities appealing to the public and arousing the interest of the public.

Part Two The PR Practitioner's Work Ethic and Personnel Training

1. The PR Practitioners' Work Ethic

Work ethic is a kind of social ideology, serving as behavior code to adjust people themselves and mutual relationships. A society should have its basic ethic, while an industry should have its ethical standard. Public relations should have certain work ethic, aiming to control the PR Practitioners' work process and standardize their professional behavior.

Early in 1923, Edward·Berners, noted expert of public relations in America, mentioned the issues of the PR Practitioners' work ethic in his first work. Afterwards, the public relations associations of different countries and the International Public Relations Association constituted the work ethic and behavior code of public relations. 《Ethic Norm of International Public Relations》 has great influence of the numerous work norms. China has also constituted relevant work ethic norms. No matter in any country, the public relations ethic norms require the PR Practitioners as following:

ⅰ. The PR Practitioners' morals

The nature of public relations requires the PR Practitioners to be of

good morals. There are two reasons for this: One hand, the public relations work is to build up good image, which requires the image builder to have good image first. Anyone of low moral quality isn't qualified to be a PR Practitioner. There are stresses on the good moral qualities of the PR Practitioners in the constitutions of public relations associations in many countries; On the other hand, the target of public relations is the public. It is inevitable to be affected by some negative phenomena and eroded by money during the contact with the public, which requires that the PR Practitioners should have good morals.

The morals of the PR Practitioners include the following aspects:

1. High social responsibility. While considering issues, the PR Practitioners should be responsible for the whole society and take the public benefits as well as the organization benefits into consideration.

2. Justice. The PR Practitioners should treat equally and act fairly to the public served, and shouldn't have any bias in favor one more than another.

3. The PR Practitioners should do anything good of others, treat others sincerely, be trustworthy, be honest and upright, and shouldn't seek personal gains.

4. Working hard and with dedication spirit. The PR Practitioners should go

upstream undoubtedly at work and be dedicated to the public relations career. Only in this way can they overcome numerous difficulties at work and make achievements.

5. Having knowledge of the law, observing the law and using the law. The PR Practitioners should have knowledge of the law, observe the law, and know how to use the law to protect the organization benefits. They should have legal consciousness. Meanwhile, they should stand out, unmask, accuse and check any violations of law and discipline instead of ignoring and allowing them to continue. They shouldn't collaborate with the evil elements, or deliberately break the law.

ii. The professional guide line of public relations. There is no doubt that 《The Professional Guide Line of International Public Relations》 has great influence. Many countries adopt the guide line directly, or constitute their own guide lines accordingly. The International Public Relations Association has been dedicated to promoting professionalization and standardization of the public relations work for a long time.

The professional and moral conducts of public relations organizations and practitioners are the guarantee to drive the public relations work to maturity and success. The professional moral standards of the public relations work include:

1. Due Diligence and Honesty

It is the PR Practitioners' basic duties to build up good organization image, create good environment for subsistence and development of the organizations, and contribute to development of public relations. Accordingly, whether the PR Practitioner is devoted to the public relations and has professional morals are very important for measurement of his or her professional morals. The PR Practitioners should love their own work, have strong sense of responsibility, exercise their social and moral responsibilities instead of doing anything contrary to their duties. They shouldn't break the law, disclose the organization secrets, or do anything bad for the organization images and reputations. Those thoughts and behaviors free and easy, with neglect of duties, no considerations of organizations or disciplines are immoral. What's more, the PR Practitioners should have honest attitude to their profession. Honesty is the life of public relations. Without honest attitude, the PR Practitioners will not get trust and support from the public, or carry out the public relations work effectively. So the PR Practitioners are required to be honest, tell the truth, lay stress on transparency and openness, not to resort to deceit, not to deceive the superiors or delude the subordinates. They should be the same outside and inside, practical and realistic instead of being opportunistic. All their actions should stand up to inspections and tests.

2. Working Hard and Effectively

Public relations is realistic. Thus, the professional moral level of the PR Practitioners depends on not only the wish to fulfill the duties conscientiously but also the perfect skill to perform the obligations remarkably. The PR Practitioners rely on their actual strength and real learning to make achievements. Diligence is the prerequisite for the PR Practitioners. Those who are lack both learning and practical ability, accomplish nothing, often make mistakes, even worse to bring damage to the public, organizations and even the society are immoral.

3. Integrity and Working in the Public Interest, Seeking No Personal Gains

The basic work of public relations is to serve for the public, organizations and society. What each PR Practitioner has is the obligations to seek an increase in the benefits of the public, organizations and country rather than the right to seek gains for themselves. The nature and feature of the PR Practitioners' work decides that they have more comprehensive social relations and grasp certain power which are useful for individuals as well as beneficial for organizations. Thus, the professional morals for the PR Practitioner to be a man of integrity and always working in the public interests, seeking no personal gains are very important. The outstanding PR Practitioners put the benefits of the country, public and organizations first. They always bear in mind that the right is endowed by people. The individual represents not only himself, but also the image of the organization. Those who take advantage of their function and power to be involved in corruption, bribery, fraud and blackmail are immoral.

4. Being Fair, Honest, Humble and United

Public relations is an exalted enterprise, to which the practitioners dedicated should have exalted morals. Thus, each PR Practitioner should be honest and upright, act on the square, be scrupulous in separating public from private interests, and never make a deal with principles. Those who are swelled with pride, jealous of the worthy and the able, and serve personal interests through trickery, struggle for the power and benefits, are immoral. Public relations work is a kind of teamwork, at which cooperation, mutual help, solidarity and friendship, mutual trust and respect are the reliable guarantee for the smooth work and successful career. The PR Practitioners should be patient, dignified, modest and abstemious in dealing with people. They should be decent in their behaviors, speeches and clothes. They should be democratic, egalitarian, generous and tolerant. They should put right when they know mistakes. 这What mentioned above are all important prerequisites for doing the public relations work well.

Ⅱ. The PR Practitioner Training

With establishment and improvement of the socialist marketing economy, the economic system reform is pushing forward the separation of the functions between administrations and enterprises. Enterprises are walking towards the market. Various alliance, cooperation and competition of the enterprises make the public relations activities develop widely, move toward maturity, and play more and more important role in social activities. As one of the core factors of the public relations activities, the outstanding performance of the PR Practitioners at work will be the key impetus to the economic development and economic system reform. Consequently, the PR Practitioner training has become an important task of current public relations work.

To conclude the practice of the public relations education in our country, and draw lessons from the experiences of the public relations education overseas, we can take the following route to train the PR Practitioners:

1. To open the public relations courses in the universities, colleges and secondary technical schools. Many domestic universities, colleges and secondary technical schools open the public relations courses in their departments or specialties of journalism, administration, business, foreign trade and tourism to educate the students in both theory and practice, which improve the structure of their specialties. In the case of insufficient education of public relations specialty in our country, many students willing to be engaged in public relations can shoulder the public relations task of some projects after learning appropriate public relations theories and taking some practical exercises.

2. Through participation in social practice to increase public relations practices.

Some public relations staff who didn't learn knowledge of public relations, but they have opportunities to participate public relations practice activities at work, after participating earnestly the activities of public relations practice many times, they gained the knowledge of public relations practice, and they study by themselves in their spare time to supplement relevant knowledge of public relations theory, they also can undertake the task of the work of public relations.

3. To open the training courses and correspondence education on public relations. Over the past few years, the public relations organizations across the country have opened many medium-term and short-term training courses to introduce the fundamental theories to the in-serve staff in the society and exchange experiences in the public relations. Some universities also open the correspondence courses on the foundation of public relations. People who accept the training courses and correspondence education have certain working experiences, and can integrate theory with practice. Therefore, it is helpful for enriching the public relations team to open to the in-service personnel the training courses and correspondence education on public relations, but the ways should be reformed to advance the training quality.

Chapter Three
Working Procedure of Public Relations

There are four procedures in the public relations work, namely public relations investigation, public relations planning, public relations implementation and public relations assessment. Public relations investigation is the premise of the work to find out the problem; public relations planning is the importance of the work; public relations implementation is the key of the work; public relations assessment is the guarantee of the work.

Part One Public Relations Investigation

Public relations investigation is the first step of the working procedure of public relations. It means that the public relations department or the PR Practitioners carry out a series of practical activities of public relations such as scientifically and accurately investigating and researching the organization's public relations history and present situation, analyzing and forecasting the trend of public relations internally and externally and testing the effect of public relations activities by quantitative analysis and qualitative analysis. Scientific methods should be adopted during the public relations investigation to inspect the organization's public relations situation step by step, understand the condition of public relations activities in order to provide scientific gist for the public relations planning and implementation.

I. Purpose and Significance of Public Relations Investigation

1. To serve for the orientation and development of the organization image. The social image of the organization is decided by the public evaluation. Though public

relations investigation, the organization can accurately understand its position in the public and the public understanding and attitude to the organization, thereby to plan the public relations activities helpful to model the expected image and improve the efficiency of public relations activities.

2. To strengthen the relationship between the organization and the public, to understand the public opinions in time. The conclusion of public relations investigation is drawn on the basis of analyzing the specific and authentic data, so it is authoritative; in addition, the public relations investigators need communicate with the subjects in different ways to acquire the data. Therefore, the process of public relations investigation is actually a communication process between the organization and the public, whereby to strengthen further mutual relationship. The more important is that the public relations investigation can monitor and learn the public views and attitudes accurately and in time, which are the public opinions. As is known to all, public opinions have great influence in modern society. Positive public opinions will be in favor of the organization development, while the negative public opinions will impair the organization image, even worse to result in the organization crisis. The organization can take appropriate measures in time to spread the positive opinions and reduce negative influence through public relations investigation and public opinions monitoring, which is significant for the organization. to build a good image

3. To provide important gist for the organization to make scientific policy. There will be no right to speak or make policy without investigation. The major task of public relations investigation is to acquire overall, true and accurate data relevant to the organization image and public desire, to learn what kind of public relations projects are not appealing to the public, to prevent the organization from being entangled with unimportant affairs and wasting precious time, human resources, material and financial resources, in order to provide reference for the management to make relevant policy and test the effect of the existing policies. Those policies made according to prudent investigation and accorded with the public desire will naturally produce positive and expected effect, and the good image of the organization will be advanced further.

4. To increase effectiveness and success rate of public relations activities. The

working plan of public relations will be of high pertinence and practicable, and will be put into effect efficiently if the public relations activities are carried out according to overall, true and accurate investigation, plus the scientific plan of the relevant countermeasure.

II. Contents for the Public Relations to investigate

i. Organization Itself Investigation

1. Investigation of the Organization Profile

Investigation of the organization basic situation covers:

(1) The nature, mission, type and scale of the organization, the managing system, structure setting and the departments in charge, etc;

(2) Operating situation of the organization, such as the developing targets, operating policy, operating strategy, the products and features of the organization, etc;

(3) Credits of the organization, such as the credits and rewards the organization gained in the history, and the special contributions the organization made to the society, etc.

(4) Culture of the Organization. It includes organizational material culture, behavior culture, spiritual culture and institutional culture, such as enterprise culture, enterprise spirit, management idea, cultural activity, etc.

2. Investigation of the Organization Strength

Investigation of the organization strength covers:

(1) The material condition of the organization, such as the area, equipment, facilities, and means to do office work, etc;

(2) The technique strength of the organization, such as the number of the artisans and the intellectual structure, the equipment of scientific research and experiment measures, and the technical level of the organization, etc;

(3) The economic strength of the organization, such as the amount of fixed assets, the amount of flowing capital, the competitiveness of the organization in the industry and the listing of the organization in the equity market, the profit per capital, etc;

(4) The benefit of the employee, such as the salary level of the organization, housing area and labour protection, etc.

ii. Relevant Public Investigation

1.Investigation of the Composing of the Public

Each organization has a multifaceted public, which relates to the survival and development of the organization, so it is critical for public investigations, the main contents cover:

(1) The internal public composing, such as the number, professions, ages, genders, capabilities, posts and professional titles, etc;

(2) External public composing, such as the number, composing, features, needs, connection status with the organization, importance to the organization and dependence on the organization, etc.

2. Investigation of the Public Need. Investigation of the public needs mainly covers: what is the expectation of the public, the attitude of the public to the organization, and what the public needs for the organization? etc.

The investigation of the public relations is one form of the social investigation, but it has different focuses from the other forms of social investigations. According to the needs of public relations administration, it investigates the public relations status of the organization, especially the public assessment on the organization image, sets the goals of the public relations, or tests the practical operation effect of certain public relations activity by collecting relevant information and analyzing various problems and their relationships. Public relations investigation is a specialized technique. It not only can manage effectively the relevant information of the organization, but also is a requisite premise for the organization to launch public relations activities.

iii. Media Investigation

It mainly covers media distribution (area, industry, type, etc), scope covered, disseminating contents, disseminating features, disseminating core, disseminating trend, disseminating effect and social influence, etc.

iv. Social Environment Investigation

Investigating scope covers political environment, economic environment, social environment, sci-tech environment and competition environment.

Political investigation covers the political structure, political atmosphere and changing trend of respective country, various policies and decrees issued or to be issued by the country or the relevant departments of the government, and the potential influence on the development of the organization caused by the policies and decrees.

Economic investigation covers the development state and tendency of the world economy, economic development strategy of the country, economic development tendency, reserves and exploitation of resources and energy, and the overall level of current national economy development, as well as the present situation and development tendency of national income, features of the social purchasing power, changing features and development tendency of resident consumption structure.

Social environment investigation covers the changes of social ideas and conduct codes, popular social trend of thought and its potential influence on the public behavior, the changes of people's values, way of act, consumption tendency, faith, cultural quality, morality norms, etc, and restrict and influence of the above-mentioned factors on the organization development.

Sci-tech environment investigation covers the technique level, technique feature, technique requirement, technique standard, technique type of the target market, the innovation trend and focus issue of the international market.

Competition environment covers the relative industry situation, the organization position in competition, the present situation and trend of competitors and the situation of their public relation activities.

Ⅲ. Policy of Public Relations Investigation

Investigation is a complicated systematical project, which requires the data to be of high authenticity. Consequently, there should be full preparations, dynamic participants and scientific and reasonable implementation procedures. Public relations investigation requires the selected subjects to be highly typical and reflect the overall situation of the whole phenomenon, so sampling survey is widely adopted.

Basic principles of public relations investigation are as following:

ⅰ. Planning in Advance

First, public relations investigation is an important complicated and regular work, which must be embodied in the quarterly and annual planning. It is a set of scientific and normative working procedures.

Second, a complete investigation planning should be drafted before a specific public relations investigation, which should cover a detailed scheme on the mission target, personnel arrangement, working process, possible problems and countermeasures.

Feasibility assessment and quality assessment should be carried out before the investigation planning is implemented. Feasibility assessment is to evaluate whether the investigation planning accords with logic and physical truth, has any problems and is feasible by adopting logic analysis, experience judgement and pilot approaches. There are three angles in quality assessment: one is to assess whether the plan reflects nicely the purpose and requirement of the investigation; the second is to assess how are the scientificalness and operability of the plan; the third is to assess whether the investigation quality led by the plan is remarkably superior to the previous ones.

ii. Being Practical and Realistic

The purpose of public relations investigation is to collect authentic data. Generally, it is common to adopt sampling investigation, questionnaire investigation, news investigation and focus interview, etc. Therefore, the selected subjects should be of representativeness and comprehensiveness, which represent the public and reflect their overall attitudes and situation. Next, the public objective attitudes towards the organization should be grasped in the investigation, which shouldn't be confused with the public speculation. Last, the investigation data collected should be comprehensive, authentic and objective, which cover various public opinions from all aspects.

Moreover, the principle of being practical and realistic requires the public relations investigators to have objective stands and not to have any bias to the public opinions on the organization. One hand, they should propagate truthfully the organization's achievements. On the other hand, they should be practical and realistic to address the existing problems, which shouldn't be covered and avoided. In a word, the data collected in the public relations investigation should reflect truthfully the target public's real attitudes.

iii. Respecting the Public

Public relations investigation is a regular work, in which the PR Practitioners represent the organization image. Hence, in the whole investigation, the investigators should have elegant manners, humble attitudes and meticulous patience, as well as respect the public life style, faith and living habits in order to get the public's support and cooperation and collect authentic information. Otherwise, the organization image will be damaged and the investigation won't be carried out smoothly.

ⅳ Pursuing Effectiveness

This policy has two meanings: first, the investigation should pursue the economic benefits; second, the investigation should be time-sensitive.

Public relations investigation is a time consuming project, which will cost a lot. Only when it is planned secientifically, arranged comprehensively, carried out diligently and thriftily, can the organization do more at higher quality with less money. Besides, the investigation should be time sensitive. Public relations investigation is carried out in a certain period of time, yet the public attitudes will change anytime with a variety of factors. The public relations investigation should be carried comprehensively and accurately, while the relative data should be collected swiftly and shortcutly. Only in this way, can the investigation report be submitted to the organization management, can the organization take corresponding countermeasures.

Ⅳ. Methods of Public Relations Investigation

Certain methods are adopted in any investigation. Investigation methods are the way to achieving the investigation goal, and scientific methods are the key premise to make scientific conclusion. The common methods adopted in the public relations investigation are as following:

ⅰ. Sampling Investigation

Sampling investigation is to deduce the situation of overall investigated subjects according to part practically investigated results. Its principle is to extract part sampled units from the collective constituted by some units to carry out experiments and observation by certain scientific procedures, measures and steps, and then, to deduce the overall situation based on the collected data in the investigation which represent the overall samples. Selecting samples scientifically is the crucial step of the public relations investigation. If the samples are not selected scientifically or representatively the investigation result will be distorted.

There are generally two kinds of sampling investigation, namely random sampling (probability sampling) and non-probability sampling (such as key-point investigation). Random sampling can be divided into random sampling, systematic random sampling (equal interval sampling), stratified sampling, and cluster sampling, etc; non-probability sampling can divided into judgement sampling, quota sampling, typical sampling and case sampling, etc.

Sampling method is most commonly used in the public relations investigation.

ii. General Investigation

General investigation is also called total investigation. It is a method to investigate all the samples at large and record the result all at once according to certain methods, uniformed project, questionnaire and standard time, such as the demographic census in our country in which the method is adopted. Unless the special needs, this kind of method is only fit for the situation of small number of the subjects and low cost investigation.

General investigation helps collect overall, accurate and full information, and its result is authentic, which is convenient for the investigators to learn the situation as a whole from a macroscopic view. This method is a best choice to get the subjects' overall information when the subject number is small. The method has an obvious shortcoming which will cost a lot and be very hard to get further information when the subject number is large. Therefore, this method is not commonly used.

iii. Medium Investigation

Medium investigation covers two kinds operating methods, one is news investigation, the other is network medium investigation.

The so-called news investigation is a method that the investigators know and study the subjects' (the public') opinions and attitudes according to the news reports released over various media.

Network medium investigation is a method that the investigators collect the subjects' (the public's and other groups') information over the network. The public relations investigators can communicate with the public by clicking to visit, transiting e-mails and communicating online. The network can not only collect the data from extensive sources, but also get the data timely due to the features of wide and fast spread of the network and its high affinity.

ⅳ. Focus Interview

This is a method to investigate through interpersonal communication. The steps are to select key groups and figures (government officer, socialites or leaders in public opinions) to interview, ask them to answer the relative questions straightly in order to investigate and understand their opinions and attitudes, and then analyze the causes led to the opinions and attitudes to explore the approach which will influence the opinions and attitudes. The reason why the focus figures are selected is that they have some popularity and social charisma which can affect the public's opinions and attitudes. There are three ways in focus interview: interview, letter and visit (investigating by letters) , interview on the phone. This method requires the investigators to have high comprehensive qualities, especially on their social skills. Moreover, how to ascertain the appropriate focus figures is a challenging task.

ⅴ. Questionnaire Investigation

Questionnaire investigation is easy to understand. It means that the investigators give out the given respondents questionnaires in which there is a group of questions designed in advance, and then collect and analyze them after they are filled in. This step must be taken to collect any first- hand public relations data in investigation. This method requires the investigators to design questionnaires scientifically and rigorously to ensure success of the investigation.

As investigation is a kind of work with strong purpose, the investigators should set a clear target and state it in pre-assumption and theory frame. Pre-assumption is the base of the questionnaire. If the founding is consistent with the pre-assumption, then it can be used as the evidence to support the pre-assumption. The theory frame consists of basic information of the investigators, motive factors, attitudes and actions, the purpose of building up which is to further study the investigated contents with some corresponding theories.

Generally, the cost of questionnaire is low, and the data collected are objective, but the response rate is hard to ensure (50% response rate is good enough). What's more, as public relations itself is a science and an art, there are usually more advanced and complicated questions in the questionnaire, which requires the respondents to have higher civilization qualities, so it is energy consuming to select appropriate respondents.

There are two kinds of questionnaire, closed questionnaire and open questionnaire according to different ways of designing the questions and answers. Open questionnaire is actually an investigation outline without answers, and the respondents can choose the answers freely. This kind of questionnaire is generally used in exploring research on some complicated issues in depth to get some constructive suggestions and valuable information, which requires the respondents to be of high qualities. The disadvantage of open questionnaire is uncertainty of answer rate and recycle rate, as well as the inconvenience in counting and analyzing the answer sheets.

The respondents can only choose the answers among the multiple choices provided by the investigators in closed questionnaire. In practice, the answers in closed questionnaire are specified and unified, and convenient for the investigators to count and analyzed, so this kind of questionnaire is widespread. The disadvantage of the questionnaire is there are possibly some questions and answers that left out by the investigators. If the proportion of the answers left out is large, the overall result of the investigation must be affected.

It can be seen from the above-mentioned that there are advantages and disadvantages of the two kinds of questionnaires in operation. The investigators should choose the appropriate one flexibly according to circumstances and requirements of tasks. Generally, the two kinds of questionnaires are both used in investigation in order to collect more objective, authentic, and comprehensive data and a better result.

Investigation questionnaire can be separated into three sections: Introduction or Lead, Investigation Project and Relevant Information. Introduction or Lead is used to illustrate the investigation meaning, purpose and explanation of relevant items, for example, who are the investigators, how to use the investigation result, and what measures taken to keep confidential (personal privacy and some sensitive issues), etc, as well as the explanation of some tasks, hints on how to fill in the questionnaire, etc; Investigation Project is the specific questions and ways to answer the questions, in which open and closed questionnaires are generally used; Relevant Information covers serial number, brief situation of the respondents, dates of the questionnaire to be used, order number of each section, etc, which will be used in counting the data.

ⅵ Observation on the Scene

Observation is to send the investigators with sensitive observation ability and analytic and judging capability to the scene to observe the respondents' attitudes and action using modern image technology with open or concealed identity, and keep the records as data. This method is often adopted because of its direct effect, but it has higher requirement on the environment.

ⅶ. Controlling the Experiment

This method is to arrange the investigators to observe the respondents' attitudes and action in an environment set up in advance to get relative information. This method is widely used in the western communication studies, as well as some investigation activities on public relations.

ⅷ Document Study

This method is to learn and analyze the relevant situation through inquiring about the achievements of investigation and study by others. The documents include publications, archives (relevant files of the government, various statistic materials, relevant minutes and big events, etc), personal data (diaries, letters, memoirs and contracts, etc). The steps of the method are taken as following: first step, to set up index, to make a document list according to the respondents; second step, to look up and record the document data according to the index; third step, to check the documents and login. Checking the documents is to eliminate the false and retain the true in an effort to get valuable documents. The checked documents should be classified according to different tasks and requirements, and then number each classified documents for future enquiry.

ⅸ. Typical investigation. There are some similarities between case study and case study, which are closely related to the typical investigation. They all go deep into "dissecting sparrows", that is, to make a thorough and detailed understanding of a particular object.

V. Procedure of Public Relations Investigation

i. Investigation Preparation

First, clear the investigation task. It means to definite the project of the public relations investigation, namely what problems to solve and what purpose to achieve. Generally, there are many investigation projects for the organization to choose. Which one to choose depends on the reality and long-run needs of the organization. There are two kinds of investigation projects, namely descriptive and explanatory projects. The former means to describe the outline and detail of the target by specific data, the latter means to explain the causal relationship of some phenomena and put forward solutions. Next, make an investigation plan. The investigators analyze the present condition and make a proper plan covering designing investigation index, selecting respondents, and arranging investigation activities according to the present image and target requirement. What's more, prepare the investigation condition, especially on personnel, material, transportation, etc.

ii. Data Collection

The main task of this period is to collect data, during which the proper methods should be adopted to ensure the reclaim rate of the questionnaire.

iii. Sorting out and Analyzing

First, sort out the data. That is to check, classify and count the collected data.

Next, analyze the investigation result. That is to show the data in diagram and do some necessary analysis.

iv. Completion of the Report

Writing an investigation report is the last step of public relations investigation, which can accurately reflect the public relations state of the organization, especially the public opinions, examine the social influence of the public relations activities, and draw some lessons on public relations from the working experience which will benefit the future work a lot.

Generally the contents of an investigation report cover: the headline (title), introduction (the consignor, host, date, reasons and targets, objects and methods of the investigation), result of the investigation and data, conclusion, suggestion, signature (investigation unit and completion date) and accessory (questionnaire, date, forms and background materials, etc).

An investigation report should be written formally according to standard formats. Here are some tips:

First, try to use popularized vocabulary and avoid jargons and terms;

Second, take the readers' stand, opinions, experience and reading habits into consideration;

Third, try to show the materials in statistics diagram or tables

Fourth, pay attention to the space proportion of each part. Deeper and further research can be carried out in a key project.

A good report should be brief in content, systematic in layout, accurate in data, rigorous in analysis, outstanding in key point and reliable in conclusion.

V. Conclusion and Evaluation

The investigators must make conclusion and evaluation on the investigation procedure and result after the report, focusing on data collection, technical means application and investigation procedure, in an effort to make it clear for the relevant staff in the organization to understand the investigation and its result better, draw lessons from the past and provide reference for the future investigation on public relations.

Part Two Public Relations Planning

Planning is scheming which is a wisdom-creating process. It is a process that public relations planners of the organization conceive and design scientifically on the project of public relations activity in advance according to the present condition, thereby to make a best activity project. It is an important step of the public relations working procedure based on objective analysis on the public and aimed at the best activity effect.

Public relations plan embodying the public relations value increases scientifity of information transiting and helps improve the objective management of the organization. Thus, some scholars think planning, as a kind of advanced work, plays the most important role in public relations. It is not only the guide to all the public relations activities, but also the core of them. The opinion is reasonable, but a little radical. Actually, public relations activities have a set of rigorous procedures, in which each step is indispensible and important. Those so-called super "ideas" are unrealistic and unpractical, so they aren't applicable to public relations activities.

I . Meaning and Characteristics of Public Relations Planning

Scientific planning is the guarantee for the social organization to make effective scheme of public relations actions

i . Meaning of Public Relations Planning

Public relations planning plays a very important role in the "four-step working method", because investigating is aimed at planning, and the implementing and evaluating are based on planning. Meanwhile, planning is of great influence and meaning for the social organization to manage its image, which can be shown in the following aspects: (1) Public relations planning is the grantee for final success. First, a careful and scientific plan helps clear up problems; secondly, a careful and scientific plan can make public relations activities develop orderly; thirdly, a careful and scientific plan can help the activities get support and cooperation from the internal departments of the organization; last, a careful and scientific plan can make the PR Practitioners confident of success. (2) Public relations planning can emphasize the image target on the organization. It can help the organization analyze the present situation, work from its strength, design a series of effective activities, and finally achieve the development target and perfect the organization image. (3) Public relations planning is a magic weapon for the organization to win in the competition. With establishment and development of socialist market economy, the competition among the social organizations is becoming increasingly intense with their strengthen cooperation, which is actually the competition in talented person and wisdom. Public relations planning is crystallization of the PR Practitioners' wisdom, which contains numerous wonderful stratagemschemes to win in the competition, so it is a magic weapon for the organization to win in the competition. (4) Public relations planning is a leap in the public relations operation. Only through planning, can a lot of public relations investigation and some basic work be refined and distilled, the organization image be remembered by the public and impress the public deeply. It is planning that makes the public operation reach a new level, so it commands the public relations operation.

ii. Features of Public Relations Planning

1. Purposiveness. All the public relations planning is carried out around the public relations purpose. The purpose is both the starting point and the end of planning.

2. Planning. Any public relations activity should be carried out designedly according to the development feature of the organization and the objective law of the public's acceptance of information.

3. Scientificalness. Public relations planning is of high specialization, so it must be based on reality and public wishes and carried out according to objective law and normative scientific procedure and methods.

4. Wholeness. The plan is to plan all the public relations activities of the organization, so the social and organizational benefits should be taken into consideration, and long-term and short-term goals should be taken into consideration.

5. Creativity. Public relations planning must break conventions, and attract the public's interests and arouse their feelings by creativity, which is the soul of public relations planning.

6. Flexibility. The organization itself is changing and developing constantly with the environment. Accordingly, public relations targets and activities should change with them.

Modern planning has developed into a stage of group planning carried out with cooperation of multi-disciplines and various human resources, and scientific planning from experience planning, which is a landmark progress.

II. Policy of Public Relations Planning

i. Policy of Being Practical and Realistic.

Any planning must be carried out according to the objective fact and subject to the objective law. In addition, the scheme should be adjusted with objective environments, organization targets and resources.

ii. Policy of Exploration and Innovation.

Innovation is the requirement of competition in organization image. Only when the public relations plan contains unique and original factors, can they attract and appeal to the public.

iii. Policy of Complying with the Public.

In modern times, the relationship between the public attitudes and actions and the organization development is a matter of life and death. Only when the organization is adapted to the public needs, consider the public benefits and get along well with the public, can it exist and develop in a sound environment.

iv. Policy of Priority of the Public Benefits.

Social organizations and individuals should first consider the public's benefits and invest in human relationships while making public relations plans. Only in this way can they win the public's trust and support. Especially when there are contradictions between the organizations' and the public's benefits, the organizations should take the public's benefits into consideration first without hesitation.

v. Policy of Being Consistent with the Whole Organization Plan.

Public relations work is a part and a branch of the whole organization work, and the planning is carried out within the frame of the whole plan. The action scheme should be inserted into and consistent with the whole plan, and subject to the whole target of the organization.

vi. Policy of Unification of Originality and Persistence.

Public relations planning is a kind of creative activity, which should be unconventional and with a new style. A successful public relations plan must contain new contents with the changing social environment. However, public relations effect must be taken into consideration while originality of public relations planning is being emphasized.

vii. Policy of Unification of Social Benefits and Economic Benefits

A good public relations plan should not only unify the public benefits and the organization benefits, but also social benefits and economic benefits. It should consistent with both the whole operation plan of the organization and social development condition. First, public relations activities must focus on economic benefits. Second, one of the purposes of public relations activities is to improve mutual understanding and adaption between the organization and its public, which are commonly based on social benefits. Third, dialectical relationship between social benefits and economic benefits should be dealt with successfully.

Ⅲ. Methods of Public Relations Planning

There are many methods in public relations planning, a few of which are introduced as following:

ⅰ. Making News

Making news means that social organizations and individuals plan, organize and conduct the events with news value on purpose under the precondition of not harming the public interest in an effort to attract the public's attention and expand the organizations' popularity and effect.

1.Policy of Making News

（1） Based on Facts. The news events in making news are not made up, but planned and arranged thoughtfully by social organizations and individuals according to absolute facts in order to make the news events more attractive.

（2） Being of High News Value. The news events planned by social organizations and individuals should be of high news value and can attract the public attention and interests obviously. The more news value the events have, the more chance there will be to be reported by the press. （3） Seizing the minds of the public. Only when the social organizations and individuals understand the public's minds, learn about their psychology, can they make attractive news appealing to the public.

2.Types of Making News

There are four types of making news according to different entry points:

（1） Propagation Medium News. Propagation medium news means that social organizations and propagation media hold intelligence games, social activities, etc together by which to expand the effect of organizations and attract media to report the news.

（2） Celebrity News. It means that social organizations establish relationship with some celebrities to attract social attention, by which to attract media to report the news and attract the public's attention.

(3) Public News. It means that social organizations establish relationship with the public to show their value and management ideas, by which to attract the public's attention

(4) Event News. It means to seize the opportunity of an event which reveals its importance for the first, and then add some colors to it skillfully to make sensational news.

ii. Borrowing Corona to Increase Reputation

It means that social organizations connect their products with reputable, authoritative and renowned organizations or events while planning public relations activities in order to achieve the effect of half the work with double results.

1. The person who borrows corona to increase reputation must of high credibility. Experts in public relations, Cutlip and Cent point out in the book Effective Public Relations: A communicator's credibility depends on his motive, credibility history and professional level, because the standards of the qualities are grasped by the target public. The higher popularity the communicator has, the more possible the public will believe him and what he initiates.

2. Authority is of great influence and persuasiveness. Authority of a person or an organization relates closely to his influence power and persuasiveness.

IV. Procedure of Public Relations Planning

Formulation of public relations plan and design of act scheme are related with establishment and perfection of image, survival and development of the organization. Therefore, PR Practitioners should work according to certain procedures when they carry out public relations planning.

The procedure of public relations planning means a series of activities covering setting public relations goals, designing activity themes, analyzing the public and selecting media, making budgets and examining plans under the precondition of investigation and research through analyzing the present situations and causes of the organization image.

1. Setting Public Relations Goals. Public relations goals are actually the ideal image status and standard for the organization to achieve through public relations planning and implementing. Setting public relations goals is the premise of public relations planning. Once the goals are set, all the work will be target-centered, and activity scheming, implementing, and effect evaluating will be carried out according to the goals.

Generally speaking, specific goals of public relations work are related closely to the problems affirmed in investigation analysis which will turn into the specific goals. The specific goals of public relations work are parts of the general objective of the organization. They exist objectively and are bound by the general objective. It is the specific goals that public relations planning should be in accordance with.

Public relations objective is a system of goals. There are two types, or four kinds, namely long-term goals, short-term goals, generic goals, and special goals.

The Short-Term Goal: It is the specification and accumulation process of the long-term goal. It has particular tasks and definite direction, and will be achieved in the short term.

The General Goal: It is set according to identity of the demands, intentions, ideas and behaviors of different types of public or the same type of public.

The Special Goal: It is set according to the particular demands of the public who share the same or similar objectives, faith, development and benefits with the organization. It has particular direction.

2. Designing Activity Themes. The public relations theme is the high summarization of public relations activities, concentrates on the main points and serves as the guide of the whole public relations activity. The theme can be expressed in a variety of ways, such as a slogan, a statement, or an expression.

3. Analyzing the Public. Any organization has its particular public. Public relations work is carried out in different ways targeting at different public, so defining the public relevant to the organization is the basic task of public relations planning. Only when the public are defined, can the organization select and make use of relevant information consciously and bring it to the particular public instead of spreading the information blindly and resulting in unnecessary cost. There are three steps in defining the public:

The first step is to identify the public's demand in interest. Public relation is a kind of mutual-benefit relationship in nature. The second step is to summarize and analyze the public's demands in different interests. The last step is to analyze the public's special demands.

4. Selecting Media. Appropriate transmitting media should be selected according to different categories of the public and their demands. Generally the following media are to be selected: ①Individual Transmitting Media. This is a kind of person-to-person transmission with a clear target, but quite a limited scope, which is applicable to some special public and key public. ② Group Transmitting Media. This is a kind of person-to-group transmission, which is applicable to a group of people with special demands or questions. ③ Mass Transmitting Media. In addition to some traditional electronic mass media, such as broadcast and television and printing media, such as newspapers and magazines, the widely used computers and Internet at the end of the 20th century made human society fully embrace the electronic age. The Internet has rebuilt a brand new mode of economy-electronic network economy, which enriches the means in public relations transmission, such as e-mails, Internet, online newspapers, online magazines, online data base, online information services, digital channels, etc. These electronic network means can be widely used in public relations activities to transmit the organization information all over the world in an effort to build a good image of the organization and solve the common problems.

5. Budgeting. Public relations have management functions each of which should have regular budget. Budgeting is necessary for public relations work. There are two ways to draw up the budget of public relations. ① Taking a Share from the Sales. It means a percentage will be taken from the total value of out-put or the whole sales as the cost of public relations. ② Target Costing. It means that a target of public relations should be set and a working plan of public relations should be made first, and then the costs on each task should be listed explicitly, finally the budgets on each activity and all the activities through the whole year should be checked and ratified. A public relations budget normally consists of the expenses on the following aspects: labor working hours, administration, professional equipment and finished products, propaganda, actual activities and sponsor.

6. Approving the Plan. PR Practitioners should take various factors into consideration, balance advantages and disadvantages, and then select the plan best for achieving the objective and realizing economic benefits maximum in many feasible plans. Therefore, the PR Practitioners should do the following work: ① Optimizing the Plan. The policy of optimizing the plan is to consider the purpose and feasibility of the plan to lower the expenses on labor, material, finance, time for the most beneficial result while selecting the plan. ② Plan Argument. It means the demonstration of feasibility after the act plan has been drawn up. Normally the relevant leaders, experts and actual practitioners will put forward some questions on feasibility of the plan, and the planners will make open reply to the questions. Generally the demonstration of the plan covers the following points: The first is to analyze the purpose of the plan to check whether it is clear and achievable. The second is to analyze the limiting factors to figure out in what conditions the plan will be feasible or infeasible. The third is to analyze the potential problems to prevent the possible problems and remove obstacles. The fourth is to evaluate the comprehensive effect to judge whether to implement the plan.

V. Methods of Public Relations Planning

Public relations planning is a creative thinking process, which will create feasible plans with the help of many methods and techniques.

i. Delphi Method. Delphi is the name of a city in ancient Greek. This method started from Rand, an American company, and was applied in the field of market prediction. The method adopted in public relations planning is aimed to ensure the quality and best effect of the planning with the aid of the experts' experiences, knowledge and comprehensive abilities in analyzing problems.

The four steps will be followed in Delphi method: 1. Letters will be sent to experts with the questions to be investigated and decided. The experts will answer the questions freely with their own ideas. 2. The experts' ideas will be counted, summed up and synthesized and a form will be made with the conclusion of the ideas, and then sent to the experts again. The experts will make further evaluation and illustration on the ideas in the form. 3. The decision making group will collect and summed up the second round of the experts' ideas and make a new form which will be sent to the experts for the third time to be judged and analyzed. The experts can insist on their original ideas and make further illustration, or change their ideas and put forward new ideas. 4. Over discussion, the decision making group will make investigation pertinently on the special ideas of some experts whom they will ask for further argument or proof

ⅱ. Brain Storming Method. The method was created by Osborne, an American creationist, in 1939. It is also called "free thinking", referred to as "BS", the original intention is the mental patient's nonsense, extended to freely think about the problem. The core of the method is to connect freely in the mind.

1. Organization of Brain Storming Method: (1) Identifying the meeting participants. Generally, 5-12 participants are appropriate for the meeting. They should be informed of the meeting theme several days in advance, and get prepared. (2) Identifying 1 meeting leader and 1-2 meeting recorders. The meeting leader should illustrate the purpose of the meeting and problems to be solved. The recorder should record all the schemes and assumptions raised in the meeting. (3) The duration of the meeting is normally no more than 1 hour, less than 2 hours at most. (4) Experts will be invited to make comments on the schemes and assumption raised in the meeting, in which some better ones will be selected, and then improved and perfected to be adopted as practical and valuable schemes and assumptions.

2. Meeting Requirements of the Brain Storming Method: ① Criticism on others' ideas is forbidden. ② All the participants are encouraged to think freely. ③ All the participants must make use of others' assumptions to enlighten their own thinking and wisdom. ④ The meeting leader, especially the high-ranking leader shouldn't express their opinions in order not to affect the freedom air of the meeting.

ⅲ. Expert Meeting

Relevant experts will be invited to have a meeting to discuss and analyze on the present problems in the organization and public relations objectives, and then they will put forward their ideas that will be summed up and made into the action plan of the organization.

Part Three Implementation of Public Relations

The implementation of public relations means the process to put the public relations plan into reality after it is adopted. The implementation of public relations is a process of action rather than a theory, which will check whether the plan is practical, reasonable and scientifical, and will play a key role to the success of the whole public relations work.

Ⅰ. Meaning of the Implementation of Public Relations

The implementing peoples of public relations should not only make efforts to shape good images of organizations, but also acknowledge the significance of the implementation of public relations.

1. The implementation of public relations is the key to solving problems. The ultimate purpose of public relations work is not to research problems, but to solve problems. Only when the public relations plan is put into practice, can the problems be solved directly, practically and specifically. It is also a public relations activity that transforms public relations planning into reality according to plan, which is accepted by the general public and the practice, and fully demonstrates the actual operation ability and professional level of public relations personnel.

2. The implementation of public relations is the touch-stone to check whether the plan is right or wrong. The implementation is a practical activity. Only in the process of implementation can the plan be check whether to be feasible, applicable to the society, and catering for the public's needs. The implementation is to disseminate the information in certain aspects to the public as planned, to arouse the public's attention, to deepen their understanding of the organization, and to form the desired attitude and behavior.

3. The implementation of public relations determines the effect of the plan. A successful implementation of public relations can fulfill the tasks in the plan completely. Otherwise, the goal of the plan can't be achieved, the relations will be worsen, either, or even run in the opposite directions. So the public relations implementation is to solve the specific problems existing in the organization of public relations, to achieve the established goals of public relations work.

4. The result of the public relations implementation is the basis for the follow-up plan to make on. No matter a public relations plan is successful or not, it will cause some influence on the society. The feedback information of the former plan implementation will be the direct material for the organization to research new problems and will have reference significance for the follow-up plans. The problem of the implementation phase is the phase that public feedback information, the achievements, the quality can be used to detect and evaluate the effect of the public relations activities and organization of the state of public relations, environmental change and intangible assets, also created new conditions for subsequent public relations work, put forward new tasks and goals

II. Policies and Methods of Public Relations Implementation

The implementation of public relations is very complicated because of its dynamic state, creativity and wide-spread influence. The implementing peoples of public relations must follow certain policies and master right methods in order not to deviate the set strategic target. The normally used policies and methods are as following:

1. The target-oriented policy and methods. This policy means the public relations activities can not deviate from the set target in the implementation of the public relations. It actually serves as a controlling means. The target orientation covers the following three aspects: The first is to control the target not to be changed willfully or overstepped in the implementation. The second is to control the development and process of the implementation. The third is that the implementing peoples use the target to guide, restrict and improve the whole implementation in an effort to fulfill the implementation as scheduled.

2. Linear arrangement. It means to arrange all the public relations activities and measures in sequence, moving towards the target step by step. Eg: The department of agriculture has evolved a new strain of hybrid paddy, which is to be introduced in the country. For this a communication program has been designed in such a way as to make the farmers adopt the new variety of paddy seeds. In adopting this new hybrid variety a farmer has to pass through four stages. 1) Awareness: The farmer learns of this existence of the hybrid paddy, which was not known to him earlier.

2) Interest: Having known to its existence, the farmer develops interest in the idea and seeks more information on the new strain for his consideration.

3) Acceptance: The farmer makes a decision to try the new variety in his own farm.

4) Trial: The farmer actually puts the idea into practice on a small scale in his farm.

3. The policy and method of controlling the schedule. It means to control the rate of process in certain procedures according to the set target in order to avoid caring for this and losing another. The control emphasize on rectify or overcome those activities different or deviated from the plan in complementation of the organization plan. There are two requirements in implementing the policy of controlling the schedule: One is to clear the purpose of the control. The other is to pay attention on the feedback information.

4. The policy and method of overall coordination. It means to keep all the parts of the work in a harmonious, unified, reasonable and complemented state in complementing the plan. It coordinates and emphasizes the cooperation among all the links, departments, and the main body of implementation and its public. There are two kinds of coordination in general. One is longitudinal coordination, which means to coordinate between the superior and subordinate. The other is horizontal coordination, which means to coordinate between the departments or implementing people at the same level.

5. The policy and method of adjustment according to the feedback information. It means to ask the implementing people to adjust, revise and remedy the plan according to the environment changes, the public's opinions and other factors while complementing the plan. No matter how objective and scientific an activity plan is, it is subjective and forecasted. Even a most scientific plan doesn't mean the reality itself. Moreover, the environment of modern times is complicated and full of changes and uncontrollable factors. Therefore, the implementing people must pay attention to and collect the feedback information in time in order to check whether the plan is adaptable to the changing situation and adjust the plan according to the feedback information.

6. The policy and method of choosing opportunity correctly. It means that the implementing people should choose the opportunity properly to disseminate the information out at the right time within the most effective period of the public relations. It is a key factor for the complementation of public relations, and will affect the overall

result. Here are some tips on how to choose opportunity correctly. First, try to avoid or take advantage of grand festivals. Second, try to avoid or take advantage of important events at home and abroad. Third, two important public relations activities shouldn't be carried out within a day or a period to avoid offsetting both effects.

III. Analysis on Obstacle Factors in Public Relations Implementation

It is unavoidable to meet various obstacles in complementing public relations plan, which will influence the efficiency of the implementing of public relations plan. There are many factors which will affect the implementation, but the major three are as following:

1. The target obstacles in complementing the public relations plan. It means the obstacles in complementation caused by the public relations target which was set incorrectly, unclearly or unspecific. If so, even though the implementation people try their best, they cannot achieve the expected result. The basic way for the plan implementers to remove the obstacles is that they should try to set a correct, clear and specific plan target, so they are required to check the plan target before implementing on the following five aspects: ① Check whether the plan target is practical and feasible; ② Check whether the plan target can be compared and measured; ③ Check whether the plan target has pointed out the expected result; ④ Check whether the plan target can be achieved within the scope of the implementation people's competence and functions; ⑤ Check whether the plan target has set the time limit . A correct, clear and specific plan target is not only the basis of the implementation people's action, but also the foundation to supervise and evaluate the plan implementation.

2. Communication obstacles in complementing the public relations plan. The implementation of the public relations plan is mainly a process of disseminating and communicating. Communication obstacles refer to the obstacles caused by improper use of the disseminating and communicating media, ways or methods in complementing the public relations plan. The common obstacles met in complementing the plan are as following: (1) The language obstacle. It means misunderstanding caused by language differences, puzzlement or faults in understanding caused by unclear language meaning and different meaning in understanding caused by polysemy, etc. Because of

the language obstacle, there will be some troubles, even disputes in communicating. Therefore, the language obstacle should be removed first when we implement the public relations plan. A successful public relations activity also means mutual exchange and mutual acceptance between different language cultures. (2) The convention obstacle. It is also called custom habits, which means the social factors with regular characteristics to adjust interpersonal relations, which came into being in a certain cultural and historical background, such as moral habits, etiquettes, appreciation tradition of the beauty, etc. We must pay attention to convention factors in complementing the public relations plan, otherwise we won't succeed in communicating. Different etiquetteand habits usually lead to misunderstanding, even frustration in communication. (3) The concept obstacle. It means the theories or ideas to guide people's actions, which belong to ideology and are accumulated, accepted and believed in under certain social circumstances. There are two kinds of common concept obstacles: One is a closed idea rejecting communication. It was rooted in feudal society, with an over 2500-year history. The other is an extreme idea destroying communication. It is commonly met in disseminating communication. (4) The psychology obstacle. It means the obstacles caused by cognition, affection, attitudes and other psychological factors. People study the psychological obstacle in an effort to understand it, know it well, take advantage of it and overcome it. (5) The organization obstacle. The concept of Organization means an open social technique system made up of many Systems. The organization obstacle in communicating is shown on the following aspects: First, too many administration levels in transmitting leading to information distortion. The more administration levels there are in transmitting, the lower fidelity rate of the information there will be. Therefore, the organization should cut down its levels and reduce the transmitting links of the information to ensure efficient and accurate communication. Second, too many segments of the organization leading to communicating disconnection. Third, the single channel caused the lack of information. Organizational barriers in this communication mainly refers to the transmission of information is basically one-way -- the situation. The importance of information transmission from the lower level to the upper level is neglected. The arrangement of the organizational structure does not consider the channels for information transmission from bottom to top, so the amount of information sent to the decision level is obviously insufficient. (6) The political obstacle. There exist different political systems, social systems, and different levels of Cold War, which hinder and limit the communication between governments of different countries. (7) The economic obstacle. Different economic conditions will affect the public on their channels, means and methods in receiving and using the information. People in different economic conditions will have different demands on information, and will accept or reject information differently. (8) The age obstacle. There are Generation Gap in old people, young people and children who have different thinking ways and experiences. Therefore different methods should be adopted while communicating with them.

Part Four Evaluation of Public Relations

It means the process to inspect and evaluate the public relations plan, implementation and effect according to the given standards relevant to promoting the popularity, credibility and harmony degree of the organization in order to pronounce judgment and put forward proposals.

I. The Purpose and Significance of Public Relations Evaluation

The purpose of public relations evaluation is to provide corresponding information according to different demands and emphases of public relations activities of the organization. Its meanings are:

(1) Public relations evaluation is an indispensable link to improve public relations work and functions as Effect Guide. (2) Public relations evaluation can strengthen the internal communication and inspire morale. It not only can make the management realize the benefits of public relations, but also make the employees know about the organization benefits and the ways to get them so that their enthusiasm is aroused and cohesive force of the organization is enhanced. (3) Public relations evaluation is a necessary premise to carry out the follow-up work. Public relations work is successive. A public relations plan must be made on the basis of the previous public relations activities and effect, otherwise the plan cannot be success.

II. The Main Contents of Public Relations Evaluation

Public relations evaluation runs through the whole process of public relations work, and each link should be evaluated. Its main contents cover: (1) Evaluating the public relations investigation. People should evaluate whether there are sufficient background materials, information, and whether the plan design, methods of the investigation, expressive way of the information and the investigation conclusion are reasonable, and the level of rationality. (2) Evaluating the plan of public relations activities. People should evaluate whether the plan is in accordance with the social law and morals, public relations target is set reasonably, the methods and procedures need adjusting, and whether the present project is feasible, etc. (3) Evaluating the implementing process and effect of the public relations plan. People should evaluate the preparations, achievement of the target and the scope and effect of dissemination. The above-mentioned contents of public relations evaluation are summarized from the perspective of the process of public relations activities. Evaluations can also be made from many other perspectives.

III. Bases of Public Relations Evaluation

(1) The coverage from the media. This includes the authority and impact of the media, coverage frequency, its quantity and quality (the quantity and proportion of the positive and negative publicity).

(2) The internal relevant materials of the organization. It covers the evaluation materials of the public relations activities from the management, shareholders and common employees, and operating and managing materials of the organization, such as statistics statements, financial statements, correspondence from the public and meeting memorandums, etc.

(3) External materials. It covers the feedbacks from the customers and relative organizations (mainly the cooperators and competitors), the attitudes of the community public and government towards the organization and their evaluation.

IV. Methods of Public Relations Evaluation

There are many methods to make the public relations evaluation. People usually use different subjects and operating ways to make evaluations by quantitative evaluation and qualitative evaluation together.

The common evaluation subjects are the public, experts, organization and PR Practitioners.

The public evaluation means to evaluate the effect of public relations activities according to the public response (some data need investigating to get). This is the most important channel of all the channels of public relations evaluation.

The expert evaluation means to invite the public relations experts to evaluate the public relations work of the organization. The experts will make valuable evaluations because of their neutral stands and rich experiences.

The organization evaluation means that the management will appoint the specific people (not the participants of the public relations activities) in the organization to evaluate the public relations work of the organization.

Self-Evaluation means that the PR Practitioners evaluate themselves.

The commonly used operating methods are comparison method and experimental method.

There are both advantages and disadvantages in the above-mentioned methods. The PR Practitioners usually adopt several methods together according to the practical needs in order to make authentic conclusion.

V. General Procedure of Public Relations Evaluation

(1) Set the Evaluation Target.

A unified evaluation target is an object of reference to examine the effect of public relations work with comparison between each other to get the result.

(2) Choose Evaluation Standard.

An appropriate evaluation standard will be in favor of evaluating and analyzing properly the public relations activities.

(3) Collect Data Widely.

The main bases of public relations evaluation are the changing information of the public inside and outside the organization since the public relations activities were carried out.

People should choose the best channels while collecting data.

(1) Evaluating the Analysis Data

People should apply reasonable evaluation methods (the choice of the evaluation methods depending on the purposes and standards of the evaluation) on comparing and analyzing the above-mentioned information to learn about the changes brought by the public relations activities, especially to check whether the projects of the activities have reached the prospected targets, and analyze the reasons why some projects haven't reached the prospected targets.

(2) Report the Evaluation Result.

Written evaluation report should be submitted to the management as their reference for the next public relations activities. People should pay attention to several points while writing the report: First, quantitative analysis and qualitative analysis should be used together; Second, the suggestions and tactics should be of operability ; Third, languages should be accurate and brief; Fourth, the conclusion should be objective and concrete.

(3) Applying the Evaluation Result.

The evaluation result of public relations activities is of great application value for the whole public relations work. Serving as a link between past and future, it can promote the efficiency of public relations work and sound public relations environment of organizations.

The application of the public relations evaluation result covers the following aspects: First, on adjusting the public relations work plan; Second, on scheming the new public relations target; Third, on improving the organization policy decision; Fourth, on improving the overall public relations work of the organization. What's more, the theoretically summarized evaluation result of public relations activities can be guide principles and operation methods of the following public relations activities. It can not only be applied on the following public relations activities, but also serve as the reference for the PR Practitioners.

Chapter Four

Image-Building of the Organization

Part One Summarization of the Organization Image

The organization image means the image and evaluation on the basis of the public's comprehensive knowledge of an organization. It is of significance for a social organization.

I. Definition and Constitution of the Organization Image

The organization image is an organic entirety, each factor of which is effective to the organization image. Each factor should make a positive role in an order to build a good organization image.

ⅰ. Definition of the Organization Image

It varies from person to person on the members' sense of identification with the organization. Yet a member's cognition to the organization is closely related to the organization image in his mind.

1. Integrity. Organizational image is the result of overall development. Take an enterprise as an example, the corporate image includes:

（1）The comprehensive factors of enterprise history, social status, economic benefits and social contribution;

（2）The personnel's quality factors such as ideology, culture, technical quality and service mode, service attitude and service quality;

(3) The management factors of product quality, product structure, management policy, operation characteristics, basic management, professional management, comprehensive management, etc.;

(4) Other factors such as technical strength, material equipment, geographical location, etc

2. Objectivity of the Organization Image. The organization image in the public's minds is the left impression after their concrete perception and cognition of the organization and the reflections in the public's minds of the organization's activities and performances. Therefore, the organization image is of distinct objectivity. A social organization should attach importance to its various activities and make efforts to do everything well so as to leave a good impression in the public's minds.

3. Relativity of the Organization Image. The organization image is affected by both the objective reference and subjective factors. Any change of the factors will effect on the organization image, so it is of relativity.

4. Stability of the Organization Image. The organization image

is the comprehensive result of its actions. Once the image

is built, it will become a metal set in some public's minds

in some circumstances both on the inside idea and on the outside

image. It won't change immediately with the different actions of the organization.

ii. Constitution of the Organization Image

The coherent image building of an organization is affected by many factors. For example, the essential factors to constitute the coherent image of an enterprise are as following.

1. The Strength Image. This is the material foundation of the enterprise. The magnificent foothold of the other factors are supported by the powerful economic strength. The factors to affect the strength image of an enterprise covers its fixed assets, total assets, flow assets, product sales and production scale, number of the employee, and advancement of the equipment, etc.

2. The Culture Image. This is the quintessence of the organization image. It is

the distinguished ideological style of the organization's production, operation and management, which takes shape on the base of the value, relying on the organization system and material system and showed as the employee's group consciousness and actions. The culture image mainly covers the organization's mission, spirit, value and its target.

3. The Talented People Image. It is the influence on the organization image from the present talented people of the organization. An organization with a galaxy of talents and orderly arrangement will do credit to the organization image. The talented people image covers the array of the talented people, their science and technology level and their management level.

4. The Brand Image. It refers to the impression left on the public by the product quality, services and logo of theorganization. The brand image is the lifeline of the organization, inferiority of which will grave damage to the organization image, consequently will threaten its survival.

5. Reputation Image. That is, the organization in the long-term business transactions and commodity exchange formed the consumers or customers to commodity producers and operators of a high level of trust. Including the organization ① whether the contract and keeping promises in the business activities. ② the courage to bear the social responsibility. ③ whether efforts should be made to do practical work for the public.

6. Competitive Image. That is, the image of the organization in the competition with the competition rules, attention to mutual cooperation, mutual understanding, equal competition. The main performance is ① whether can grasp the friction point in the competition. ② whether the competition contradiction can be handled correctly. ③ looking for opportunities for cooperation.

II. The Characteristics and Meaning of the Organization Image.

ⅰ. The Characteristics of the Organization Image

1.Objectivity

The organization image exists objectively. The image is built on the basic condition and action of the organization. People cannot evaluate the image without considering the objective performance of the organization. Yet, the organization image is embodied by the products and services of the organization, which leave certain impression on the public and reflected objectively.

2. Relative Stability

Once the organization image is built, when the relative factors stay the same, no matter its idea or image will have its mental einstellung in certain public's minds under certain circumstances. Therefore, the organization image has its stability, but it is relative rather than absolute. Otherwise, if a relative factor changes, or after a public relations activity, the organization image will change, even change radically. Therefore, an organization should try their best to gain the public's recognition and praise in order to build a good image and a relatively steady image.

3. Subjectivity

The organization image is of subjectivity, because it is the Public's opinions and perspectives towards the organization. The publics themselves are quite different. There is great variability in the public's social statuses, values, modes of thinking, cognition abilities, aesthetical standards and life experiences, etc. Therefore, different people will have different impressions and evaluations on the same organization, just as the old saying goes, "Both parties claim to be in the right. " In addition, the organization employees will build the image and spread it initiatively, permeating their own ideas, attitudes.

4.Propagation

Propagation is the bridge between the organization and the public. An organization must have the aid of propagation in building its good image in the public. The public get to know the organization image via the information from various channels. When the public get to identify with the organization image, the propagation is successful. Otherwise, if the organization image cannot meet the public's expectation, the propagation is unsuccessful. The public have selectivity in accepting information because of the great amount and diversified channels of the information. Therefore, it is very important for an organization to take seriously and make good use of the public media and other propagating means in building a good image in the public.

5. Integrality

The organization image, as an entirety, is made of complicated factors. Some factors, such as the qualities, functions, packages and brands, etc, the external images of the organization are easy to be known by the public; other factors, such as the culture, objectives and spirits, etc, the invisible images are difficult to be apperceived by the public. Yet, all the factors are interdependent and interrelated as a whole, and contribute to building the organization image. As for some organizations, they say turkey to one and buzzard to another, and lead to imperfect images. Thus, an organization should take each factor seriously in an effort to build a good image in the public rather than placing particular emphasis on one side, and neglecting the other.

ii. The Significance of Building an Organization Image

The feature of the market economy is competition, the highest level of which is the competition of organization images. The organization who has an good image will gain the support from the public, possess the market, get continuous profits and be the winner in the fierce competition. The wide significance of building a good organization image is as following.

1. The Organization Image Is an Indipensible Part of Intangible Assets.

Intangible assets, as important economic resources are significant parts of the organizational assets, existing as the form of knowledge rather than the material form. The intangible capital in the global value chain will gradually determine the fate and wealth of the enterprise,Francis Cell, director - general of the world intellectual property organization, said at the world intellectual property report 2017. It hides in the appearance, feeling, function and overall attractiveness of the products we buy, determines the success rate of products in the market, and intellectual property is the means to maintain the competitive advantage of intangible capital. The boss of the Coca Cola Company has ever said that the big banks would have come to extend credits initiatively to the company if it had been burned into ashes overnight, as they know there are still $ 3. 6 billion intangible assets in the company. Thus, it is clear that the intangible assets play more important role than the tangible assets. Natural disasters can destroy the tangible assets, but they cannot destroy the value of the tangible assets. The intangible assets are of very high value in many famous organizations of the world. Apple sells a $ 810 iphone 7, with 42 % of its sales revenue to apple, showing a high return on intangible capital in the industry. The intangible asset is so influential, because it represents the organization image, which decides the value of the intangible asset. The intangible asset is manifested in the form of the organization image. The higher cognition degree, the better reputation, the more harmonious atmosphere, the more accurate fixed position the organization has, the greater value and value added ratio the intangible asset will be of.

Toyota Motor Corporation has continuously perfected its organization image to sustain and protect its intangible asset. When the maintenance center of Toyota Motor Corporation gets the maintenance telephone call from the customer, a worker will be assigned to drive a car in good condition to the customer's. He will leave the car with the customer for daily use, and drive the broken car away for maintenance. After maintenance, the car will be refueled full and returned to the customer. It is the thought to serve for the customer heart and soul that multiplies the value of Toyota's intangible asset. Therefore, an organization must attach importance to its image to develop and keep up its intangible asset continuously.

Part Two Organization Images Building

I. Classification of Organization Images

We should get to learn the organization image from different angles because of its multiple levels and dimensions.

1. An Particular Image and a General Image in Terms of The Contents of the Organization Image

A particular image means an image left in the public on a particular aspect or several aspects, or the image left in some people by the organization. For an example, an enterprise with good services will leave with some customers the image of the First-Rate Service Enterprise; a charity donation of an enterprise will leave with the public the image of the philanthropic enterprise. The particular image is very important for the enterprise, for it is impossible for the public to know an organization all-around. An organization often leaves a particular image with the public, and some people often support an organization due to the particular image. For example, song fans support some star singers, and ball-game fans support some star players. Therefore, the particular image is the point to break through for the organization to improve its image.

A general image means the total image having been contributed to by all the factors and the total of all the images.

2. A True Image and a False Image in Terms of the Authenticity of the Organization Image

A true image means the image in accordance with the physical truth of an organization. A false image means the image with inconformity to the physical truth of an organization. There are many reasons for the false image to take shape, such as distortion in propagation, or subjectivity and one-sidedness of the public assessment. It should be illustrated that the true image is not good for certain, yet the false image is not bad for certain. Some good images take shape by the false data submitted to the superior authorities from some enterprises. Of course, such kind of good images are false. An organization should be surely inspired to build a true and good image instead of a false and bad one. A true image is good for an organization to gain the public understanding and trust and strengthen the drive to build a good image.

3. A Tangible Image and an Intangible Image in Terms of the Visibility of the Organization Image

A tangible image means the organization image that can be felt by the sense organs of the public including the product images, building images, mental attitudes of the employees, substantial images, etc. An intangible image means the sense images that take shape by the abstract and logic thinking of the public. Although such kind of images are invisible, they are the highest level and nearly the nature of the organization image. The intangible image is often more valuable than the tangible image for an enterprise.

To take MacDonald, Coca-Cola and Sony as examples, their intangible assets, such as the credits, are much more valuable than their tangible assets, such as their machinery equipments and workshops.

4. An Actual Image and a Self-Expected Image in Terms of the Reality of the Organization Image

The actual image of an organization is the image generally accepted by the public, which is the public cognition and assessment on the organization. The organization's history, founders, current leaders, management and operation levels, etc are the main factors contributed to the actual image of the organization. The self-expected image is also called the ideal image of the organization, which means the expected image to be built in the public. It is the target set by the organization itself and the direction for itself to strive towards.

5. An Internal Image and an External Image in Terms of the Formation of the Organization Image

The internal image of an organization means its internal employees attitudes to the organization and judgement on the organization. The external image of an organization means its external public attitudes to the organization and judgement on the organization. Generally speaking, the internal image of an organization is the base of its external image. If the internal employees have a good cognition and a positive assessment on the organization, the external public will have a good impression on the organization. Therefore, an organization should pay more attention to its relationships with the internal public to build a good internal image.

II. The Principles and Methods of Building an Organization Image

i. The Principles of Building an Organization Image

The principles are the guiding thoughts to comply with when an organization makes and implements its image strategy, which are the behavior codes in building the organization image.

1. The Principle Based on Quality

The product image of an organization is crucial to building a good organization

Chapter Four
Image-Building of the Organization

image. In addition to the unique trademark, an organization must rely on its good quality, reasonable price and considerate service to gain the public trust. Quality is the lifeline of an organization, is the key to building a good organization image.

For example, in order to talent shows itself in the peer competition, Singapore Airlines formulated a series of standards of service and require all staff strictly enforce: (1) treating of all the passengers equally with care and courtesy, to impress all passengers in small service details. (2) to modify other airlines' practice that passengers cannot get the seat number when they are booking tickets, only before boarding, they can get the boarding card with the seat number at the airport. Using the computer booking system all over the world, passengers can get the seat number on the plane at the same time when booking any flight ticket in any country. (3) let each of the crew remember all the names of the passengers in advance ,passengers only need to be attached to the seat number on the boarding card, the crew in the cabin door,and directly call the passages name ,guiding passengers to condemnation, the passengers are respected by attention, deepened to the company impression. Improved the image of the organization. (4) in order to reduce the fatigue of passengers during the intercontinental flight, the flight attendants sent a pair of nylon soft shoe covers and sunshading glasses to each passenger for passengers to rest. Also sent a beautifully printed menu above, in English, French and German languages with three full meal dishes, other details of the service is thoughtful and comprehensive. (5) when passengers finish their pleasant trip, the company prepares a package of beautifully decorated toilets for each passenger, including toothbrushes, toothpaste, soap, combs and two bottles of cosmetics, which are printed with Singapore Airlines logo. If the passengers want to write letters to their friends, they can be mailed free of charge to all over the world by Singapore Airlines; If passengers fill in a form with their name and address, the information will be put in the company's computer, and a number of days later, the company will send the ten or twenty passenger coupon within a year on the coupon purchase priority ticket, if baggage passengers can not pay, sometimes also will send passengers some Singapore Department Store coupons. Through a series of active public relations service measures, Singapore Airlines has won a reputation on international routes, won customers, and is far ahead in the fierce international competition.

2. The Principle of Regarding Reputation as Life

The reputation of an organization is the core index and the life of its good image. An enterprise or a product with good reputation will build a firm image base in the hearts of customers. A wise entrepreneur would rather suffer loss in his finance than his organization reputation, which is the life and irreplaceable wealth of the organization. Any organization should insist on the Reputation Above All principle in building its good image.

The Boeing 747, a British Airways flight 008, was ready to fly from London to Tokyo, Japan, and delayed takeoff for 20 hours. In order not to delay passengers waiting for this flight back to London in Tokyo, British Airways helped them to transfer to other airlines in time. 190 passengers happily accepted the British Airways arrangement to fly to London by other companies. But one of the old Japanese ladies, Otake Xiuko, said nothing would change her to take other flights, she just want to take flight 008. Out of credit, No. 008, which was originally planned to have another flight arrangement, had to fly back to London as soon as it arrived in Tokyo. In this way, only one passenger was carried on flight 008 from Tokyo to London, with a range of 13000 kilometers. Otake Xiuko enjoyed 353 seats on the machine, as well as the thoughtful service of 6 crew and 15 attendants. It is estimated that the flight has lost at least about $100 thousand in the British Airways. On the surface, British Airways is really a big loss, but from the deep point of view, the British Airways has changed a good organization image that money is hard to buy.

3. The Principle of Laying Stress on the Overall Situation

It is an all-round operation for an organization to build a good image, which depends on the entire characteristics. The so-called entirety mainly covers four aspects: The first is the all-round target of the organization image; the second is the organization related with various aspects; the third is the image building relying on all the staff's efforts; the fourth is the various methods applied in building the good image. Therefore, an organization must lay stress on the overall situation and make a unified public relations policy to coordinate its internal activities in order to get the support from all its departments and their co-operations when the organization launches any public relations activity in society.

4. The Principle of Laying Stress on Propagation

The action, strength and endeavor of an organization are the sources of its good image, but they are not enough. An organization must lay stress on effective propagation in its public relations activities. It means the organization must publicize itself through proper channels and make advantage of the channels to leave its true and good image with the public. Only by focusing on the spread of organization, public relations will be better and better, the organization image will be more vivid.

ii. The Methods of Organization Image Building

1. Planning the Organization Image

Planning the organization image includes the following three stages, namely investigating the current image, designing the image framework and arguing the image scheme.

2. Analyzing the Elements of the Organization Image

Different organizations will meet the social demands on different aspects and levels, so the public will have different impressions and assessments on different organizations. Therefore, the organization should pay attention to the analysis of its own image elements, and focus on the shaping of image elements. Here only take the organization as an example, mainly introduces the following several elements:

(1) The Product Image

The product image means the organization image reflected from the products or services of the organization. It is the basic factor constituting the organization image. It is the products that through which the public get to know the organization and the organization have its public. In terms of the modern product image, we have tangible product images including quality, function, packages, and trademarks, etc, and intangible service images including the hotel services, pre-sales, in-sales and after-sales services of the products, etc. The quality image is the most important of all, for quality is the highest standard for users to assess an organization, and it is the life of the enterprise.

(2) The Operation Image

The operation image is the image expressed through the operation and management activities of an organization. It reflected in a series of operation and management activities, such as the operation style, management efficiency, personnel system, and employment condition, etc.

(3) The Staff Image

The staff are the main body of an organization. The staff image is the image expressed through the employees' conducts, qualities, abilities, and attitudes, etc. It covers the images of the organization controllers, public relations practitioners and typical figures who are all the embodiment of the organization image. Therefore, it is an important aspect of the image building project to build up a team of high-quality leaders and employees.

(4) The Environment image

The environment image is the image expressed through the facilities of an organization and its environment. It functions as settings and decorations of the organization, and constitutes the hardware of the organization image. The environment image concludes the location, building complex, decorations, showcase arrangements and product display, etc, which constitute part of the modern office civilization, production civilization and commerce civilization.

(5) The Culture Image

The culture image is the image expressed through a series of culture factors of an organization, which constitutes the software of the organization image. It includes the values, managing philosophy, historical tradition, ethics, etiquette, slogans, flags, dresses and various propaganda materials, etc, of which the values and managing philosophy are the core of the culture image and play a guiding and decisive role.

(6) The Identity Image

The identity image is an image displayed by the organization through the logo and recognition system, which can help the public to identify and remember the image of the organization. It includes organization name, product brand, trademark, micro - record, advertisement, subject word, typical music, font, color, etc. In addition, there are some elements, such as organizational strength, management level, efficiency, property, credit records, business policies, tax status, peer competition, acceptance of supervision, community relations and so on.

3. The Organization Image Building

(1) The Staff Image Building

The staff image is expressed in professional ethnics, professional training, cultural accomplishment, manners and speech and service attitudes of the employees. It is the representative, exhibition and embodiment of personalization of the organization image.

The main ways to build the staff image are: First, to improve the employees' overall qualities and make them realize the importance and methods of image building; Second, to foster the employees to devote to work and connect their future with the organization development closely. Each member should care for the operation, benefits and reputation of the organization; Third, to relate the employees' contributions with their remunerations and encourage them to make efforts and excel in work; Fourth, to encourage the employees to develop noble sentiments, entrepreneurial spirits and right values to make the organization full of vitality.

(2) The Leadership Image Building

The leadership image is the impressions left with the internal employees and external public by the political thought levels, knowledge structure, working experience, decisive capabilities and opening and pioneering spirits of the organization leaders.

The main ways to build the leadership image are: First, to build up a reasonable leadership team made up of the leaders with multi-structured knowledge and reasonable-structured age; Second, to apply the policy of "Only Using the Talented"; Third, to feed back the working performance in time, to examine the leader achievements and conducts and to commend the excellent leaders; Fourth, to foster the leaders' service consciousness and make them cognize their own roles and responsibilities.

(3) The Product Image Building

The target of building the product image is to build the image with the internal quality agreed with the external

quality and to meet the customers' demands.

The major ways to build the product image are as following:

a. To think highly of the product design and to use new thinking, technology and material to develop unique products.

b. To supervise quality seriously and stipulate the quality standards and targets clearly to ensure the best quality of the products.

c. To lay stress on the image building of the product surface to meet the aesthetic demands in appearances, colors, packages and decorations of the products.

d. To make the best of propagating means to spread products in popularity. Let more public understand of products, use products, laying a good foundation for improving the reputation of products, brand strategy

(4) The Brand Image Building

A brand is a part of a product and a combination of a name, a term, a pattern and a logo, which are different from the other sellers' products. It is called a trademark after registration and an intangible wealth with not only economic value but also credit value.

The major ways to build the brand image are as following:

a. To raise the brand awareness.

b. To make a strategy and centralize the human, financial and material resources of the organization to build the brand.

c. To make persistent efforts from cultivation of the brand to its maintenance.

d. To carry out a systematical engineering of the brand, laying stress on the external image, scheming, and internal image building.

(5) The Service Image Building

Service image refers to the service attitude, service mode, service quality, service level and the impression formed by the consumers and the public to the organization. With the development of society, people are paying more and more attention to the service while enjoying the products. The goal of service image building is to establish a service attitude sincerity, enthusiasm, service skills skilled, superb, service process timely, fast, service project perfect, meticulous, service style novel, unique image.

The major ways to build the service image are as following:

a. To raise the first-rate service consciousness, which requires the employees of an organization to regard all their work and activities as the opportunities to serve for the public.

b. To provide perfect service facilities and conditions to meet the material requirements of the first-rate service.

c. To make considerate service projects and contents.

(6) The Competition Image Building

Only the organization which is brave to compete and good at competition can survive and develop in the economic market. The target to build the competition image is to build the image of the organization which can keep to the competition rules and focus on mutual cooperation, mutual understanding and equal competition.

The important ways to build the competition image are as following:

a. To make certain what is the focus of competition. Currently, the focus of competition lies in price, cooperation, advertisements, trademarks and technology, etc.

b. To deal with the contradictions in competition properly. It is normal to have contradictions in competition with people in the same trade and competitors, but the key is how to keep calm and deal with the contradictions cautiously.

c. To seek for the cooperation opportunities in competition. On one hand, someone may be your competitor, on the other hand, he may be your cooperation partner.

(7) The Credit Image Building

The credit image is the public trust and assessment on the work effectiveness, product qualities, technology levels, service attitudes, personnel qualities and the overall strength of the organization, which come from the social responsibilities of the organization. The target of the credit image building is to make the organization trustworthy, responsible for the pubic and brave to shoulder the social responsibilities.

The major ways to build the credit image are as following:

a. To comply with contracts and keep words in production and operation and to observe the professional ethics.

b. To shoulder the social responsibilities bravely.

c. To try to do something concrete for the public, maintain the consumers' legitimate rights and interests and provide the public with material and spiritual assistance.

(8) The Environment Image Building

The environment image means various environments in the life, production, work and operation of the organization. For the public, the organization image is a window for them to know and identify the organization image; For the employees, the organization image is the office environment and living environment; For the organization itself, the organization image means its spirituality and management level.

The target of the environment image building is to make a beautiful and decent, clean and orderly environment with unique character.

The major ways to build the environment image are: First, try to beautify the environment, which covers the work in five aspects: ① Beautify and green the courtyard and factory; ② Clean the office and workshop and make them in order; ③ Design the sculptures and decorations reasonably ④ Design the building complex coordinately and beautifully in style and character; ⑤ Treat the sewage, waste gas and sediments effectively. Second, underline the specific character of environment. The environment of the organization should be unique and specific, and embody the image character both in layout and decorations.

Chapter Five

Public Relations Etiquette

Part One The Outline of Public Relations Etiquette

Etiquette refers to behavior norms and codes of conduct that people should abide by in life and work. It reflects a person's cultural rearing, and is a etiquette and ritual established by people in communication. Public relations etiquette mean the necessary etiquette and rules of the PR Practitioners in the public occasions, and their necessary courteous receptions and respects for the public. As techniques of propagation and communications, public relations etiquette are the etiquette and rites for the PR Practitioners to follow in the public relations communications. The research targets of public relations etiquette include self-esteem and other-respect of organizations and skills of etiquette-application.

I. The Important Role of etiquette in the Public Relations

It is not only good for the organizations to communicate with the public, but also good for them to build good images to follow etiquette in the public relations. It can serve as the following three roles.

1. "Passport". Generally speaking, the organization representatives and PR Practitioners who understand and follow the etiquette are welcomed by the public, so the etiquette can work as passports and be good for them to communicate with the public and finish the public relations tasks smoothly.

2. "Lubricant". Etiquette can serve as beautiful words, dress, and postures to build up a friendship bridge between the organizations and the public and be good for further communications.

3. "Cornerstones". etiquette of the PR Practitioners can reflect not only the individual's quality, but also the organization's overall image, and make the public be pleased to contact with the organization.

II. Principles in Etiquette

Etiquette reflect not only the individual's self-esteem, morality and education, but also the respect to the partner in contact.

There are four principles in etiquette: the Respect Principle, Moderate Principle, Honest Principle and Self-Disciplined Principle, of which the Respect Principle is the most important and fundamental.

1. The Respect Principle (also called the Public-Respect Principle). First, public-respect means to respect the counterpart's individuality, status and position. Only when you consider and solve the problems in the counterpart's position can you be easily understood and supported by the public. Second, public-respect means to respect the counterpart's points of view and requirements, and try to satisfy him. Even though you have different opinions, you should try to explain honestly and ask for his understanding. Last, public-respect means equal treatment, mutual benefits and courtesy demands reciprocity.

2. The Moderate Principle. It means the two parties should follow certain codes and customs to show the etiquette in socialization and try to be natural and moderate. We should show our etiquette in accordance with specific conditions in the public relations activities.

3. The Honest Principle. It means to be honest in the public relations socialization with undivided attention on the association and consideration from the counterpart's position.

4. The Self-Disciplined Principle. It means the two parties in the public relations socializations should be strict with himself and lenient towards the counterpart, and try

to treat the counterpart tolerantly.

Ⅲ. Some Common etiquette in Public Relations. Etiquette means to indicate respect, greeting and wish to the counterpart in socialization. It is the specific regulation of politeness in words, behaviors and manners. Etiquette reflects a person's inside beauty. Its essence is respect to others. The following are some common etiquette of public relations.

ⅰ. The Etiquette of Appellation

Appellation is the first etiquette while meeting each other in public relations socialization. We should pay attention to three points: First, the words should be appropriate for the counterpart's sex, age, status, position, nationality, culture and other backgrounds. Second, the tone of speech should be modest. Third, the voice should be beautiful. Fourth, we should dress each other respectfully, and dress ourselves modestly. We can call nicknames if we have close relationships with each other.

ⅱ. The Etiquette of Introduction

Introduction is the basic way to know each other in the public relations, including self-introduction and introducing others.

1. Self-introduction. There three points to pay attention to: First, the words should be polite and moderate, modest and comfortable. Second, we should introduce clearly our personal data in brief works. We should use body languages and assistant language properly. Third, extend your respect and modest to end your self-introduction.

2. Introducing others. There are four basic etiquettes: First, Pay attention to the introduced personal data, and introduce them in order (hosts after guests, men after women, oneself after others). Second, we should use body language and assistant language politely and properly. Third, we should choose moderate information in introduction to start the common topic. Fourth, be careful to avoid individual privacy in introduction.

ⅲ. The Etiquette of Compliment

Another important etiquette while meeting is compliment. There are many ways to express compliment, such as nodding, smiling, waving and so on. We should pay attention to the following two points:

1. Being moderate. It is appropriate to gesture or nod to your friends in the public occasion, while you shouldn't call their names loudly. Men should behave as gentlemen and be considerate in front of ladies.

2.Following Local Customs. Customs vary from country to country. Wherever you are, you should follow the local customs. So you should learn about local customs in different places.

ⅳ. The Etiquette in Conversation

1. Being concentrated. You should listen carefully keep eye contact to show your concentration on the conversation and say some simple words to keep the conversation going.

2.Using civilized posture. 'You shouldn't look around in conversation. You should show your amiableness and sincerity in conversation.

3. No interrupting. It is impolite to interrupt others in conversation. Therefore, you should say sorry and ask for permission, then cut in with your words if necessary.

4. Repetition avoidance. You shouldn't repeat the same topic in the public relations conversation. You should try to seek for the common interested topic to keep the conversation going .

5. The contents choice. Although there are a wide range of contents in conversation, they should be theme-focused. If the counterpart says something impropriety, you should try to change the topic skillfully, and get down to your business intentionally.

6. Politeness. You should say hello and ask for permission if you want to be involved in the others' conversation. You should greet him if someone wants to be involved in your conversation. Whoever you are talking to, you should behave politely in the public relations socialization.

7. Time management. The conversation for the first meeting shouldn't be long. When someone is busy with his work, you should make a long story short. If you visit someone in the evening, you should respect his habits and private time, and try to have s short conversation.

8. Distance keeping. It means the psychology and space distance. The two parties in the public relations socialization represent specific organizations, each has his own

interests. It is crucial for them to keep distance to have a mutual-benefit conversation and promote mutual development.

V . etiquette in a banquet

A banquet is a common public relations activity organized carefully for welcoming, thanking, congratulating and contacting. The etiquette in a banquet are not only the regular customs but also the embodiment of individuals' qualities and self-cultivation.

1. The host's etiquette. The basic etiquette during the banquet are as following:

(1) Ask the guests to be seated in order; (2) Greet the guests and start the meal; (3) Propose a toast; (4) Entertain the quests carefully, introducing the dishes and persuading the quests to drink properly, etc; (5) Ask the guests to have a rest in the parlour to drink some tea or eat some fruit after the meal.

2. The guest's etiquette. (1) Be punctual for the banquet; (2) Pay attention to your dress and appearance; (3) Greet the host decently; (4) Do as your host wishes.

3. Etiquette while having the meal.

(1) Please take the seat or leave from the left of the chair; Please don't use your hands to support your chin or put your arms on the table; Please don't clean tableware with napkins or play with the tableware.

(2) The guest should stop eating and talking, and clap your hands duly when the host proposes a toast.

(3) Please wait a moment when the soup is hot; Please don't make any sound while eating, or talk to others with food in your mouth; Please leave for coughing or spitting, or cover with a handkerchief and turn outside.

(4) You shouldn't loose your belt or tie, or roll up sleeves, or take off clothes during the meal.

(5) You shouldn't just pick up your favorite dishes and look unhappy with other dishes.

(6) You should taste slowly while drinking and limit to 1/3 your capacity for drinking ; You shouldn't smoke while drinking; You should lower your glass to your host's while proposing a toast.

(7) You should be calmed down and handle properly when something unexpected happened during the meal.

(8) You should put your napkin on your chair if you leave midway, and fold up your napkin and put it on the right of your dish when the meal is over.

(9) You should ask the ladies and the elder to take first while eating fruit or drinking tea in the parlour.

(10) The guest should thank the host sincerely for his hospitality while saying goodbye to each other; The host should thank the guest for his coming; The guest should ask the host to stay and shake hands saying goodbye when the host sends the guest out.

ⅵ. Etiquette in Visit

In addition to meetings, banquets, visit is a common and convenient way for organizations to contact each other. The most important etiquette in visit is to show your politeness and respect.

1. Being polite and considerate. You should ask for the host's permission before your visit, make clear the appropriate time, inform the number of visitors; Be punctual for the visit; Greet the host and his family members politely.

(1) Dress decently and first put away your glasses, hats, gloves, scarfs, etc while entering the room.

(2) Pay attention to your sitting position.

(3) Ask for the host and ladies' permission before smoking, and ask them to do the first.

(4) Please don't visit the host's yard and bedroom without permission; Don't touch the host's books and furnishings while being showed around.

(5) You shouldn't kick the host's cats, dogs and other pets.

2. You shouldn't arrange too many contents in your visit. You shouldn't prolong your visit to settle some problems unsolved in negotiation, for it's simply a visit to show your politeness.

3. You should pay a visit at the host's convenience. 10 a. m. -4 p. m. is the best time.

ⅶ. etiquettein Reception

Reception is a very important activity in public relations. It decides the public first impression on the organization, further to affect its reputation and image whether the reception is warm, polite and considerate. Here are the tips for reception:

1. Prepare carefully. The PR Practitioners should get themselves ready in consciousness, appearance, dress and behavior; Beautify the environment to receive the guests sincerely and warmly.

2. Welcome sincerely. You should first greet the visitors warmly, ask them to be seated, drink tea, then ask them in detail the information such as the names, status, purposes and demands, etc. Then you should decide and adjust the reception standards, procedures and ways quickly. Different visitors need different counterparts to receive. The daily reception work should be done accordingly and sincerely.

3. Serve considerately. It means to provide convenience for the visitors. Especially for the visitors or representatives from afar, you should provide accommodations and food, arrange visits and workshops, help them buy return tickets, etc, in an effort to help them finish tasks and make them feel easy at home.

Ⅳ. Etiquette in Public Relations Concerning Foreign Affairs

ⅰ. Etiquette in Meeting and Seeing off in the Contacts Concerning Foreign Affairs

1. You should prepare considerately before the international public arrival. Try to have a grasp of the situation and get prepared, then you won't feel sorry.

2. Confirm the reception standard and greeting order before international conferences. According to the customs, people follow the reciprocity principle. In multi-national contacts, people arrange the order according to the first letters of their English names of each country, or their arrival priority. National flags are usually hanged for grand situations of international public relations activities.

3. While meeting, the superior of the host should shake hands with guests first, and introduce his team members one by one; The greeters should greet guests, nod, smile and shake hands to show their respects.

4. The host should arrange to present flowers to the guest, if the visitor is a VIP. A lovely child or a vigorous girl is usually chosen to be the presenter. You should take

customs, taboos and flower languages in different countries into consideration before presenting flowers.

5. The greeters, especially the head of them, should accompany the guests to their rest places. If there is an escort, the head should introduce them to the guests after a short rest. Introduce the schedules and living environment, and help the guests solve temporary problems.

6. After the international public relations activities, the hose should arrange to buy the guests their return tickets, and see them off.

ii. Etiquette in the Banquets Concerning Foreign Affairs

1. Etiquette in Chinese Food (referring to the above-mentioned etiquette in banquets)

(1) Avoid as taboo. For example, avoid the number "13" when you invite westerners for dinner; the dinner should be arranged after sunset when you invite the Islamic guests during Ramadan. (2) Dress up to show your attention to the social activity. (3) The host should suit the convenience of guests. Just introduce the names and features of dishes rather than persuading them to eat or drink more.

2. Basic etiquettein Western Food

(1) The seat order. The woman should be asked to sit on the right on the man for the two; and in the middle of the two men for the three; the seat near the wall should be left for the senior for two men or women. The seats should be arranged between men and women. The male guest of honor should be seated on the right of the hostess, and his madam on the right of the host. Follow the host's action, unfold your napkin, then fold it to2/3 and lay on your lap; put your napkin on your chair before your leave for something temporary.

(2) How to use your tableware. The tableware should be taken from outside to inside, with the knife in the right hand, and the fork in the left. If you want to have a rest, then put your knife and fork in the pattern of "八", or 3:40 hand clock on your plate; after the mean, they should be put in the pattern of 4:00 hand clock on the plate, with the napkin folded in square on the right of the plate. Generally, only when you take soup, can you use spoon; and use spoon for assistance when you take noodles. You

shouldn't play with your knife and fork while speaking.

(3) Rules and Principles for Business Meals

Firstly, dress decently. Suits and shoes should be tidy and clean, with ties for men in formal occasions. Ladies should wear dresses and high heels. Casual clothes are not suitable for any formal occasion. Secondly, "Ladies first. " Ladies should be seated first and have a taste first. Thirdly, be seated elegantly. You should take a seat from the left, with 10 cm between your body and the table. Be seated straight, with your back leaning against your chair back to show your adaptability and self-confidence. Men should be seated with knees apart slightly and hands on the legs or the chair arms. Ladies should be seated with knees holding together and hands on the thighs, or with crossed legs and hands between the waist and thighs, or on one chair arm. Fourthly, the guests should stop eating and respond with applause when the host toasts the guests. Fifthly, rules for drinking. Strong alcohol should not be taken; drinking amount should be controlled to 1/3 of your daily drink; please don't smoke or shake glasses while drinking. Hold the glass with your thumb, index finger, and middle finger holding the leg of the glass, and the small finger under the bottom.

Normally, people drink red-grape wine with cold dishes, white-grape wine with fish, eggs and roast meat. Generally, the host will toast the guests in order of importance; the younger and inferior should lean their bodies to the older and superior, with glasses lower to the latters' to show their politeness and respect.

iii. Gifts in Public Relations Activities Concerning Foreign Affairs.

Giving gifts is very common in socialization. Giving gifts in public relations is to show your friendliness, such as best wishes, congratulations, miss, care, encouragement, appreciation, etc. Here are the tips for giving gifts:

1. Select carefully. Please select gifts according to the interest of the recipient as well as the theme in your public relations contacts. Try to avoid the taboos of the recipients according to their nationalities and customs, for people in different countries and regions have different understanding of animals, plants, flowers and colors, etc, and have different taboos.

2. Be innovative and practical. The gifts should be beautiful, innovative and

practical. What matters more is the signification of the gift than the its cost.

3. Respond politely. The recipient should open the gift in front of the giver and say "Great", "Beautiful", "Very nice", "It is my favorite. Thank you very much. " to show your politeness and sincere appreciation, no matter what kind of the gift is.

Part Two Social Skills in Public Relations

Ⅰ. The Outline of Personal Interaction

ⅰ. The Significance of Personal Interaction in Public Relations

Interaction is also called "communication" or "informational communication". It means the process to contact each other, exchange information and communicate ideas between people in socializing activities. It is the process to transfer information from one person to another. The significance of personal interaction in public relations are as following:

1. To spreading information. One of the most important functions of public relations is to propagate and communicate. A good interpersonal relationship will build up the PR Practitioner and his organization's reputation and image, which good for natural communication between the two parties.

2. To pave the road and bridge. With further interactions between the PR Practitioners of the organizations, the two parties will understand each other better and increase their credibility, which will pave the road and bridge for their future personal interactions and further development.

3. To build up image. A good image of an organization is intangible wealth. The PR Practitioners attitudes, eloquence, appearance, knowledge, morals and professional levels, etc will leave a deep impression on the counterpart in interactions between both individuals and organizations in the public relations, which will affect the entire image of the organization itself.

4. To cohesion strength. "Internal unity, external development" is a target of

public relations activity. If an organization has both internal and external harmonious interpersonal relationships, all will be of one mind, then anything will be easy to deal with.

ii. The Factors Effecting Personal Interactions

People have some relationships with others in one way or another. There are many factors to affect personal interactions.

1. Selectivity

(1) In terms of subjectivity, demands and interests of individuals are very important factors to affect theirs selectivity in personal interaction, according to which they will make "standards" to select their counterparts. "Things of a kind come together. People of a mind fall into the same group"; in addition, the moods and emotions of the PR Practitioners will also affect their choice.

(2) In terms of the counterparts, whether they are attractive is also an important factor to affect selectivity in personal interactions. If a person is of good professional skills and morals, it is easy to satisfy the counterpart's demand for personal interactions; if a person is attractive and graceful bearing, he is easy to be the choice of others to contact with.

2. Effectiveness

(1) "The effect of the first reason", namely "the first impression", usually affects personal interactions. The more specific and truer data you get from the counterpart at first meeting, the more likely you are to further your relationship.

(2) "The effect of close reason", namely "the similar terms", means the two parties have the same or similar situations in time and space, and they are likely to further their personal interactions. For example, relatives, friends, town fellows, colleagues, same-aged people, people sharing the same interests, habits, etc are pleased to talk with each other.

3. First Entry

First entry means that people tend to judge the counterpart and deal with affairs according to their experience from previous interpersonal relations.

4. Entirety

It is a process for people to get to know each other, from the first impressions to the whole recognitions, from the superficial appearances, dresses and adornments and behaviors, to the inside qualifications and professional skills. Thus PR Practitioners shouldn't judge others hurriedly and try to avoid holding a part as the whole.

iii. Rules and Principles to Follow in Personal Interactions

1. To respect others. As the old say goes, "You honor me a foot, I will in return honor you ten feet", people not only hope but also need to be respected. Anyone likes to communicate with the one who respects others.

2. To observe disciplines and obey laws. You must observe disciplines and obey laws in personal interactions. Your speeches and behaviors shouldn't break the laws or violate social morals.

3. To treat others equally and sincerely. You should treat others equally and sincerely, no matter he is poor or rich, beautiful or ugly. You shouldn't judge a person by his appearance, dress or social status.

4. To keep your commitments. As an old saying says "Faith moves mountains", it is very important to keep your commitments. Any opportunity won't be given to a person or an organization who usually breaks his promise. Therefore, you should keep your promise and try to meet others' demands in personal interactions. If you are not sure about something, you should ask for further discussion later; if you are incapable of something, you should say sorry and decline others politely.

iv. Morbid Mentality in Personal Interactions

1. Self-contempt mentality. This kind of person will look down upon himself and lack of confidence, so he cannot bring his advantages and merits into play. Self-contempt person will have no his own idea, just listen to others and chime in with others.

2. Coward mentality. Such kind of person is introverted, usually lack of experience. It is hard for a coward to achieve his goal, and the coward psychology will be the rope to bind his mind and behavior.

3. Suspicious and jealous mentality. This kind of person tends to doubt others, think others untrustworthy. He is likely to think they are speaking ill of him whenever he sees others talking, so he usually gets into trouble. Such psychology will hurt oneself

as well as others.

4. Negative mentality. This kind of person usually talks back to show his doing something unconventionally. He will argue for the sake of arguing no matter what others say. He tends to confuse what is right or wrong, true or false, thus easily disgusts others.

5. Exclusive mentality. This kind of person likes to do something within his own scope and refuse to expand his mind. 6. Game-playing mentality. Such kind of person likes to join in the fun on occasion, change about and talks through his hat, so it is hard for him to make sincere friends.

7. Greedy mentality. This kind of person makes friends just in order to "use the other for his own ends, so he usually makes the friends who are useful for him and who can bring him benefits. The person like that usually "burns the bridge after crossing it" and likes to gain extra advantage by unfair means, so he is easy to get damaged in his own personality.

8. Unconcerned mentality. This kind of person is unconcerned about anything or anyone unrelated with himself. He usually speaks in harsh words, with proud and aloof attitudes, so that he keeps others away from him and loses more friends.

Ⅴ. The Methods to Conquer the Morbid Mentality in Personal Interactions

1. Please conquer the self-contempt mentality, recognize and appraise yourself correctly.

2. Keep positive spirits of being "dare to try not afraid of failure".

3. Adjust your mood and discard the depressed mood.

4. Choose a moment and go easy.

5. Choose a familiar time, place and content to talk about.

6. Discard the "self-protection" mentality and take part in social activities actively.

7. Open your mind, clear up your prejudice and associate with others freely.

8. Respond others' words in time and praise their achievements.

9. Do more and talk less; go straight to the heart of the matter at the critical moment.

10.Keep modest and hopeful.

11. Work dependably and play the role happily behind the scene.

12. Dress yourself up suitably and raise your voice.

ⅵ. Basic Social Skills of Public Relations

1. Keep stable. A PR Practitioner should try to keep stable in his speech and deportment, coherent in his conducts. He should neither have many "faces" nor be in consistence in his words in public relations occasions.

2. Be together with the organization. A PR Practitioner represents an organization, so he should have the faith to "share the same fate" with the organization in his speech and deportment.

3. Seeking for identical. You should try to look for common ground with the counterpart and narrow the distance between each other.

4. Self-training. A PR Practitioner should teach himself from all aspects to improve his social skills, and show himself at appropriate time to attract the public.

Chapter Six
Graduates' Public Relations Image Building

Part One Graduates' Public Relations Image Building

Ⅰ. Meaning of Public Relations Image Building

ⅰ. Image

Image itself means shape and appearance including both the external image and internal characteristics, such as disposition. A person's image includes his or her external images, such as his or her appearance, posture, conducts and so on, and his or her rich internal images, such as his or her disposition, accomplishment, bearing, nature, language emotion and so on, which constitute the parts of a person's integral image. What we are discussing about is the integral image including both the external and internal images.

With popularization of public relations, the word "image" has been widely used in various propagating media. We not only talk about a person's or a group's image, but also the image of an enterprise, an organization, a government, a brand, or a trademark and so on. "Image" is as increasingly popular as "public relations". As the pillars of society, graduates should try their best to build good images.

ⅱ. Image Building

A person's look, stature and skin color are inborn, but his or her appearance, bearing, conducts, attitudes, dresses, emotions and abilities are acquired and can be refined. People can improve their integral images by learning, training and cultivating, the course of which is image building which is imperceptible.

With development of society, people keep on beautifying their life, but first they should beautify their self-images. The aim of public relations etiquetteis to build good images of graduates, which help increase their social attractions and contribute to their success.

iii. Public Relations Image Building

The public relations image means the integral impression left on the social public by an individual, a group or an organization in public relations activities; or the integral assessment, viewpoint or attitude towards an individual, a group or an organization in public relations activities. The public relations image of a graduate means the integral impression left on the social public by a graduate individual or group in public occasions, social contacts or public relations activities. The public relations image of a graduate is the focus of the public concern.

Graduate images are actually influenced by their external performance and behaviors. The public have their ideal images of graduates in their minds, namely the images of knowledge, civilization, sense of responsibility and justice, vitality, their best behavior, and wide popularity of the public. The improvement from the actual images to the ideal images is the process of image building.

II. Graduates Should Pay Attention to the Public Relations Image Building

i. Urgency of Graduates' Public Relations Image Building

First, Graduates will face new competition, challenges, tests and opportunities of the 21st century. How to participate in the competition, address the challenges, stand the tests, seize the opportunities and promote themselves with good images are serious problems for them to consider carefully. How to build good public relations images has been a heated topic on campus in universities and has been listed in the agenda of higher education. Some graduates couldn't conduct themselves properly on public occasions so that their images have been damaged in the latest few years. Recently, many universities have launched various activities on self-cultivation and image building aiming to call on the graduates to realize the importance and urgency of public relations image building. From the " self - cultivation" education activities carried out by Peking university students, to the university of Shanghai, Hubei institute of nationalities and other universities that carry out the discussion of college students image which to show that college students should pay attention to the image of public relations has been urgent.

Second, college students are a special group. What they do and what they say will be tagged by social personages, affecting the social evaluation of college students. Third, for college students collectively, good college students' image is intangible wealth, invisible call, can form strong cohesion, attract them together, form collective sense of honor, and work together to create the best image. The image of a good college student is a potential power of infinity. Fourth. For the individual of college students, a good image is a good life and a good image is the bright future. To shape the image is to shape the life and design the future. The image of a person in the society is a part of a person's life, and the personal image itself is the epitome and reflection of his life and its future.

ii. Public Relations Quality Development and Public Relations Image Building

A person's public relations image depends on his or her public relations quality, so he or she should try to develop good qualities on the following aspects:

1. The behavior must be correct. You don't have to be like the ancients, you can't stand like a bell, sit like a bow, but at least you have to stand and sit correctly.

2. Observe public civilization. Don't speak loudly in public places, for example, don't spit, don't bring inconvenience, such as the elevator rail station right to left, don't put the whole body when take the subway from the ride against the rotary rod and so on.

3. Be polite to people. As it goes"courtesy costs don't blame", China is a state of courtesy, as college students, we should understand, learn, use etiquette and have respect to the elderly, show care for the young person, have righteousness to the friends , and show tolerance to avengers which is real etiquette.

4. Do more exercise. The ordinary life of college students is lazy and they sit

in front of computer all day, which not only damages eyesight, but also affects the physical health of college students. If college students have enough knowledge but have no healthy body to support their actions, they can't do what they want to do. No organization likes people without health, so college students need to do more exercise and have a healthy body.

5. To Develop Good Morality

A graduate should love his country, the people and science. He should be of hard working spirit, unity and cooperation spirit and pioneering spirit. He should be honest and upright, stress credibility, modest and polite.

6. To Develop Good Character

A person's character is not inborn, it is changeable with education and training. A graduate should unceasingly optimize his character with his education, and try to be optimistic, open-minded, self-confident, enthusiastic and lively, and be on his best behavior and of sense of humor in socializing.

7. To Improve Social Skills

With development of our country, there are more and more associations between different areas and with foreign countries. A graduate should develop his social skills to be adapted to the modern open society. A graduate should be good at communications and exchanges with people from different areas, of different nationalities, skins, ages, classes and characters in an effort to build up good social networks of public relations.

8. To Improve Emotional Quotient (EQ)

Comparatively, a graduate is with high Intelligence Quotient (IQ), which means he is intelligent, has abilities to cognize objective things, to acquire knowledge to remould the objective world and has powers of observation, imagination, thinking and decision. IQ is essential for success, but as an important factor of impelling personality, EQ is another important factor for success. EQ is the ability of the reining emotion and its relative psychology and behaviors. Many graduates with low EQ couldn't control their emotion or concentrate on their study and work, because they are usually haunted by psychological distress or mental disturbance. So a graduate should develop his EQ to set a correct ideal target and be persistent to make efforts for it. He should be confident, refrain himself and try to develop health psychology and good habits.

9. To Adjust and Perfect the Knowledge Structure

As the global trend of science and technology becomes more and more integrated, a single "specialized" talent has not adapted to the requirements of the new century. College students' career choice is diversified, and the demand for "compound" talents is constantly improving. The knowledge structure of college students needs to be adjusted and improved. In addition to the basic knowledge and professional knowledge of college students, the study of comprehensive knowledge should be strengthened. University education must improve the cultural taste of universities; The cultural quality of college students must be improved. Only comprehensive knowledge of college students can improve the overall quality and create a good public relations image.

10. To Strengthen the Public Relations Consciousness

Public relations consciousness is the internalization of the standards of public relations codes and behaviors, as well as the reflection of public relations practices in people's minds. As a civilized idea of modern society, public relations consciousness is proportional to public relations image building. The stronger public relations consciousness a person has, the better public relations image he will build, and vice versa. Just as Yu Ming Yang, the professor of Public Relations in Shenzhen University, has ever said, "The competition of public relations must be the competition of the public relations practitioners' qualities, and the core of which is public relations consciousness." Only when the graduates strengthen their public relations consciousness, can they build good public relations images in society.

III. To Build Public Relations Images from the Beginning of Campus Life

Besides study, there are many rich and colorful activities on campus in literature, art and sports, as well as my associations. Undergraduates should actively take part in these activities to demonstrate themselves and improve their qualities, practice their social skills and build good public relations images. There are also various social public good activities outside the campus which the undergraduates should take part in, such as the activities of youth volunteer, offering love to society, donating money to the Hope Project, respecting the old and caring for the young, social survey, and so on. Undergraduates can steel their character and will, broaden their networking scopes and it pays to build good public relations images.

Part Two Relationships between the Graduates' Job-Hunting and Public Relations Image Building

With more and more intense competition, the society and employers have more and more strict requirements on graduates who have to meet the employers' demands on knowledge structure, professional foundation, competence, and good public relations images as well.

It is obvious that public relations images play a very important role in job-hunting, which is the process of self-promotion. Public relations image building is the prerequisite and most effective way in self promoting.

I. External Public Relations Image Building in Job-Hunting

The outside image means a person's appearance and bearing, namely his expressions, dresses, postures and styles, etc.

i. Appearances, Postures and Dresses

A person's look and body are genetic and inborn, but they can be dressed up to good appearance with decent make-ups and dresses. So a graduate should dress properly in job-hunting, and a girl should make up slightly. The clothes should be clean, tidy and formal, and appropriate to the position you are applying for. Dressed and personal adornments can reflect a person's character, interests and tastes. In this sense, dresses and personal adornments are a kind of culture and civilization. Graduates should choose the dresses and adornments according to their status, sex, age, and stature.

ii. Statures, Expressions and Styles

A person's stature, expressions and styles are changeable, and can be trained in daily life. A graduate's stature, expressions and styles can pass on some messages which can effect on the result of the interview.

A graduate should look kind and natural, talk and behave gracefully at interview. He should have eye contact with the interviewer, and answer questions politely with a smile on the face. He should be concentrated and shouldn't look around. Faced with difficult questions, a graduate should calm down to think over, and try to demonstrate his points in a way neither servile nor overbearing. The etiquette of expressions is to keep smiling. A smile on the face can send a signal of friendliness, kindness and optimism, as well as a graduate's confidence, positiveness and devotion to work. Smile can be regarded as a magic weapon for self promoting and a beautiful silent language.

II. Internal Qualities and Self-Cultivation

A person's external qualities and self-cultivation are not as obvious as his external image, but they can be perceived through the senses, and reflected by a person's speech and deportment, attitude, mood behavior and conversation, to be reflected clearly College students should try to cultivate good temperament and improve their cultural accomplishment in school. In the job application as far as possible to show the vulgarity of the temperament and good cultivation, which will be very conducive to the success of the job

A graduate 's behavior cultivation is more important at interview, because it can be observed straightly rather than be read in his resume like other qualities in politics, morality, culture and so on. A graduate's speech and behavior will leave a lasting first impression on the interviewers. An undergraduate should make efforts to cultivate himself to improve his cultural qualities and temperament on campus.

Here is an temperament to show this:

A gentleman is looking for an office boy. About more than 50 people came to call, but this gentleman just picked up a boy. One of his friends asked him, "why do you like the boy?" He did not bring a letter of introduction, nor did anyone recommend it. "You are wrong," the gentleman said, "he brought many letters of introduction. He rubbed the dirt off his foot at the door and closed the door after he entered the door, indicating that carefully. When he saw the disabled old man, he immediately got up and gave way to show that he was kind and considerate. When he entered the office, he took off his hat first and answered my questions. He was decisive and proved that he was polite . Everyone else walked over from the book I had deliberately put on the floor, and the boy bent over and picked it up and put it on the table. His clothes were neat, his hair was well combed, and his nails were made clean. Don't you think these are the best letters of introduction? " This case fully illustrates the importance of behavior cultivation in the job application.

III. Application of the Public Relations Expressions at Interview

Conversation and inquiry at interview are the process of communications between the interviewer and the interviewee, and self-promoting as well. A graduate should make use of the chance to apply the public relations expressions to leave a good first impression.

The so-called public relations expressions mean the words or phrases which can produce the following effects while being applied to pass on messages: (1) to cause the interests of the other party; (2) to make the other party feel pleased and identify with what you said; (3) to leave a good impression; (4) to touch the other party with catching words; (5) to achieve success with original ideas.

There is a story abroad: a blind man begging on the roadside to beg people. He placed a note in front of him, which read: "my eyes are blind. Please give me some money!" the pedestrians on the road walked by him, and few people gave alms. One of the poets passed by, and the blind man begged him. The poet said, "I don't bring money today, but I can write a poem for you. " In the paper the blind poet wrote: "sunshine so beautiful, but I can't see!" pedestrians hurried past saw this short poem and were touched by it, and gave the blind some money. The previous piece of paper was not enough for money, and the next note did not raise money but let the pedestrians take the initiative. The latter language is the popular language of public relations. This story gives us a lot of inspiration. We should pay attention to the use of public relations language in job application.

i. To Use Polite Expressions through the Interview.

Politeness is very important at interview. Polite expressions reflect not only the respect on the other party, but also the self-cultivation of the interviewee. No matter what the result is, a graduate should speak politely through the interview.

ii. To Implement the Sincerity Principle.

Sincerity is not only the principle of the public relations expressions but also an important principle of public relations. The sincere attitudes and expressions will be perceived and thought highly by the two parties of conversation. Some study suggests that sincerity is regarded as the most important personal quality by graduates. Sincerity is the basic principle in exchanges and communications, and a prerequisite as well to gain mutual trust.

iii. To Use Compliments Properly

Choose a proper opportunity to show your appreciation or admiration on the employer, interviewer or the examiner with compliments, which will please the other party and leave a good impression on the employer. The point is that your compliments should come from the bottom of your heart rather than flattery.

iv To Be Polite and Modest

A graduate should be polite and modest, and pay more attention to the art of speaking whenever you ask or answer a question in a new organization.

v. To Be Confident and Answer Questions Technically

You must be self-confident at interview. If you can answer the interviewer's questions confidently, it means you have taken the first step to success in self-promoting. If you answer the interviewer's questions shyly and cowardly, it means you are self-abased. Self-abasement is unhealthy, will weaken your will, courage and confidence, and leads to failure. You should be self-confident rather than self-abased at interview.

vi. To Be a Good Listener

You should be polite enough and try to be a good listener at interview, which means to be concentrated on listening and grasp the key points of the questions, then think them over and respond contrapuntally and actively.

vii. To Be Realistic and Down-to Earth

You should be practical and realistic at interview. It is wise enough to take the attitude of being realistic to state what you really understand and admit what you don't know. It is acceptable and trustworthy to be honest and frank enough.

Ⅷ. To Keep the Words Brief and Clear

As time is limited at interview, you should try to make your answer to the point, brief and clear. You should speak mandarin without dialects and accents. You should try to attract and impress the interviewers with honest, wise and humorous expressions in proper tempo and tone.

Part Three Skills for Graduates' Job-Hunting

Ⅰ. Basic Requirements for Graduates' Job-Hunting

Generally speaking, people can achieve success in society only when the three factors-"policies, capability and opportunity" function comprehensively. It is very important for graduates to make advantage of the policies-"fair competition", "job-hunting by self-determination", "two-way choice", etc to sell themselves in human resources markets.

ⅰ. Getting Ready and Seize Opportunity

"Good luck happens when preparedness meets opportunity". It's a skill to get oneself ready and seize opportunity to sell oneself successfully.

1. Knowing yourself. Only when you know yourself can you be self-confident and succeed. A graduate should know his current situation and make clear his own position in the particular environmental system, such as whether his major is a "long line" or a "short line", "popular or unexpected"; whether his academic record is good or bad; what is his advantages over others, etc. Then he can ascertain his target, level and scope in his job-hunting and competition.

2. Knowing others. A graduate should know the national situation, employment policy and graduate situation as well as himself, such as the demand for graduates in

economic development, the employers' demands and requirements, and his competitors' situation. Otherwise he may lose the opportunity of employment.

3. Showing yourself. A graduate should seize opportunity to show his talents and skills to sell himself at interview. He should show his good self-cultivation, deportment and image to attract employers to accept him.

ii. Expressing Oneself

Anyone in public relations has to rely on his own talents and make use of possible opportunities to express himself to leave good impression on the relevant public and to be accepted by them. How to express your own emotions, data, opinions and achievements to build a good image and develop good interpersonal relationship? Here are some tips to refer to:

1. To hold up the principle of being "realistic and down-to-earth". Graduates are at the best time of life, they have bright future. As a graduate, he should stick to the principle of "being realistic and down-to-earth", not only introduce his levels on knowledge, skills, morals, and merits, etc, but also his development potential and short-term and long-term goals at interview, so that the employers can have a better understanding of you.

2. To make good use of the first few minutes to introduce yourself. As the old saying goes, "Opportunity seldom knocks twice", it is very important for a graduate to seize the opportunity and make good use of the first few minutes to make a good self-introduction, and leave a good and lasting "first impression" on the employers.

3. To build a good image for yourself. A good image is very important at interview. In addition to your abilities and talent, you have to dress properly, pay attention to your non-verbal languages and be at your best behavior to stand out at interview.

4. To speak clearly and attractively. To some extent, a person's voice can represent his disposition and self-cultivation. At interview, a graduate should pay more attention to his speed, tones and tunes while speaking, and show your confidence and vitality.

5. To speak skillfully. A graduate should follow the "moderate principle" to express himself in an orderly way at interview. It means that he should provide moderate amount of his personal data as well as self-appraisal. He should neither sing his own praises nor

improperly belittle himself. Here are the tips for you to follow the principle:

(1) Choose appropriate words to express yourself orderly, and make yourself understood clearly.

(2) Pay attention to the other party's response, try to adjust your words to meet the other party's desire.

(3) Try to avoid the undesired words, such as "hum" and "um", which may affect your coherence and logicality, and upset the other party.

(4) Try to avoid or limit your usage of the words such as "but", "maybe", "probably", "seem", etc, which may damage your credibility with the body language such as "lowering head".

(5) Try to avoid using some obscure terminologies and unpleasant appellation, and not to illustrate a formal affaire in a joking tone, which will leave a bad impression of you.

II. Skills for Job-Hunting

i. Basic Requirements for Interview in Job-Hunting

Graduates should pay attention to the following points:

1. To get enough preparations. As an old saying goes, "Readiness is all", a graduate should train himself to build a good image in different aspects before interview. He should take part in different imitated interviews on campus; play an interviewee in front of a big mirror to check his dress, expressions, eye contact and manners, etc; record his speech to check his voice and tunes. Only in this way can he gain experiences before interview and reduce his nervousness.

2. To pay attention to the beginning. Just as an old saying goes, "There isn't a second chance to create the first impression", it is very important to seize the opportunity of the first meeting and leave a good "first impression". First, you should greet the host politely at interview; then, say "hello", "smile" and "shake hands" ; next, start with "beg your pardon" to make a brief self-introduction and lead to conversation; last, pay attention to your walking posture, standing posture and sitting posture, etc.

3. To be a good listener. You should listen to the host attentively with eye contact

and smile, respond in the words "right", "reasonable" and "is it" to show your attention and politeness.

4.No interruption. You should not interrupt the host. Even if you have something to explain, you should ask for permission and beg pardon for your cutting in. For example, "Beg your pardon, Mr. Lee. May I cut in with an explanation here?"

5. To be patient. You should be patient to answer questions orderly, in detail and according to the facts at interview

6. To look into the future. While answering questions, you should look into the future of your position and career to show your love to the job, your enthusiasm and creativity.

7. To take leave politely. You should show your appreciation for the chance of interview and thank the host at the end of the interview, then take leave politely. For example, "Thank you, Mr. lee, for giving me the chance to introduce myself here today. I really appreciate it. " "Thank you for your consideration, Manager Lee. May I leave now? Good-bye! "

ii. How to Face the Challenge of Interviewers

Temperaments, interests and styles vary from person to person, so the interview and how to answer the interviewer officer's questions become complicated. The interviewee should try to understand the interviewer officer's thinking and speaking styles and manners at the very beginning, so as to address his challenge properly.

1. In front of a "modest" officer. Some interview officers seem to be modest and amiable to shake hands with you, but they are actually strict and insightful. You should be alert and honest enough to express your viewpoints, and shouldn't be overbearing in front of such officers.

2. In front of a formalist officer. Some officers are inflexible and seem indifferent of any changes to the situation. Such kind of officer is usually introverted, stubborn and persistent in principles. He has certain frameworks in his conduct. You should try to say something appealing to stimulate him and arouse his interests to talk more. Then you will listen to him patiently and pretend to be an old friend of him.

3. In front of an experienced officer. An experience office will do everything

politely and considerately, but you can feel distance in his politeness. They seem to be enthusiastic, but sometimes to be indifferent. You should speak less and be cautious, especially when you talk about your abilities, wishes, requirements and feelings. You should ask him "What do you think of it?" after your self-introduction. Although he won't express his attitude, he hopes to be respected. Once he makes a decision, it will be lasting and hard to be change. Thus it is very important to leave a good first impression of being steady, firm, intelligent, efficient, responsible and trustworthy.

4. In front of an "egoistic" officer. Such kind of officer usually speaks affectedly with arrogant expressions in his eyes to make himself unique. You should be brave enough, and shouldn't take account of his attitude. You should be polite enough to have a pleasant conversation with him. Remember to be brief to the point.

5. In front of a quiet officer. This kind of officer usually sits there quietly, observes you and waits for your actions. Sometimes, even though you have spoken a lot, he still just keeps quiet like a mute. You shouldn't be scared by him, instead, you should be brave enough to express yourself and give full play to your special features.

iii. Skills for Preparations of a Self-Recommendation Letter

A self-recommendation letter is not as direct or concrete as a face-to-face interview. The host cannot know the applicant further by reading his letter, but the self-recommendation letter (including the personal dada uploaded on the Internet) has its advantages and is irreplaceable. First, you can introduce yourself accurately, thoroughly and orderly in the self-recommendation letter through illustration of words, diagrams, pictures, particular wording and designing. In addition, you can spare lots of time and energy to contact more companies to collect employment data as your reference to make decisions. Thus it is a good way for job-hunting to send your self-recommendation letter or upload your personal data on the Internet. Here are some tips for your reference:

1.To know different employers' requirements for applicants Different employers have different requirements for applicants in gender, age, body, eyesight, address, school records, etc. Only when you know the requirements and think you are in accordance with them can you send your self-recommendation letter and wait for your further chances.

2. To prepare your data carefully. You should prepare your data carefully and analyze which of them are objective or subjective. For example, your school records, social positions, awards and credits are objective; your characteristics, interests and hobbies, talents and potentials are subjective. If you have any strong points that are being cried for by the employer, you can underline them to outstand yourself.

3.To ask for recommendation from your teachers or departments of the university. If you have a recommendation letter from your teachers or Employment Guiding Centre of the university with personal signature or office stamp and the words "The case is true, agree to recommend. " on it, then the employer will think you are trustworthy and have a good impression of you. Many universities have opened their websites and uploaded the graduates' personal data, which can increase credibility of the data.

4. To write a brief application letter for a job. You should write a brief application letter after the self-recommendation data with a few hundreds of words to apply for a position clearly and politely, illustrating "with attachment of personal data or pictures, etc. Finally write your address and contact number, then you can send the self-recommendation letter out.

iv. Skills for Filling in the Application Form for a Job

There are various forms for graduates to fill in, ranging from the "talents seeking form", "questionnaire" to "diagnosing form". Here some tips for your reference.

1. Sort out different forms to make sure the form style and your focuses.

2. Be cautious of your data selection, wording and content tailoring.

3. Fill in the form carefully with beautiful and skillful calligraphy.

4. Be brief and clear. You'd better fill in the form with too many contents in the order of time so as to be read clearly. In a few words, while filling in the application form for a job, a graduate should be careful, cautious and realistic. What's more, you should be brief and to the point in words. Then you will be a successful applicant.

Chapter Seven
Management of Public Relations Crises

It is really challenging for public relations when an organization gets involved in crisis. As crisis is ominous and incidental, fewer people would rather care about it and get ready to deal with it. It is advisable for organization leaders and qualified PR Practitioners to take precautions for the possibilities of crisis. Once in crisis, they can respond and address challenges according to flexible plans. Management of crisis has been an important practical task in public relations work.

Part One Summary of Public Relations Crisis

I. Concept, Classifications and Features of Crisis

i. Concept of Crisis

Crisis means the serious malignant event that endangers an organization's existence and development, namely the emergency that has a big impact on an organization's existence and development.

The so-called emergency only refers to the malignant event in a narrow sense, which is unfavorable for an organization. There are two classifications of emergency in a narrow sense, namely common emergency and grave emergency. Common emergency refers to the public relations disputes in commercial activities of enterprises, including the disputes within an enterprise, disputes with consumers and disputes between different organizations. Grave emergency refers to grave accidents in production and operation (such as grave work accidents and environment pollution accidents), decision failure in production and operation, serious losses from natural disasters, and so on.

ii. Classifications and Features of Crises

1.Classifications of Crises

In regard of reasons, crises social organizations can be divided into the following categories:

(1) Crises caused by subjective factors, such as grave accidents in quality, environment pollution, building collapse and food poisoning caused by ill management.

(2) Crises caused by objective factors, such as earthquakes, fires, floods and other unexpected natural disasters.

(3) Crises caused by the public misunderstanding, such as serious crises in public opinions, medium criticism, behavior conflicts and so on.

2.Features of Crises

There are four features for any kind of crisis:

(1) Sudden. Any emergency is unexpected and results in serious loss and trouble for an organization. It is unpredictability of crises that makes it really hard for people to deal with them.

(2) Swift and violent. Any crisis is swift and violent, with serious impact and rapid expansion.

(3) Serious. Crises are harmful to not only organizations but also society. They will damage to organization images, have impact on production and operation, resulting in "Image Crisis" and huge economic losses of the enterprises.

(4) Sensitive. People tend to be sensitive to crises, so crises are easy to be the focus of news media and the hotspot of the public, which will arouse negative social opinions and make it more difficult to solve the crises.

II. Concept and Classifications of the Public Relations Crises

i. Concept of the Public Relations Crisis

The public relations crisis means the serious conflicts between an organization and the social public, or the opinions obviously unfavorable to an organization. Although the public relations crisis is different from the serious accident crisis of an organization, they are closely connected with each other. Although the public relations crises are not presented as sudden malignant events, the losses caused by them are hard to measure and remedy. The intangible losses will lead to tangible losses, even worse to endanger the organization's existence and development.

The reasons for the public relations crises are:

(1) Failure to solve the sudden malignant crises of the organization. There are negative public opinions unfavorable to the organization

(2) Ignorance of the role of public relations, which results in the increasingly serious conflicts between the organization and the public.

(3) The public misunderstanding from being unaware of the truth, which leads to unfavorable public opinions and behaviors.

(4) Communication crisis caused by poor communication of the organization information, such as mistakes, failure to communicate, or communications inconsistent with the facts,

(5) Trust crisis caused by the social opinion leaders' agitation.

ii . Categories of Public Relations Crises

Public relations crises can be divided into the following categories according to the nature.

1. Public Relations Crisis Caused by Disasters

Public relations crisis refers to the organization crisis caused by natural calamities or irresistible social disasters, such as mountain torrents, lightening stroke, earthquake, and the like. Disaster crises take place suddenly and are independent of man's will. They usually destroy the production and operation of the organization, and do great damage to the public relations and images of the organization, consequently lead to public relations crises.

It is the PR Practitioner's important responsibility to call on the staff to hold together to overcome difficulties and encourage them to struggle for maintenance of the organization image.

2. Reputation Crisis

Reputation crisis refers to the crisis that seriously damaged the enterprises' reputation and images. This kind of crisis is usually resulted from the enterprise's failure to perform the contract or inferiority in products or services which endanger the consumers' benefits.

Reputation crisis is presented in public relations as the public trust and support losses on an organization which endanger the existence of an organization.

3. Management Crisis

This kind of crisis is usually caused by the management fault or poor management of an organization. The reason many businesses are suffering a lot in finance is the long-term hidden fault in their management and decision. The issue must be addressed immediately, otherwise the production and operation of the enterprise will be worsen, even go bankrupt.

4. Credit Crisis

Credit crisis means that the enterprise has lost the trust from financial organizations and cannot get necessary turnover fund, thus the enterprise cannot run smoothly and finally is driven into crisis. The so called "debt chain" between various enterprises is a kind of credit crisis, which is a secondary crisis, following management crisis and reputation crisis.

5. Quality Crisis

Quality crisis means an organization is inferior in working staff, equipment and management and isn't competitive. Many enterprises suffering from quality crisis couldn't introduce innovative technology or develop new products, consequently are passive in competition, or faced with being merged or bankrupt.

6. Image Crisis

Image crisis refers to the crisis caused by the organization scandals, such as being accused of bribes, tax evasion and other unlawful acts. Image crisis is a kind of nature crisis, so the organization should take measures to address it immediately.

Part Two Prevention of the Public Relations Crises

According to some survey, it is inevitable for a modern enterprise to suffer from different kinds of crises. No matter what measures an organization takes, it will suffer a lot once crisis happens. Accordingly, it is advisable to find out signs, make scientific analysis and take precautions against crises, namely to manage the public relations crises.

Management of public relations crises is also called public relations crisis handling or crisis public relations, which means an organization makes use of various resources and takes various feasible measures to prevent, limit and eliminate crisis or negative influence caused by crisis. Management of public relations crises makes use of the knowledge and skills of public relations and management to scientifically address the potential or existing crises of an organization according to the principles and methods of the two disciplines.

I. Analysis on the Reasons of Public Relations Crises

The reasons of the public relations crises can be divided into two categories, namely the internal reasons and external reasons of an organization.

i. Internal Reasons of an Organization

(1) Fault in decision-making. It means that an organization couldn't make correct managing and public relations strategies according to the present situation and developing trend of the market. Fault in decision-making is an important reason for management crisis.

(2) Poor management. It means the serious problems in quality of products and services caused by poor management in foundation work, unscientific methods and means in management, incomplete regulations, and the like.

(3) Inferior quality of an organization. It is an important factor for all the other crises except for the disaster crisis. It first refers to the inferior quality in the leaders and staff of an organization. It is the quality of human resources that makes a decisive role for an organization.

(4) Fault in public relations strategy. It means an organization couldn't make its public relations strategy according to the public relations policy on the basis of objective facts, couldn't pass on the authentic information to the public, which resulted in the

damage to the image and reputation of the organization.

ii . External Reasons of an Organization

(1) Irresistible power. It means the external power or sudden natural disasters beyond the organization control, which will affect normal production and operation of an enterprise, such as earthquakes or coups

(2) Policy or system factors. The policy and government system of a country have great impact on organizations. For example the general office of the State Council on the strict implementation of the notification of public building air-conditioning temperature control standards (Guo Ban Fa 2007 No. 42) documents issued which caused a big crisis for many air conditioning companies .

(3) Social factors. Social factors refer to the obstructions from the social malpractices and unhealthy tendency, which affect production and operation, and disturb the normal economic order of the society.

II . Process of Public Relations Crises

Crisis is a kind of unsteady and abnormal situation, the process of which can be separated into four periods.

(1) Latent period. It is also called "pre-crisis" period, during which some factor leading to crises have come into being. If the factors haven't been find out or eliminated, they will contribute to crises. Therefore, all the supervisors and PR Practitioners of the organization should be cautious enough to find out the crisis signals and try to eliminate the negative factors and prevent the crisis in the latent period.

(2) Outbreak Period. An accident will be the blasting fuse and make the crisis evident after the latent period, then the crisis steps into the outbreak period. If people can see beyond and make some preparations, they can foresee and control the speed, magnitude, directions and lasting period of the crisis and reduce the damage to the minimum.

(3) Processing period. This is the period to address the crisis, during which the staff members should be focused on crisis accidents. The workers should make correct decisions, take resolute actions in emergency to address crisis.

(4) Recovery period. After the crisis, the organization image has been seriously damaged. The organization suffers in a passive situation of being investigated and examined by relevant departments from the government and being interviewed and reported by the media. The organization has to do self-analysis and self-criticism, and take measures to clear up messy situation and rebuild the organization image.

III. Precautions against Public Relations Crises

There are two links in precautions against crises: one is to forecast the crisis, which means to find out "germination" of crisis; the other is to make countermeasures to deal with crisis in advance.

i. Crisis Warning

Enterprises are more inclined to meet with crises in market economy. The reasons are as following: First, enterprises are faced with much more fierce competition full of risks. Second, enterprises have more autonomy in management under the macroeconomic control, regulation management and supervision of the government. Third, consumers and press media are more sensitive to the existing problems of enterprises, so any crisis accidents of enterprises won't be secrets for the public.

Although the environment is complicated for enterprises, it is advisable for an enterprise to make precautions against crises, make use of crises and take a turn for the better. Preparations should be made on the following aspects:

1. To Make Psychological Preparation of Strain

Both the leaders and PR Practitioners of an organization should be conscious of crises and make psychological preparations of strain. Only in this way can an organization make crisis warning, foresee the potential crises in organization activities and take countermeasures.

2. To Establish the Crisis Warning System

The PR Practitioners should coordinate relevant departments to establish crisis warning system on the following aspects to capture some crisis signs.

(1) To enhance collection and analysis on the information of public relations and enterprise operation in an effort to grasp the public feedbacks to organizations in

time.

(2) To keep a close eye on the economy policies of our country and the system reforms in economy, politics and education in order to operate the organization in harmony with the social background.

(3) To communicate with the VIP clients frequently and make them become the steady supporters of the organization.

(4) To usually analyze the competitors' business policy and market demand trend.

(5) To make regular self-diagnose, analyze the situation of operation and public relations, make objective evaluation on the organization image, find out the disadvantages and take necessary measures.

(6) To carry out various investigations, research and forecast the potential crisis accidents and try to eliminate the crisis factors in the latent period.

3. To Set up an Alarm Line

The PR Practitioners or managers in each subsidiary company can notify the relevant departments and staff members via the alarm line once they find out something uncommon to ask whether they have ever met such kind of problems and their experiences in an effort to take proper measures to avoid the similar problems.

ii. Crisis Response Plan

It is crucial to take measures to solve problems once accidents happen. A crisis response plan must be made before crises to get ready for emergency.

The so-called crisis response plan is a plan for emergency providing a set of schemes of human resources, materials, methods and measures required in addressing the emergency. The crisis response plan has ever been compared to "flashlight" with which people can deal with crises orderly.

Generally, a comprehensive crisis response plan includes the following contents:

1. To Establish a Crisis Response Team

The first task to make a crisis response plan is to establish a crisis response team, in the core of which there are organization leaders, technical experts, public relations directors and legal advisor, plus other relevant members according to various crises.

Once any crisis happens, the team members in charge will shoulder responsibility to deal with the crisis, while they should be prepared for response to crises at ordinary times.

2. To Study out the Crisis Response Plan

The crisis response team is responsible for studying out the crisis response plan. The plan should be inclusive of any possible crises and countermeasures, which are compiled as a crisis response plan manual. The manual is a guideline to deal with various crises. Although it varies from enterprise to enterprise, all the manuals should be detailed enough to deal with crises.

Generally speaking, the following preparations should be taken into consideration in the crisis plan:

(1) To make a crisis response booklet. Crisis response measures can be compiled into easy-to understand booklets given out to staff members to establish the employees' sense of crisis and make them understand the possibilities and response measures of crises.

(2) To study out the news plan of crisis response. How to deal with news press seems very important for an organization once crisis happens, for it matters the public concern and opinions. The coverage the news press will have great impact on the organization image. A special in charge is preferable to contact with the news media.

(3) To confirm the speaker in advance. A speaker should be confirmed to represent the organization to introduce to the public the crisis process and efforts made to address the crisis. The speaker should make public the crisis fact in time to make the public understand the fact and make rational analysis on the crisis.

(4) To confirm and contact the rescue organizations. The PR Practitioners should confirm the possible rescue organizations, such as emergency centre, police station, firehouse, and nearby community, etc, establish friendly relationships with them and inform them the possible aids the organization will ask for once crisis happens.

3. Crisis-Imitating Drills

The crisis response team can carry out practices and drills in given certain crises to test the team members' responsiveness, decision making ability, their crisis-addressing knowledge and psychological endurance.

The crisis response plan and drills are only tools prepared for dealing with crises, the relevant departments and staff members should cooperate with each other and apply the plan to address crises flexibly.

Part Three Dealing with Public Relations Crises

Ⅰ. Principles to Manage Public Relations Crises

Management of public relations crises means the process of the PR Practitioners' taking measures to deal with the public relations crises caused by emergent accidents to safeguard the good image of the organization

It is inevitable for an organization to be faced with various challenges in the market-oriented economy and information times. It is an important project in public relations practices to manage crises and deal with unexpected accidents. People should observe the following principles in managing crises:

1. Quick Response

Any crisis happens suddenly and spreads rapidly leading to the press media and social public's concern. The organization suffering in crisis should respond quickly and take countermeasures to manage the crisis, meanwhile they should make public the truth, try to win over the public sympathy and reduce the losses from the crisis.

2. Being Honest and Frank

The organization in crisis must be honest and frank to disclose the fact of the crisis in an effort to gain the trust of the public and the press media. The more facts it conceals, the more doubtful the public and press media will be.

3. Humanitarianism

In most cases, any crisis will lead to great losses of lives and properties, which will draw great attention of the public. Therefore, humanitarianism principle should be adhered to in crisis management.

4. Safeguarding Reputation

The role of public relations in crises is to safeguard the organization reputation, which is the aim of crisis management. Reputation is the life of an organization, and will definitely be damaged in crises, so the PR Practitioners should make efforts to reduce the damage to the reputation in crisis management, and try to gain the public understanding and trust. The aim of following the above-mentioned three principles is to safeguard the organization reputation.

II. Procedures of Public Relations Crisis Management

Once crises happen an organization should quickly take actions to reduce the damages to the minimum. A scientific procedure is crucial to efficient management in crisis.

i. To Establish an Organization Specializing in Crisis Management

All the social organizations should join up to establish a centre to make decisions, manage crises and communicate, whose director should be a leader of an organization. The public relations organization in the centre should be responsible for helping the director make investigations and analysis, contact with others, disclose information and make strategies, etc.

If any organization gets into crisis suddenly, they can ask the experts in public relations to make a think-tank to help them make decisions and manage the crisis.

ii. To Master the Overall Crisis Situation Rapidly

The relevant staff member should have on-site investigation to find out the real situation of the crisis accident:

(1) The crisis type, time, site and source.

(2) The influence scope, casualty and injury, loss of properties, negative effects on the organization and society caused by the crisis. The effect from the taken measures and possible social influence.

(3) The crisis trend and opportunity to address the crisis.

(4) Who are the public involved in the crisis? How about their communications with the organization and how the organization will respond them.

Chapter Seven
Management of Public Relations Crises

iii. To Insulate the Crisis Rapidly

The staff members should do as the following tips to insulate the crisis in investigation:

(1) Personnel Insulation. It means to divide the personnel into two teams once crisis happens-one is in charge of the crisis management, the other is in charge of daily work. People shouldn't neglect either of them.

(2) Crisis insulation.

It means to restrain the crisis scope, prevent it from expanding, and isolate the crisis area from the normally working area. Actually actions should be taken in crisis warning period to insulate the crisis and reduce losses.

iv. Countermeasures Taken to Address Crises

Having established the crisis management centre, the director of which should take charge of analysis on crisis data and study out the countermeasure plan. The plan usually includes the following contents: (1) To make in-depth analysis on the crisis background, source, trend and illustrate the consequence and impact on the public. (2) To set public relations target to address the crisis. (3) To make basis countermeasures to deal with the crisis and confirm the information, principle and channels of crisis communication. To study out the afterward disposal and work out the schedule of crisis management.

According to the previous experience and some experts' views, different countermeasures should be taken pertinently towards different public once the crisis happens.

1. Internal Countermeasures

(1) To circulate a notice of crisis, call on all the staff members to make concerted efforts to survive the crisis and take measures to control the crisis.

(2) Notify the sales department to stop selling such products if the accident is caused by inferior quality of products. To call back the unqualified products, send quality control team to test the unqualified products, figure out the reasons and take measures to improve the product quality.

2. Countermeasures to the Victims

No matter the victims of the crisis accident are inside or outside the organization, their family members or relatives should be notified at the earliest time. The organization should do everything possible to rescue the victims and settle the problem arising thereafter.

(1) How to console the victims and their family members is a sensitive and important task in crisis management. The staff members should be cautious enough to listen to their complaints and dissatisfaction in communicating with them, should shoulder responsibilities according to the facts and try their best to meet their reasonable demands and offer necessary services. The staff members should pay attention to the way of notifying their family members when there are casualties and injuries in the crisis in case of serious strike to their family members.

(2) It is very important to tell the victims and family members about the truth and show sympathy and condolence to them. The staff members should discuss with victims and family members on compensation for their losses.

3. Countermeasures to Press Media

Press media usually focus on crisis accidents and their development. How to contact with press media after crisis accidents is one of the PR Practitioners' important tasks.

(1) To disclose the truth of accidents to press media and make clear the organization's attitudes and acts in response. A senior is preferable to represent the organization to introduce to the press media the course and reason of the accident and the measures taken, being taken and to be taken.

(2) There should be enough communications leading to unified understanding and statement of the accident in the organization before announcement.

(3) There should be explanations to the journalists to ask for their understanding if there is something inadvisable to disclose. Please don't say "no comments" to refuse to respond.

(4) It is necessary to establish a temporary reception centre to receive the journalists and disclose development of the accidents and afterwards measures.

(5) Mistakes in disclosed information must be corrected promptly. The PR

Practitioners should keep track on the coverage of the accident, correct mistakes if there are any and provide the true data.

4. Countermeasures to the Superior

（1） Report the crisis accidents realistically to the superior.

（2） Report the progress of the situation regularly and ask for guidance, support and assistance.

（3） Submit the general report to the leader after the crisis management, which includes the management process, solution methods and future precaution measures.

5. Countermeasures to Business Partners

（1） Pass on the crisis information realistically as soon as possible

（2） Circulate a written notice of the measure being taken.

（3） Send a representative to explain the situation face-to-face if necessary.

（4） Pass on the handling process information regularly to the cooperators.

（5） Explain to the cooperators the crisis management process in written form afterwards.

6. Countermeasures to Consumers

（1） To hand out to consumers the written materials in explaining the outline of the accident through retailers and other channels.

（2） To explain the crisis truth, handling process and future precaution measures via press media.

（3） To warmly meet and receive the visiting representatives

（4） To compensate for the losses of consumers.

Ⅴ. Conclusion, Inspection and Publishment

It is indispensible work of the crisis management in the last period. The work team of the crisis management should inspect and assess the whole crisis management, report the result to the board of directors and shareholders and make it known to the public.

Ⅲ. Strategic Problems to Be Paid Attention to in Crisis Management

There are many uncontrollable factors contributing to crises, so the PR Practitioners should be sober, decisive and flexible in crisis management. Here are some tips in strategies in crisis management.

1. To Get the Dominant Role in Public Opinions

Once upon the crisis happens, the organization should communicate with the public at the earliest time in case that some speculations and unrealistic coverage from some press media will affect the public judgement. Before identification of the accident truth, the organization should take the published information as the only authoritative source and introduce the public some background information, preliminary situation and measures taken to take ground of the public opinion and get the dominant role in public opinions.

2. To Cooperate with the Public, Societies and Authority Organs to Address Crises

It is an effective strategy to cooperate with the pubic, societies and authority organs to enhance the organization's credit in the public. It is the basis of the strategy for the organization to keep close relationships with them in normal times, because it is easy to get the public's trust and sympathy if they act on behalf of the organization.

3. To Disclose the Practical and Effective Actions in Time

In addition to the accident, the PR Practitioners should focus on the practical and effective actions taken by the organization. Especially in the accident leading to casualties and injuries, they should prominently make publicity to the efforts made and actions taken to save the victims.

4. To Organize the Leaders to Confront the Accident Personally

It will build the good image of being brave to shoulder responsibilities, capable, decisive and honest to manage the crisis to organize the leaders of the organization to come to the accident site and manage the crisis.

5. To Designate a Press Spokesman and Speak in Once Voice

At the begging of the crisis, the public and press media are easy to speculate the situation and lead to negative opinions because of the unclear situation and confused information sources. The organization should designate a representative as the press spokesman to introduce the realistic situation of the crisis and measures to take; the team members of crisis management should be sober enough to analyze situation, make correct decisions and speak in one voice.

Chapter Eight

Government Public Relations

More and more enterprises have been cognizant of the important role of public relations in their popularity enhancing, image building and profit making. The government, the core of the national superstructure should attach great importance to public relations, which will benefit the social stabilization and be the necessary requirement of opening to the outside world and developing the market-oriented economy.

Part One Connotation and Characteristics of Government Public Relations

I. Connotation of Government Public Relations

The so-called government public relations means a kind of administrative function that the national administrative organs apply a variety of propagating and communicating means to establish mutual-understanding, trusting, cooperative and lasting relationship with the public in an effort to build a good image of the government. The definition concludes at least the following three meanings:

(1) The government public relations is the relation between the government and the public. The government is the subject of the public relations, the organizer and initiator of the public relations activities, the effect of which depends on and affect the government. The public is the object of the public relations and activities. The public

will evaluate the government image and the effect of the government public relations.

(2) The government public relations aims to build a good image. Although there are many contents of the government public relations and different direct targets of various activities, the only one final target of them is to build a good government image.

(3) Propagation is the way and means of the government public relations. Different propagation and communication methods are the links between the government and public, so whether the social disseminating media are advanced and disseminating channels are smooth will directly affect the effect of the government public relations activities.

II. Characteristics of the Government Public Relations

The government public relations is of the nature of general public relations, while it is of the characteristics different from other kinds of public relations.

i. Special in the Public Relations Purpose

Rather than aiming to make profits as other social organizations, especially enterprises, the direct and essential purpose of the government public relations is to improve administrative effects by building a good image. The government serves for the public, so their authority must be built on the basis of the public trust and support, otherwise the relationship between the government and public will be destroyed, which will cut down the policy effects.

ii. Special in the Public Relations Subject

The subject of the government public relations is the national administrative organs, who are completely different from various economic, cultural and political organizations in nature. First, the government has great power. It can make policies, issue decrees, controlling national armed forces, police, prisons and other strongly armed organs. Second, the government is unique in society. It is over any social organization and unrestricted by any competition rule. Last, the government is of a huge system and complex structure. It has a complete system from central to local. Further more, it has an extensive range of administrative jurisdiction, from the residents' necessities of life to economic development, from national defense and foreign affairs to environmental ecology.

iii. Special in the Public Relations Object

The object of the government public relations is greatly extensive and incomparable. Its basic object is the citizens, actually the entire social public. In addition, the international public is also its object. Further more, the government's public is made of different groups of different interests. The government must take their different opinions into consideration when it makes policies or issues decrees. Meanwhile, different groups or organizations have their own public who are among the government's public, so the government public are quite complex in structure.

iv. Special in the Public Relations Means

Propagating is the means of public relations activities. Compared with other organization public relations, propagation of the government public relations has the following incomparable advantages in backgrounds:

1. The Government with Enormous Information Resources

The government organs are the place converged with various data. If the society is compared to a machine, the government is the operator of the machine, has the advantage to get timely and accurately the information of operation of different parts on the machine. In addition, the government functions as a coordinator of the society. One hand, it can collect various data through its organizations on different layers; on the other hand, different organizations actively provide data to the government. Therefore, the government has enormous information resources.

2. The Government Controlling the Public Medium Directly or Indirectly

One hand, the government, the unique social organization, has great amount of public propagating media. Taking our country as an example, our government manages newspapers, radio and TV stations, so it can make use of them to propagate for the government in public relations activities. On the other hand, the government can indirectly dominate the public media. Taking the USA for example, the government can indirectly control the public media through the law, policies and regulations on news investigations, etc. In this way, the government can mater the discourse power and ensure the public relations plan to be strictly implemented and the public relations target to be smoothly reached.

3. Rigorous and Rapid Propagation within the Government

Although the government is huge and complex in structure, it is rigorous in organization. Any information can be passed on accurately and rapidly within the organization no matter vertically or laterally.

4. Government Public Relations' Synthetic and Cross Use of Various Propagating Channels, Means and Carriers

Most government policies are first implemented as documents within the organization of the government, and then they are propagated by the public media. Sometimes the policies are implemented in both ways

5. Effective in the Government Information Propagation

There are four links in information propagation, namely from information sources to propagators, to media, to contents, and to the public. Obviously, the government has absolute advantages in information sources and media-rich in sources, large in media number and various in propagating means, which ensure the effect of the government information propagation.

Part Two Significance and Functions of the Government Public Relations

Ⅰ. Significance of the Government Public Relations

The government public relations is a series of administrative actions to coordinate the relations with the public, aiming to give play to the role of the government. Its significance in management can be summed up as following:

ⅰ. Favorable for Image-Building

The first task of the government public relations is to build a good image, with which in the public, the government will be trusted and supported by the public, and the government activities will get the public understanding and cooperation. The government makes efforts to narrow the gap between the ideal image and the actual image by means of social propagation, networking and guidance of public opinion, etc.

ii. Favorable for Policy-Making

The government must understand the people's feelings and demands through public relations activities, such as public opinion survey when a policy is being made, especially some important guidelines, policies and reforming measures are to be launched.

iii. Favorable for Decree-Implementing

The government has to rely on the public understanding, trust and support to effectively implement its policies, so it has to do much propaganda work to get the public to admit and accept a new decree or policy. Otherwise, a new decree or policy will be hard to be accepted by the public, which will be the barrier in the government public relations.

iv. Favorable for Coordinating the Internal Relationship

Essence of the government public relations is to coordinate the relationship with the federation of trade union through propagation, for the improvement of the administration efficiency has close relationships with both the external social environment and internal organizational environment. Without a good internal organizational environment, there will be frictions between the different departments, upper and lower levels, and civil servants, leading to unnecessary losses, mutual distrust and irresponsibility, which will reduce the administration efficiency. Therefore, it is an important step of improving the administration efficiency to communicate information by all means to coordinate internal relationship, which is also the purpose of public relations activities. Only when an organization has harmonious internal relationship with all in one mind and close contact with external, can it have extensive cooperation and favorable administrative environment.

II. Functions of Government Public Relations

The purpose of the government public relations is to build a good image of the government, around which all the practical activities and work carried out are within the government functions.

i . Information Exchange

Information, a form of social universal connection, being widely penetrated in all areas of life, has been the premise for each organization to act and develop in the era of knowledge economy. Whether the government can get information, the amount and quality of the information will be the crucial factors for the government to make policies.

The function of the government public relations in information exchange are shown in the following aspects:

1. Information Exchange within the Organization

In relation to the government public relations, the organization is composed of leaders and civil servants. The leaders' images will affect the external image of the whole government as well as the internal cohesion and solidarity. Therefore the leaders' abilities in organization, decision, coordination and management are the contents of information exchange of the organization.

The civil servants are the working staff in different departments of the government, the relationship within whom, and that between whom and the public will affect both the inside and outside environment.

2. Information Exchange in Policies

It is very important for the government to understand policies timely, comprehensively and accurately, for the government administration of a country or an area often depends on the policies made by them. Therefore, it is necessary for the government to exchange the information of investigating whether policies are correct, how the policy making levels are, how the policies are implemented and understanding the public assessment on the policies.

3. Information Exchange in Organization Installation and Working Efficiency

In the contact with the government, the public consciously or unconsciously have different opinions on the government's organization installation and working efficiency. Some think the organization installation is reasonable and they work efficiently with fewer procedures and flexible mechanism; while others think the organizations are over staffing and they work inefficiently with miscellaneous procedures. No matter what the public opinions are, the government should collect, reorganize and analyze the relevant information.

ii. Consultation and Suggestion

It means the PR Practitioners of the government provide their leaders with reliable information of social public situations and trustworthy opinions. Their consultations and suggestions cover the following aspects.

1. Consultation and Suggestion on General Situation of the Public

This is the routine work of the government public relations. The consultation provides the government with general situation between the government and public, such as the civil servants' belongingness, the public assessments on the government's image and the media's opinions on the government, etc.

2. Consultation and Suggestion on Specific Situation of the Public

It means the PR Practitioners of the government provide relevant situation instructions and suggestions on some special activities to be held by the government.

3. Consultation and Suggestion on the Public Psychological Changes and Trends

It means the government put forward their opinions on the public psychological changes and trend analysis according to their long-term observation on them and accumulation of them, combined with the medium and long term planning and the reports submitted to the controllers.

iii. Communication and Coordination

The government's communication with the public means the government as the subject of public relations communicate ideas and information with the public by various means and in various ways, in an effort to improve mutual understanding and trust between the government and the pubic and create more favorable environment and condition for the government work. The significance of communication between the government and the pubic lies in:

1. Requirement of Democratic Politics

It is the nature of modern democratic politics that the public take part in the management of national and social affairs. The public have to "know politics" in order to participate in and discuss political affairs and supervise the government work, which requires the government to pass on relevant information to the public timely and roundly. Only in this way can the public understand more about political affairs; on the other hand, the government also can understand more about the public opinions, suggestions, demands and voices, which can be adopted and become the basis of policies and decisions.

2. Requirement to Increase the Government's Transparency

The government has to connect with the public closely to gain their trust and support. It is an effective way for the government to open their political activities, increase their work transparency and clear the communication channels.

3. Requirement to Enhance the Government Function

It is important guarantee for the government to increase their working efficiency to ensure the information smooth going, timely and accurately. If decisions, planning and arrangements cannot be passed on to the public timely from the government, their implementation will be affected. If the government cannot mater the feedbacks from the public, their following work will be affected. Therefore, the government must make use of modern propagating means and media to keep contact with the public closely.

Coordination means that the government as the subject of public relations try to adjust and straighten out the relationship between the government and the public through consultation, adjustment and communication in order to create appropriate environment and conditions for the government to carry out all work. In relations to social management, the entire society is a huge organizational system, in which there exists a set of serious working nets and orderly procedures. All trades and professions, groups, social stratum and classes work around the core of the government administration system, and all subsystems have complicated relationships and stakes with the government. The government function of coordination is obviously important in dealing with the relations with them. The government should coordinate the relations between the following parties: (1) To coordinate the relationship between the government leaders and its civil servants; (2) To coordinate the relationship between different departments in the government; (3) To coordinate the relationship between the government and the public.

iv. Building a Good Image

Government image covers the following three aspects: First, government value.

It refers to behavior codes and motive power of the government permeated in the aim, developing target and actions of the government. Second, government behavior. It covers managing level, service level, working efficiency, devotion to work and honesty in performing their official duties, etc. Third, social developing target. Only when the government sets a favorable and practical social developing target and propagates it to make it permeated into the public, can it get the public identification, support and good assessment.

Public relations is art to build images, so is the government public relations. The government image is significant for its survival and development. A good image is prerequisite for the government to gain the public trust and support.

Part Three Principles of Government Public Relations

The principles of government public relations mean the codes to follow and the requirements to meet in the government public relations activities.

Ⅰ. Realistic Principle

Realistic principle means the government should pass on information practically in public relations activities, establish mutual trust relationship and build a good image in the public inside and outside the government through two-way information exchange inside and outside the government.

Ⅱ. Opening Principle

The public cry for "Openness" and "Transparency" in government work. Political rights should be open to the public equally in the democratic society. The public are entitled to understand and participate in the political affairs, which is the base of democratic politics. In addition, it is of real significance in preventing and fighting corruption in our country to keep the government work open to the public.

The government work should be open, but it doesn't mean to open without principle. The PR Practitioners should handle well the relationship between the opening and the confidential with firmness in principle and flexibility in policy. First, they should differentiate different publics, with whom to communicate in different means, to whom to open different contents to different extents. Second, they should differentiate different time, conditions and occasions. Last, they should differentiate different limits between the law and institutions.

III. Interest Principle

Interest is the basis to build and maintain good public relations. Interest relationship is the nature of public relations. The interest here means the interests between the government and the public. How can we handle well the relationship between the government and the public in government public relations?

The public in government public relations can be divided into the domestic public and the foreign public in terms of nationality who have different interest relations with the government, which means different principles should be followed in government public relations activities.

Further, the domestic public can be also divided into three categories in terms of amount, namely the broad masses of people, some masses of people and groups and a few masses of people and groups.

Towards the first category of public, the principle to put the public interests first should be followed and the public interests should be taken into consideration at any time in government public relations. The government should think what the public opinions will be, how they will evaluate on them and whether they are in accordance with the public interests before they make any policies, laws and implement any projects. Only when the government put the public in their heart, solve problems practically for them and serve for the people heart and soul can they get the public understanding and support in their public relations activities.

Towards the second and third categories of public, the government will put the interests of the broad masses of people first without hesitation if their interests are contradicted with those of the broad masses of people; the government will take all their interests into consideration if they are not contradicted in interest.

Towards the foreign public, our Chinese government adopts the mutual-benefit principle with both benefits of China and foreign countries into consideration in diplomatic activities rather than the national-benefit-first principle adopted by many other countries, which is proved to be very successful.

All in all, the government shouldn't generalize its actions in dealing with the benefit relationships with the public due to its complexity.

Part Four Integral Principle

It means that the government public relations organizations or practitioners should study and estimate the government public relations from the whole point of view, namely to start from the whole and try to cooperate with each other for the integrate effect of the government. Government policies reflect national interests, so government organs at all levels shouldn't have any special interests away from the whole national interests. The integral principle must be followed in the government public relations because of the integrity of the government work.

The integral principle involves extensively, but it mainly covers the following areas:

First, the government should deal with outside public relations from the whole point of view. In any specific public relations activity, the government is faced with part of the public and the work members shouldn't confine themselves merely to facts as they are. They should combine some interests with the whole interests, partial and local interests with the integral interests.

Next, the government should deal with inside public relations from the whole point of view. Although different organs in the government have different functions and working scopes, they work to the highest interests of the public. Therefore, all the government organs and civil servants should cooperate with each other and try to effectively perform the function of the whole government system.

Here are some tips on implementation of the integral principle in the government public relations:

(1) To be aware of the integral image in mind, enhance the integral consciousness and bring all the members' competence into full play.

(2) To make a unified public relations policy, unify all the actions and paces and cooperate closely.

(3) To manage correctly the relationships between individuals and organizations, inferiors and superiors, parts and whole, and lay stress on the overall situation and entire target.

Part Four Modes of Government Public Relations

Due to different objects and specific targets, the government will carry out public relations activities in various modes, the major of which are as following:

I. Propaganda Mode of Public Relations

The mode of propaganda means that the government makes use of the public media or other propagating channels to actively pass on the information of their work or activities to both the inside and outside public in time, and publicize the government in its service aims, service projects, working targets and various policies, etc. At present, the government does self promotion mainly through the following channels:

i. To Hold Press Release

It is also called press conference where an organization will invite some journalists to attend and a designated person will declare some important information and be interviewed by journalists. Here are some features of press conference: (1) It is formal, ceremonious and credible; (2) It is good for an organization to release information comprehensively and objectively: (3) The propagating effect of press conference is closely related with its supporters and announcers' levels.

At present, press conference has been a popular form for many countries' governments to release their information. It has been a system for our central government to hold press conference ever since the Thirteenth Congress of the Party. It has been found that it is good to open the government work, inform the public of grand events, improve the relationship between the government and public and build a good image of the government.

ii. To Make Use of Press Media to Conduct Propaganda

In terms of mass communication, press media such as radio, TV, newspaper and network, etc, are the most effective means to disseminate information. Further, the government has their own advantage to use press media, as the government is the gathering place for information sources, which means press media will contact the government actively to get information. What's more, the government is authoritative and has the discourse power of press media, which makes press media easy to propagate according to the government's intention.

iii. To Use Government Public Relations Advertisements

The government public relations advertisement means the government organization buys space of printing media or time of electronic media to conduct propaganda in language or other ways without any interference of editors. In comparison with other advertisements, the government public relations advertisement has two unique features: (1) Different targets: Consumers are the targets of general advertisements, while the targets of the government public relations advertisements are the domestic and foreign public in various areas, the former of which is more wide-ranging. (2) Different purposes: General advertisements aim to promote sales of certain products or services, while the government's aim to communicate with the public in terms of the government's policies, law, decrees and some social focused on topics on economy, education or public welfare, etc, in an effort to communicate feelings, deepen understanding and gain the public praise; the former is profit-oriented, while the later is more commonweal –oriented.

iv. To Hold a press conference

It means the government make comprehensive use of words, pictures, material objects, illustrations, power points, videos, acoustics, and demo on spot, etc to propagate the government's policies, law and decrees. This form is direct, audio-visual, interesting and practical, which is easy to attract the pubic and offers an opportunity for the government to understand the pubic and exchange ideas with them.

II. Consulting Mode of Public Relations

This type of public relations means that the government tries to collect social information by seeking advices and asking for opinions from both the inside and outside public. This type of public relations functions as " government think-tank" with the aim to provide scientific evidence, design proper or optimized theories, policies and methods for government administration and to forecast some situations. Its working means are as following:

ⅰ. Opinion Poll

Opinion poll means to collect, reorganize, add up and report the public opinions timely and accurately by means of modern scientific methods and mathematical calculating methods, and determine the changes of social pubic opinions. It functions to reflect different opinions, attitudes, views and estimates from the public of different social classes on somebody, certain policy or any social issue, in an effort to provide evidence for different levels of government to make decisions and improve administrations.

ⅱ. Petition Letter

Petition Letter means the social public visit departments of the government or write them letters covering comments, suggestions, or put forward requirements, petitions and complaints. Petition letter is convenient for the government to collect information, feedbacks of the public and accept surveillance.

ⅲ. Interview

Interview, as a frequently-used method in the government public relations, is to collect data in words by talking with the interviewees. Interview is usually carried out face to face, with the investigators putting questions to the respondents and the interviewers keeping the minutes of replies, responses of and impressions left by the interviewees. Interview can be conducted as collective one, namely symposium, and individual one, with advantage of keeping secret.

Ⅲ. Intercommunicating Mode of Public Relations

This mode of public relations means the government carries out public relations by associating with the public. The government can contact directly with the public to pass on information and collect data in formal occasion where they appear to be serious, or an informal occasion, such as tea party, cocktail party, etc where they appear to be amiable and easy to touch the public and communicate with them, building the image of People First and People Cherished.

IV. Defensive Mode of Public Relations

It is also called crisis management, which means the government works out pertinent measures by analyzing the upcoming crisis according to the situation, with which the government can resolve the crisis in good order and recover the good image and credit of the government once the crisis happens. This mode of public relations functions as warning and preventing to eliminate the negative trend in the bud and reduce the bad effect of crisis to the least.

V. Rectifying Mode of Public Relations

It is also called remedy mode of public relations or crisis management, which means the government adopts correct measures to address or rectify the crisis with negative effect on the government public relations or benefits. There are following three steps in the procedure of rectifying mode of public relations:

i. Hands-on management to understand the situation

This is the first step of rectifying mode of public relations, as well as the common point for domestic and overseas government to handle issues successfully.

ii. Analyzing the Situation, Searching for Countermeasures

The second step is to analyze the situation to find out the reasons for the problem, and then work out remedy measures with relevant departments and working members.

iii. Putting the Countermeasures into Effect to Defuse the Crisis

This is a very important phase in the procedure, which is to take actions to put the countermeasures into effect and defuse the crisis. Without this step, the previous steps will be short of success.

There are many other modes of government public relations in addition to the above-mentioned five modes. The most important for the government public relations practitioners is to develop strong consciousness of public relations, as well as mastering these methods and techniques.

第一章
公共关系概述

第一节 公共关系发展史

一、公共关系的萌芽

现代意义上的公共关系起源于美国。19世纪中叶,美国风行一时的报刊宣传活动是现代公共关系的起源。当时美国出现了一种廉价的报纸,因为一便士就能买到,所以又叫"便士报"。它以普通大众为主要对象,印刷发行了大量以通俗为主的新闻。因为这样的报纸只需一便士就可以买到,所有购买量很大,这类"便士报"强调舆论的独立性,追求趣味性和刺激性,再加上价格低廉,所以很快风行一时,读者很多。当时,很多公司和财团看准这一机会,便纷纷雇人写煽动性新闻,为自己做夸大和虚假的宣传。而报刊为了迎合市民读者的心理,也乐于发表。在这种配合下便出现了当时的报刊宣传活动。菲尔斯·巴纳姆是这一时期最有代表性的报刊代理人,因制造轰动性舆论宣传而闻名于世。这种宣传运动的特点是宣传自己,单纯追求轰动效应,以欺骗公众利益为代价。假如披露真相会对组织产生不利的结果,就立刻调整组织自身的形象和行为,而不是极力去掩盖真相。所以它在公共关系历史上被称为"一个可耻的乞讨"。因此,有人称这是公共关系历史上一个不光彩的开端。

二、公共关系的职业化

19世纪末,美国进入了资本主义的垄断时期。由于垄断资本家肆意、贪婪地榨取劳动者的血汗,使得阶级矛盾不断激化,劳资关系异常紧张,从而引起了社会的强烈不满。在这种情况下,美国的新闻界首先掀起了一场揭露资本家恶行的"揭丑运动",报刊上刊登大量揭露和抨击资本家及政府丑行的文章,这种强大的舆论攻势致使许多大组织和资本家声名狼藉。垄断财团面对这种情况或者使用高压手段,或者使用贿赂手段试图平息舆论的攻击。但这些手段都未奏效,反而起了火上浇油的作用,更加引起公众的愤慨。于是,有人提议组织应该以"说真话""讲实情"来获得公众信任,这种主张被越来越多的工商界开明人士支持。艾维·李就是这一思想的主要代表。艾维·李曾是一名记者,他根据当时的情况,总结巴纳姆式报刊宣传活动的经验教训,提出了"说真话"的全新思想:一个组织要想获得良好的信誉,不是依靠向公众封锁消息或者以欺骗来愚弄公众,而是必须把真实情况披露于世,把与公众利益相关的所有情况必须告知公众。在这种环境下,艾维·李把"讲真话""公众必须被告知"规定为公共关系的基本原则并在美国创办了第一家正式的公共关系事务所,开展对外服务。从此,职业化的现代公共关系正式问世,艾维·李也被人们誉为"公共关系之父"。艾维·李虽是现代公共关系的创始人,但他的公共关系工作却主要是以感觉、经验和想象作为依据,而不是以科学的调查研究方法为手段,也没有系统的公共关系理论指导,因而他的公共关系实践活动被认为"只有艺术,没有科学"。

三、公共关系科学化

美国著名的公共关系学者爱德华·伯内斯(Edward L.Benays)是真正为公共关系奠定理论基础,使现代公共关系科学化的人。伯内斯在1923年出版了公共关系方面的理论著作《舆论》和教科书《公共关系学》,并于1923年首次在纽约大学开设公共关系课程。终于使公共关系的基本理论和方法形成一个较为完整的体系,使公共关系走向了科学化的阶段。伯内斯第一次提出了"公共关系咨询"的概念,明确肯定了公共关系的重要职责之一是向组织提供政策咨询,整个公共关系活动过程应当包括从策划、实施、反馈最后到重新评估等8个基本程序。他特别强调公共关系工作的针对性,要求公共关系人员应以公众态度为出发点,了解公众的喜好以及他们对组织有什么期待和要求，只有在确定了公众的价值观和态度这一基础上，才能进行组织的宣传沟通工作。伯内斯力求把社会科学的研究成果运用到公共关系实践当中，认为公共关系的沟通活动只有在一定的科学理论的指导下才能发挥威力。20世纪50年代以后，卡特利普、森特和杰夫金斯等一大批公共关系专家和大师，又继续伯内斯公共关系科学化的进程。他们出版了一系列公共关系的重要著作，提出了著名的"双向对称"公共关系模式。各类公共关系组织也相继地在世界各地涌现出来，公共关系专业的硕士学位、博士学位相继设立，公共关系不断吸纳各种新兴学科的知识并采纳先进的科技手段，使得公共关系很快成了一门具有丰富内容的独立学科，公共关系实务也获得了深入发展。当今世界，公共关系作为一种传播活动和管理职能，在经济、政治、文化、教育、科技、卫生、体育和军事等领域中发挥着巨大作用，成为各类非经济组织所必不可少的一种工作。20世纪80年代实行改革开放以来，公共关系也开始被引入中国市场。

四、公共关系在中国的发展

公共关系在中国也获得发展。1984年，广州白云山制药厂率先设立公共关系部，开始开展公共关系活动。1986年11月，中国第一家省级公共关系协会——上海市公共关系协会成立；1987年6月22日，中国公共关系协会在北京成立；1991年4月26日，中国国际公共关系协会（CIPRA）在北京成立。从公共关系在西方国家和我国产生和发展的历程可以看出，影响和推动公共关系发展的基本社会条件如下：1）商品经济的发展和市场竞争的形成。2）现代社会交往的发展。3）生产社会化的客观要求。4）政治民主化的发展。5）近现代管理科学的发展。6）教育的普及和公众文明程度的提高。7）工业技术和大众传媒的发达。

公共关系在中国经过多年的发展，目前已在社会经济诸领域得到广泛应用，无论政府、组织、组织还是个人，均已认识到公共关系的必要性与重要性。网络信息化的进步和信息技术飞速发展，为公共关系提供了一个良好的发展环境。中国社会主义市场经济快速扩大，中国公共关系事业不断发展，社会组织内部的公共关系部门日益增多，各类专业的公共关系机构逐渐在公共关系市场上确立了自身的地位，开始步入更加职业化和专业化阶段。

第二节 公共关系定义

一、什么是公共关系

许多人都试着把公共关系严格定义为高质量的形象塑造。然而公共关系与宣传并非同义词。宣传只是公共关系人员所使用的很多策略之一，也许最好的办法是把公共关系作为挂毯，许多零件错综复杂交织成一个整体布局。

首先我们来搜索一下公共关系的定义

那么什么是公共关系？借用一个流行的20世纪50年代的电视游戏节目的话，那就是64000美元的问题。不幸的是，没有明确的答案。公共关系的现代实践首先是20世纪初，研究者们才认真的开始研究并且开始定义。在21世纪之初，公共关系研究者开始从自己研究的角度去定义公共关系；而且每个人都认为自己的定义是好的。而且学者们也不断问不同的人一个问题：你认为什么是公共关系？当被提问者回答"我不知道"，或者答案是模糊的，学者们也不感到惊讶。事实上，这确实是一个难题，即使那些每天从事公共关系实务的人也很难用一个准确的定义来描述他们做什么。

这种混乱在调查会计师、律师和公共关系从业人员的时候得到了充分的说明。之所以选这三组人员是因为他们有共同点——他们与客户的顾问关系。每个组都被问及职业及其在组织内部的职位。尽管会计师和律师清楚地了解自己的角色，公共关系从业人员却并不了解。这引起了研究者提出一个问题：如果公共关系从业人员对于他们自己是谁以及在做什么都不清楚，为什么要指望别人理解？

甚至专家们关于什么是公共关系职业也没有得到任何共识。由于长期人们对公共关系进行所谓的消极的解释，许多组织使用委婉语来代替公共关系，如："公共事务""公共信息""传讯"或"社区外展"来形容公共关系工作。比如，博森·马斯泰勒公司，这是一个世界上最大的公共关系机构，在自己网站上介绍自己的公司为"全球观感管理公司。"

其他组织，特别是政府机构，试图隐藏他们的公共关系从业人员所做的一切行为，比如嫉妒对手和热心的削减预算，从而给他们自己安上一些看似无害的头衔，例如："特别助理"或"信息管理"。一个州的代理人员为了避免被审查，努力删除在北卡罗来纳州政府电话簿的清单。"公共信息办公室"的员工在接电话时候被指示重复办公室的分机号码而不是说"这里是公共信息办公室"。

二、公共关系的定义

1976年，公共关系的开拓者和学者雷克斯·哈洛为了消除一些关于公共关系的困惑，总结472个定义。从中提出了他自己关于公共关系的定义，强调公共关系作为一种管理功能，有助于建立和维持相互沟通、理解、接受，与合作组织与公众之间。

其他学者也曾试着用几个字来界定公共关系的含义，在《公共关系管理》一书中，教育者托德·亨特和拉姆斯E.格鲁尼界定公共关系为："社会组织与公众之间的管理沟通。"

公共关系从业者之间能达成共识的是关于公众的定义：公众是这样的一个群体，他们在特定情况下有着共同的利益和价值观——尤其是他们有共同的可能愿意采取行动的利益和价值观。

关于公共关系的定义很多，我们这里只选择几个来说明。比较早的并且被广泛接受的是美国《公共关系通讯新闻》中给出的定义："公共关系是一种管理职能，它可以用来评估公众态度、检测个人或者组织的政策、活动是否与工作利益一致，并负责设计与实施旨在争取公众理解与认可的行动计划。"

其他学者也给出了一些关于什么是公共关系的定义。美国著名的研究公共关系权威卡特利普和森特在《有效公共关系》中下了这样的定义："公共关系是一种管理职能，它确定、建立和维持一个组织与决定其成败的各类公众之间的互利关系。"

最早从事公共关系学教育的莱克斯·哈罗博士，搜集了将近500个关于公共关系的定义后，得出这样的定义："公共关系是一种特殊的管理功能。它帮助一个组织建立并保持与公众之间的交流、理解、认可与合作；它参与处理各种问题与事件；它帮助管理部门了解民意，并对之做出反应；它确定并强调组织为公众利益服务的责任；它作为社会趋势的监视者，帮助组织保持与社会变动同步；它使用有效的传播技能和研究方法作为基本工具。"

英国的公共关系协会认为：公共关系是一种积极的、有计划的以及持久的努力，以建立和维护一个机构与其公众之间的相互了解。

美国的爱德华·伯内斯认为：公共关系是一种处理一个团体与公众或者是决定该团体活力的公众之间的关系的职业；公共关系就是投其所好。

美国普林斯顿大学教授希尔兹指出："公共关系就是我们所从事的各种活动、所发生的各种关系的通称，这些活动与关系都是公众性的，并且具有其社会意义。"

中国的学者赵建华等认为：公共关系是一个社会组织在运行中为使自己与公众互相了解、相互合作而进行的传播活动和采取的行为规范。

范铨远等学者认为：所谓公共关系，是一个社会组织为了促进相关的公众对它的理解、合作和支持，而采取的一系列有计划的努力和活动。

还有的学者认为"公共关系是组织管理机构经过自我检讨与改进后，将其态度公诸社会，借以获得顾客、员工及社会的好感和了解的经常不断的工作""公共关系就是内求团结、外求发展""公共关系使公司得到的，就是那些在个人称为礼貌与德性的修养""公共关系就是要争取对你有用的朋友"等等。

王乐夫先生认为：公共关系是一种内求团结、外求发展的经营管理艺术。它运用合理的原则和方法，通过有计划而持久的努力，协调和改善组织机构的对内对外关系，使本组织机构的各项政策和活动符合广大公众的需求，在公众中树立起良好形象，以谋求公众对本组织机构的了解、信任、好感和合作，并获得共同利益。虽然公共关系的定义五花八门，但本书认为总的来说，仍然可以把各类说法归结为从静态和动态两个角度来理解什么是公共关系。

当公众与组织产生关系的时候，公众被称为利益相关者，这意味着他有你组织的股份或者在某方面潜在涉及您的组织利益。事实是，只要是人，他们都会用不同的视角来看世界。这就是为什么最好避免在定义公共关系时产生关于措辞是否确切的争论，相反，应该去关注行业本身的各种元素。在这里人们发现了共识。任何全面的公共关系定义都具有以下内容：

——公共关系是一项管理职能。一个组织和公众对其成功的重要的关系必须是组织的领导最关心的问题。公共关系从业者提供顾问的时间、方式，并提供重要的沟通方式。换句话说，从业人员不只是士兵服从命令；他们还是将军，帮助制定政策。像所有的管理人员一样，他们必须能够衡量他们的各种项目成功度。

——公共关系涉及双向沟通。在沟通中不仅仅是告诉人们一个组织需要什么。还包括聆听人们所关心的事情。这种倾听的意愿是建立关系过程的一个重要组成部分。

——公共关系是有计划的活动。公共关系是"计划过的"活动。以一个组织的名义所采取的行动必须经过精心策划，而且要和组织的价值观和目标一致。因此一个组织和公众对其成功的重要的关系是一个组织最关心的问题，这些行动还必须与公众的价值观和目标一致。

——公共关系是一个以研究为基础的社会科学。正式和非正式的研究使组织能有效沟通，并充分地了解环境所面临的问题。公共关系从业者和教育工作者也通过各种专业和学术刊物与同行业中的其他人来分享他们的知识。

——公共关系是一种社会责任。一个从业者的责任超出组织目标。因为从业人员和他们所代表的人们在社会中发挥建设性作用。

这样一个共同的主题贯穿整本列表：即关于管理的概念。有远见的、管理良好的组织知道他们必须与公众保持良好的关系，这对他们的成功至关重要。一个1 992次研究中，试图确定公共关系的卓越性，在研究中指出，一个组织与这些公众建立良好关系可以通过诉讼、监管、组织抵制等形式为组织省钱，或通过与这些团队建立友好关系减少损失。同时，研究表明一个组织培养与消费者、捐助者、股东和立法者的良好关系，可以赚更多的钱，。因此，培育这些良好的关系是公共关系从业者应该扮演的最重要的角色之一。

第三节　公共关系的特征、特点与原则

一、公共关系的基本特征

公共关系的基本特征可以概括为以下六点：

（一）对象为公众

公共关系是指一定的社会组织与其相关的社会公众之间的相互关系。公共关系是以组织为支点，建立组织与公众之间的良好关系。

社会组织必须坚持着眼于自己的公众，发展与他们的良好关系，才能使组织得以顺利发展。

（二）目标为美誉度

塑造形象是公共关系的核心问题和公共关系活动追求的目标。但是美誉不是由组织主观认定，而是由公众来认可、评价。只有通过公共关系活动与公众建立良好的关系，赢得公众的理解和支持，才能达到以美誉为标志的组织形象的建立。

（三）原则为互惠

公共关系是在商品经济的基础上产生的，它要取得一定的利益公众的支持。既要完成本组织的目标，又要让公众受惠。只有这样，才能够合作长久。

（四）长远为方针

良好的公共关系的形成和组织形象的塑造，不是一朝一夕就能建立起来的。即使建立起来了，也还需要不断地加以维护、调整和发展。公共关系活动需要长期不懈的努力。如果急功近利，只会适得其反，酿成大错。

（五）手段为传播

公共关系主要是通过各种信息传播媒介和沟通方法，去建立和维持组织与公众之间的交流，去了解和影响公众的意见、态度和行为。这是公共关系有别于其他工作的显著特点。

（六）信条为真诚

社会组织在与公众进行传播沟通时必须传播真实的消息，对公众的态度应当是真诚的，组织的各项活动也必须诚心诚意。只有真诚才能取信于众，只有真诚才能够赢得合作。所以，真诚是公共关系活动的基本信条。

二、公共关系主要特点

公共关系是为了使组织在社会公众中树立良好的组织形象。要求在信誉建立过程中，力争超过竞争对手。公共关系的对象研究是内部和外部的相关机构的各种关系。

公共关系不是短期的，它关注的是长期效应。组织通过各种公共关系策略的实施，占领市场，促进销售，树立良好形象。

公共关系强调的是对公众的真实性和平等性，坚决反对不平等或不择手段，采取欺骗的方法盈利。这样才能树立组织的公众形象，促进销售。在一定程度上，公共关系也是一种间接促销。

公共关系采用的基本方法是协调关系，也就是内外结合、双方沟通。组织内部的各种关系得到协调，能帮助组织在良好的环境中求得生存和发展。一个组织必须做到双方沟通，为组织的发展做好信息收集工作，使其更好地了解公众的需求。在此基础上，组织还须及时向公众传递其经营信息。

三、公共关系活动原则

公共关系在活动过程中需要遵循以下基本原则：

（一）实事求是的原则

求实原则要求公共关系在活动中实事求是地进行传播沟通活动。它主要包括以下几点：

第一，公共关系计划方案的制定是建立在实事求是的市场调查基础上的。

第二，向内外公众传播信息必须实事求是。

第三，评价事件必须客观公正。

第四，应当在公共关系活动中尊重民意。

如果对实事求是没有准确的把握，开展公共关系活动就失去了生存的基础和成功的条件；如不能真实地传递和公平地评价信息，就无法达到与公众的相互了解。公共关系是一项应用性、实践性很强的工作，不实则虚。如果采取回避的方法，就会使组织失去信誉，严重的甚至会影响到组织的生存。

（二）创新的原则

公共关系是一门经营管理艺术，只有不断创新，才能保持其旺盛的生命力。公共关系的促销策划、广告策划、传播策划等等，如果不能够做到别出心裁，与众不同，就不会给公众留下深刻、难忘的印象。

如果公共关系活动不能够刻意求新，就会陷入人云亦云，依样画葫芦的境地，公共关系活动就会浪费人、财、物等资源。

公共关系活动提倡："想人家没想过的，做人家没做过的。"

（三）公众利益至上的原则

公众利益至上的原则既是公共关系活动的重要原则，也是公共关系人员应该遵循的职业道德。组织只有时时、处处为公众利益着想，坚持公众利益优先，才能得到公众的好评，才能使组织自身获得更大的、长远的利益。

但是公众利益优先原则，并非是要组织完全牺牲自身的利益，而是要求组织在考虑自身利益与公众利益关系时，始终坚持把公众利益放在首位。

（四）互利互惠的原则

公共关系是以一定利益关系为基础的。它主张关系的双方在交往或合作中应该共同获益，共同发展。凡是有损组织关系对象的事情，最终必将损害组织自身。因此，维护组织公共关系对象的利益，也就是维护自身的利益。互利互惠的原则，强调组织与公众之间利益的平衡协调，"和自己的公众对象一同发展"。

另一方面，只有互利互惠才能建立最稳定、最可靠的关系。在商品经济社会里，没有互利互惠就没有平等的基础，就不可能建立正常、平等、互利、互惠的社会关系。

第四节　公共关系的要素

公共关系活动是一种双向沟通活动。整个公共过程实际上就是组织和公众借助公共关系传播而达到相互理解的过程。由此可见，公共关系是由三个要素组成的，即社会组织、公众和公共关系传播。组织是公共关系的主体，公众是公共关系的客体，公共关系传播是组织和公众联系的纽带与桥梁。由于公共关系活动是由这三个要素相互作用而成的，因此，我们首先要考察这三个要素。

一、社会组织

社会组织是人们按照一定的原则和方法有计划、有目的地建立起来的具有共同利益的集体或机构，如组织、学校、医院等。社会组织有多种类型。从业务性质来看，社会组织有经济类和非经济类之分，经济类组织是以追求经济效益为中心的，它的典型形式是组织。非经济类组织是追求社会效益为中心的，如社会福利机构、学校等。从规模来看，社会组织有大中小型之分，这主要是就社会组织的人力、物力和财力等要素的规模而言的。此外，社会组织还可以从地区、从所有制等进行分类。由于社会组织是公共关系的主体，所以，有多少类型的社会组织就应该有多少类型的公共关系。本书主要研究组织的公共关系问题。

二、公众

公众是公共关系的客体或对象，它是与组织相联系的各类个人、群体和组织的总和。作为公共关系对象的公众必须具备以下三个条件或属性：第一，相关性，即他们必须与特定的组织有关系或联系。公众总是相对于一定的公共关系主体即组织而言的，离开公共关系主体谈公众是没有意义的，在逻辑上也是不成立的。另一方面，这里的"联系"有特定含义，它是指公众的意见态度观点和行为具有实际的或潜在的影响或制约，而且组织的决策和行为也对这些公众的利益具有实际的或潜在的影响。所以，并不存在笼统意义上的公众，也不存在广泛意义上的公众。不同的组织有不同的公众。第二，整体性。由于组织在运行过程中要与许多方面发生关系，这些方面都会成为组织的公众，因此，组织的公众是一个综合体。以一个企业组织为例，它的公众包括内部职工、顾客、原材料供应商、社区、政府、银行，等等，这些公众对组织而言形成一个整体。当然，公众具有整体性并不是说每次公共关系活动都要把它们的全部作为对象。事实上，就每次公共关系活动而言构成公众的只是一个或几个部分。但就总体公共关系活动而言，我们必须具有全面、系统的观点去协调组织与整体公众的关系。第三，同质性。如上所述整体性是就所有公众而言的，它是总体公共关系活动要考虑的对象。对于每次公共关系活动而言，就应该考虑公众的同质性。所谓"同质"是指具有类似或相同的利益、态度、观点、需求等。只有同质才能形成集合体，才能对组织产生一种压力。因此，在进行具体的公共关系活动时应该分析同质公众，这些公众往往面临同样的问题。例如对于环境污染而言，同一个社区的公众构成同质总体，因为他们都深受环境污染之苦，组织的公共关系活动应把他们作为公共关系对象。由此可见，同一组织不同的公共关系活动也有不同的公众。综上所述，作为公共关系对象的公众必须具有相关性、整体性和同质性，而且不同的组织有不同的公众，同一组织不同的公共关系活动也有不同的公众。然而，虽然组织之间或公共关系活动之间公众的差异可能很大，但是对大多数组织或大部分公共关系活动而言，有一些公众是共有的。杰弗金斯认为这些基本公众主要有以下七类，即社区人员、本组织的员工、原材料供应商、商业经销商、财务公众、消费者或用户以及有影响的人士。组织在进行公共关系活动时必须认真地分析公众。这是因为：第一，分析公众进而确定公众可以识别和了解公共关系活动将要涉及的所有有关个人、群体或组织，这样便于制订有针对性的公共关系方案，提高公共关系效果；第二，分析公众并将他们按重要程度排序，有利于在公共关系预算或资源许可的范围内确定优先原则或取舍原则，因为不同公众对组织公共关系的重要程度是不同的；第三，如果不分析公众或不确定公众，其结果将是缺乏针对性，达不到预期目标，本想赢得太多公众而结果则往往因分散了精力和经费而适得其反。因此分析公众、确定公众应是每项公共关系方案的重要组成部分。

三、公共关系传播

它是组织和公众联系的中介，是借助于一定的媒介，根据一定的原则，采用一定的方式在双方之间进行沟通。公共关系虽然是管理职能但不是管理职能的全部。它不是万能的，其作用主要表现在两个方面：一是给高层管理部门和人员担任顾问，另一是将组织或高层管理部门的行动或决定告诉公众。公共关系的作用是：当政策顾问参与决策制订公共关系工作方案、说服最高管理部门接受方案取得中层管理人员的合作、争取其他雇员的合作及演讲发表演说，为别人撰写讲稿、为会议选择讲演人等。

以案例"小燕子"的一封信来说明：日本奈良市郊区有一家旅馆，外在环境优美，招待客人热情，很吸引顾客。但美中不足的是每年春季，许多燕子争相光临，在房檐下营巢安家，排泄的粪便弄脏了玻璃窗和走廊，服务员小姐擦不胜擦，使得旅客有点不快。旅馆主人爱鸟，不忍心把燕子赶走，但又难以把燕子粪便及时、彻底清除，很是苦恼。一天，旅馆经理忽然想出一条妙计。他提笔写道：女士们，先生们：我们是刚从南方赶到这儿过春天的小燕子，没有征得主人的同意，就在这儿安了家，还要生儿育女。我们的小宝贝年幼无知，我们的习惯也不好，常常弄脏您的玻璃和走廊，致使您不愉快。我们很过意不去，请女士们、先生们多多原谅！还有一事恳求女士们和先生们，请您千万不要埋怨服务员小姐，她们是经常打扫的，只是她们擦不胜擦。这完全是我们的过错。请您稍等一会儿，她们就来了。您的朋友：小燕子。这显然是以小燕子的名义写的向旅客们解释、道歉的信。旅馆经理把它张贴到显眼的地方。客人们看了这封公开信，都给逗乐了，不仅不再提意见，而且还对这家旅馆更感亲切，并留下了美好的印象。

本案例充分了说明主体与客体可以通过适当的沟通方式，消除误解，赢得公众的理解和支持，树立组织的良好形象。

社会组织、公众和传播沟通是公共关系学中三个最基本的概念，因为它们表达了公共关系现象中的三个最基本的要素。

第二章
公共关系从业人员

公共关系从业人员，这是对从事公共关系工作的职业人员的普遍而又常见的称呼。公共关系从业人员英文为PR Practitioner。在欧、美国家，对公共关系人员的称呼有PR Practitioner（公共关系从业人员）、PR Man（公共关系人员）、PR Officer（公共关系官员）等称呼。公共关系作为一种职业，对从业人员有着特殊的要求。公共关系从业基本素质和能力可以通过规范化的条例表达出来。

第一节　公共关系从业人员的基本素质与基本能力

公共关系工作涉及层次比较多，比如管理策划、公众分析、新闻传播甚至形象审美等等。这无疑需要从业人员具备管理、心理、新闻传播、形象设计与审美等多学科的知识和能力。

一、公共关系人员基本的素质

公共关系人员是公共关系活动的主体。如果我们把公共关系活动看成是塑造组织形象的工作，那么，这个工作需要公共关系人员来做。更具体一些说，塑造组织形象，需要对传播媒介进行操作，这些操作必须有公共关系人员的介入。一切公共关系活动都需要由人来组织，而公共关系人员则是组织公共关系活动最合适的正规人选。没有公共关系人员的努力，再好的公共关系策划都是无法实现。一切公共关系工作的成败得失、有效程度和创造活力，在很大程度上取决于公共关系人员的素质条件。

公共关系从业人员素质包括社会文化素质、心理素质和自然素质三个方面。

（一）社会文化素质

社会文化素质包括思想政治观念、道德行为规范和科学文化知识等。作为公共关系从业人员，其社会文化素质应具有以下基本内涵：

1. 政治素质与道德素质。政治素质与道德素质是公共关系从业人员开展公共关系工作的前提。它集中表现为：高尚的职业道德，包括精益求精的工作作风、认真踏实的工作态度以及忘我的牺牲精神和高度的责任感等。

公共关系工作具有很强的目的性。任何组织开展公共关系工作起码是为了获得较高的知名度和美誉度。公共关系从业人员往往直接代表组织与外界往来，他们在协调与处理各种公共关系时，首先应该作风正派、行为严谨、品质优良、道德高尚、不谋私利、不徇私情。高水平的思想政治素质与伦理道德素质，不仅能使公共关系从业人员个人而且能使其所代表的组织在社会公众中树立良好的形象与声誉，甚至能弥补公共关系从业人员其他素质条件的缺陷。如果公共关系从业人员缺乏良好的思想政治素质与伦理道德素质，那么公共关系工作的开展就失去了前提条件。不但公共关系工作不能正常开展，整个组织的社会形象也会遭受破坏。因此公共关系从业人员素质的首要部分，必须是较高水平的思想政治素质与伦理道德素质。

2. 科学文化素质。科学文化素质是公共关系人员开展公共关系工作的基础。随着时代的进步，世界在飞速变化，组织与组织之间激烈的竞争，无时无刻不在向公共关系从业人员的科学文化素质发起挑战。作为公共关系从业人员，应该认真审视自己的科学文化知识结构，充实、完善和更新自己的科学文化知识体系，提高自身的科学文化水平。

公共关系从业人员应该掌握以下知识：

（1）公共关系专业知识。公共关系学是公共关系实践的理论概括，它总结出了公共关系的基本规律、程序，介绍了具体公共关系活动的基本技巧、方法，是公共关系从业人员从事公共关系活动的理论指南。公共关系从业人员只有掌握公共关系的基本原理和方法，遵循公共关系的基本规律，灵活运用公共关系技巧和方法，才能有效地达成公共关系工作的目标。

（2）与公共关系密切相关的知识。公共关系从某种意义上讲是一种管理活动,它借鉴了管理学中行为科学的许多理论;公共关系以传播为手段,须大量运用人际传播、大众传播技术;公共关系工作直接面对社会、面对人,须研究人的心理、态度、行为。由此可见,公共关系是一门涉及管理学、市场营销学、传播学、社会学、心理学等学科的综合性边缘应用学科,公共关系从业人员应该了解与其密切相关的这些学科的知识。

(3)开展特定公共关系工作所需的专业知识。如果公共关系从业人员要为商业组织开展公共关系工作,就必须了解流通领域的基本常识、商业竞争的规律;如果一个组织要开拓国际市场,就需要了解国际公共关系知识、国际市场营销知识、国际市场竞争的基本格局和对象国的政治、经济、文化、风俗习惯等方面的知识。只有掌握好相关工作的专业知识,才能在公共关系活动中取得良好的公共关系效果。

(二)心理素质

心理素质,也就是个性心理品质,是公共关系从业人员做好公共关系工作的关键。在心理素质方面,对公共关系人员的要求大致有以下三个方面:

1.自信的心理

自信,这是对公共关系人员职业心理的最基本的要求。一个人有了自信,才会产生自信力,在从事公共关系工作中才能游刃有余,吸引更多的公众,最终创造出奇迹。

古人云:"自知者明,自信者强。"充满自信的公共关系人员,敢于面对挑战,敢于追求卓越,他们自信能超人,自信能胜人,因而自强不息。这样的公共关系人员塑造的组织形象,必然是良好的形象。如果公共关系从业人员缺乏自信,则塑造的组织形象也是缺乏卓越的平庸的形象。

公共关系工作是一种复杂的程序,公共关系人员虽然能在一定程度上预测到工作的结果,但还是需要冒一定的风险,这就需要有自信。当然,这种自信是建立在周密的调查研究、全面了解情况的基础之上,而非盲目自信。当一个组织遇到危机时,缺乏自信的公共关系人员通常会显得手足无措,一片慌乱,即使有很好的转机,这样的公共关系人员也难以把握;而充满自信的公共关系人员,面对这种情况,使组织转危为安。就像法国哲学家卢梭所说的那样,"自信心对于事业简直是奇迹,有了它,你的才智可以取之不尽,用之不竭。一个没有自信力的人，无论他有多大才能，也不会有成功的机会"。

2.热情的心理

从事公共关系工作的人员应有一种热情的心理。公共关系工作不是一种简单轻松工作，而是一种需要人们付出大量智力和体力劳动的艰辛的工作。很多公共关系人员头脑中几乎都没有八小时工作制的概念，他们有的只是加班加点超负荷工作习惯，没有极大的热情，没有全身心的投入，是做不好公共关系工作的。拥有热情的心理，才能使公共关系人员兴趣广泛，对事物的变化有一种敏感性，且充满想象力和创造力。一个对什么都没兴趣、对一切都漠然的人，是无法胜任公共关系工作的。这样的人在做公共关系工作的时候，就不会主动，往往处于被动式中，其工作效果十分有限。公共关系人员也需要凭借热情的心理，来与各种各样的人打交道，结交众多的朋友，拓展工作的渠道。缺乏热情的人，既不能接受别人，也不可能为别人所接受。

3.开放的心理

公共关系工作是一种开放型的工作，从事这种工作的人需要有一种开放的心理。公共关系工作是一种创造性很强的工作，这种工作要求人们以开放的心理，不断接受新的事物、新的知识、新的观念，在工作中敢于大胆创新，做出突出的贡献。具有开放心理的人，能宽容、接受各种各样与自己性格不同、风格不同的人，并能"异中求同"，与各种类型的人建立良好的关系，这是公共关系工作十分需要的。公共关系人员有开放的心理，就能在很多方面表现出一种高姿态，冷静地对待和处理工作中所遇到的困难和挫折，而不会斤斤计较一时一事的得失。

（三）自然素质

自然素质，即先天遗传的生理素质，包括解剖生理特征和生理机能特征。自然素质包括有健康的体魄，很强的适应力和快速的反应力，超负荷的承受力、适应能力、抵抗能力等等。公共关系从业人员的自然素质要求"自然美"，如身体健康、五官端正、四肢健全无畸形、身高符合现代审美标准、身手敏捷、灵巧、抵抗能力、负荷能力和适应能力强。

公共关系从业人员还要具备以下意识：

1.形象的意识

形象的意识是公共关系意识的核心。公共关系活动中，最重要的是珍惜信誉、重视形象。现代组织都十分重视组织形象。良好的组织形象，是一个组织的无形资产和无价之宝。组织的形象必须是真实的，而非虚假的；组织的良好形象，必须以组织的良好行为和优质产品或服务为基础，而非编造出来的。公共关系从业人员必须具备强烈的塑造形象的意识，时时刻刻像保护眼珠一样维护组织的形象。

2.服务公众的意识

形象是为组织的特定对象所塑造的，这些特定对象必然与组织有着某种联系，他们是组织的公众。离开了公众，孤立的组织形象是毫无意义的；忽视了公众，组织的生存就会受到威胁，自然也就更谈不上组织的进一步发展了。任何组织的公共关系工作都必须着眼于公众。当组织利益与公众发生冲突时，满足公众利益应该是第一位的。现代公共关系教育的先驱、美国著名公共关系学者爱德华·伯内斯早在1923年就指出：公共关系工作是为了"赢得公众的赞同"，"公共关系应首先服务于公众利益"。公共关系从业人员必须具有服务公众意识，能时时处处为公众利益着想，利用条件、创造条件来为公众服务，努力满足公众方方面面的要求。

3.真诚互惠的意识

真诚互惠的意识是公共关系的功利意识。否认公共关系工作的功利性，这是自欺欺人。一个处在当今竞争社会中的组织，需要有一种竞争态势，但在我们社会主义国家，这种竞争不应是"你死我活"或"大鱼吃小鱼"，而应是既竞争又合作，共同发展，共同前进。任何组织也都想通过公共关系工作，追求自身经济效益和社会效益的最佳统一，但这种追求，必须建立在彼此尊重、平等合作、互惠互利的基础上，而非建立在欺骗他人、坑害公众的基础上。公共关系从业人员在进行公共关系工作的时候必须培养真诚互惠的意识。

4.沟通交流的意识

沟通交流的意识，实际上也可以说是一种信息意识。组织为了塑造良好形象，更好地为公众服务，以实现其目标，就必须构架一个信息交流的网络，来掌握环境的变化，保护组织的生存，促进组织的发展。从更高的层次说，沟通交流的意识是现代社会的民主意识。公共关系活动是一种具有民主性的经营和管理活动。组织为了塑造能为公众所接纳的良好形象，以求得公众对组织的支持，就必须倾听公众对组织的各种建议和批评；组织为了推销自身的良好形象，提高知名度和美誉度，就必须运用交流的技巧，将自身所作所为宣传出去。而这一切都必须依赖于一种民主精神、民主意识。

5.创新的意识

塑造组织良好形象是一个创新的过程。组织的良好形象一旦塑造起来，就需要相对稳定。但相对稳定并不等于一成不变，它应是一种积极的稳定，即在稳定中孕育发展，包含发展。只有在发展的基础上才能实现真正的稳定，同样，也只有在稳定的前提下才会有真正的发展。既然组织的良好形象需要发展，那么，就必须有创新、有突破、有超越，既超越自己，又超越其他组织。至于组织良好形象塑造过程中的每一个公共关系活动，其策划与设计也需要有创新。公共关系是一门具有创造性的艺术，那么，它必然具有审美价值。很难想象组织的良好形象是不美的，是丑的。唯有美的形象，才能为人们所欣赏、所接受；唯有美的活动，才能为人们所参与、所投入。

6.立足长远的意识

塑造组织良好形象，不是一朝一夕的事，而需要通过长期努力，不断积累，才能取得成功。公共关系活动与广告或推销不同，如果说后者更多地着眼于眼前，注重较为直接的效益，那么，前者从根本上来说，立足于长远，追求长期的效益。任何急功近利，只关注眼前利益的组织都不会获得长期的发展。

二、公共关系人员的基本能力

公共关系是一项实际操作能力很强的工作。1999年，国家劳动与社会保障部提出公共关系的职业能力特征是：较强的口头与书面语言表达能力，协调沟通组织内外公众的能力，调查、咨询、策划和组织公共关系活动的能力。公共关系人员的基本能力，大致可以概括为五个方面的能力：

1.表达能力

包括书面表达能力和口头表达能力，"能说会写"是公共关系从业人员的基本能力。公共关系人员担负着对内外传播的任务，要撰写新闻稿件、演讲稿、咨询方案，起草活动方案，编写刊物，这些都要求公共关系人员具有一定的文字功底。口头表达方式是最便捷的沟通手段，从事公共关系工作，要与各类公众打交道，要求公共关系人员能清晰无误地传播信息，和公众进行言语沟通。

2. 交际能力

是指通过人际交往传递信息、增进了解、强化感情的能力。缺乏人际交往能力的人，往往在工作和生活中诸事不顾，困难重重。公共关系人员是社会组织的代言人，是组织形象的体现者，肩负着沟通公众、树立形象的重任，只有具备一定的社交能力，才能立于不败之地。社交能力是各方面能力的综合体现，如推销本组织的能力，与人相处的能力，吸引、改变、影响他人的能力，还包括通晓并遵守社交场合的礼仪规范能力。

3. 组织能力

是指有计划、有步骤、有目的地开展和完成某项具体活动的能力。一个活动的完成包括调查、策划、组织人力、物力以及进程把握等环节，这是对公共关系人员组织能力的检验。公共关系活动往往和组织活动分不开，如各类庆典活动、新闻发布会、新产品推广等。公共关系人员要自始至终合理统筹、合理安排，圆满完成任务。

4. 应变能力

是指应付突发情况的能力。世界上任何事物都处在千变万化之中，公共关系工作莫不如此。公共关系人员会经常遇到一些突发事件，公共关系人员必须在突发事件中处乱不惊，紧急应变，这就要求公共关系人员必须具有驾驭环境、坦然应变的能力。

5. 创新能力

是指公共关系人员在公共关系工作中具有创新的思维，工作内容创新，手段创新。任何一种公共关系工作都要求公共关系人员充分发挥思维创造能力，设计出具有新意的公共关系活动，吸引公众，激发公众的兴趣，使公共关系工作富有新意。

第二节 公共关系从业人员的职业道德及公共关系人员的培养

一、公共关系人员的职业道德

道德是一种社会意识形态,是人们调整自身及相互关系的思想意识和行为准则。一个社会要有一个社会的基本道德,一个行业也要有一个行业的道德准则。公共关系工作也必须具有一定的职业道德,以约束公共关系人员的工作过程,规范其职业行为。

1923年,美国公共关系学专家爱德华·伯内斯就在他的第一本公共关系著作中提出了公共关系从业人员的职业道德问题。此后,各国的公共关系协会、国际公共关系协会,制定了公共关系的职业道德和行为准则。在众多的职业准则中,《国际公共关系道德准则》的影响最大。我国也制定了相关的职业道德准则。不论哪个国家的公共关系道德准则,对公共关系人员都有以下要求:

(一)公共关系从业人员的道德

公共关系工作的性质决定了公共关系从业人员必须具备良好的道德品质,这是因为:一方面,公共关系工作是塑造良好形象的工作,这就要求塑造形象的人首先自己要有良好的形象。一个没有道德品标准的人,是没有资格从事公共关系工作的。许多国家的公共关系协会,在会章中都特别强调公共关系工作人员必须具有优良的品德;另一方面,公共关系工作的对象是公众,在和公众交往的过程中难免会受到社会上不良行为影响和金钱物质方面的诱惑,这就要求公共关系人员自身要有良好的品德,才不会被腐蚀,成功地完成公共关系工作。

公共关系人员在道德方面,主要包括以下内容:

1.高度的社会责任感。也就是公共关系人员在考虑问题时,不仅要重视所在组织的利益,而且要重视公众利益,既对组织负责也要对公众负责,担负起社会的责任。

2. 公正。公共关系人员要在工作中对于自己所服务的社会公众一视同仁，平等相待，不能厚此薄彼。

3. 与人为善，诚恳待人，守信用，不谋私利，作风正派。即在工作中对待公众要态度诚恳，遵守承诺，不见利忘义。

4. 埋头苦干，有奉献精神。公共关系人员在工作中，要不怕困难，知难而进，有为公共关系事业献身的精神，这样才能克服工作中的重重困难，在公共关系事业上有所成就。

5. 知法、守法、用法。公共关系人员要知法、守法，还要懂得运用法律保护组织的权益。除具有法律意识外，还应在遇到有违法乱纪的行为时，能勇敢地站出来予以揭露、控告或制止，决不能听之任之，更不能同流合污、知法犯法。

（二）公共关系职业准则

在所有的公共关系道德准则中，《国际公共关系道德准则》无疑是影响最大的。很多国家直接采用此准则，或以此为范本制定自己的职业道德准则。长期以来，国际公共关系协会就致力于推动各国公共关系工作职业化和规范化。

公共关系组织和人员良好的职业道德品行，是推动公共关系工作走向成熟和成功的保证。公共关系工作职业准则主要包括以下内容：

1. 恪尽职守，真诚待人。公共关系人员的根本任务是为组织塑造组织的良好形象，以及为组织的生存和发展创造良好的环境，同时为公共关系事业的发展做出贡献。因此，衡量一个公共关系人员是否具有高尚职业道德，最重要的是看他对公共关系事业是否尽心尽力、尽职尽责，有良好的职业道德。公共关系人员应热爱本职工作，对工作尽心负责，有强烈的职业责任感，能充分履行本职工作应尽的社会责任，有很强的道德观念，不参与任何本职工作相悖的事务，不违背国家的法律制度，不泄露组织的机密，不做有损于组织形象、信誉的事。而那些玩忽职守、自由散漫、无组织无纪律的思想和行为，都是不道德的。另外，公共关系人员在对待职业的态度上要体现出诚实的态度。真诚是公共关系的生命所在。缺乏真诚，就不能取得公众的信任和支持，就不能有效地开展公共关系工作。这就要求公共关系人员真诚待人，讲真话，讲实话，注重透明，注重公开，不弄虚作假，不欺上瞒下，做到说话、办事、做人表里如一，实事求是；不投机取巧，一切行动都经得起检查和考验。

2. 不断学习，努力工作。公共关系是不断由实务构成的。而公共关系实务能否成功主要取决于公共关系从业人员的能力和水平，公共关系人员职业道德水平如何，不但要看有无自觉履行职责的愿望，还要看有无出色履行职责的过硬本领。公共关系人员干好工作凭实力，凭真才实学。不断学习新知识是公共关系人员应该做好的。如果公共关系从业人员整天不学无术，在工作中常出差错，不仅自己形象受损，而且会给公众、组织乃至整个社会带来损失，都是不遵守职业道德的表现。

3. 廉洁奉公，不谋私利。服务于社会、服务于组织、服务于公众是公共关系工作的基础工作，每个公共关系人员只有为公众、组织、社会谋福利，公共关系工作才能做成功，公共关系人员不能利用手中的权力为私人谋取利益。公共关系人员的工作性质和特点，决定了他们拥有较广泛的社会关系并且掌握着一定的权力。这些关系和权力，不仅对组织有利，而且对个人也有用。因而廉洁奉公、不谋私利的职业道德，对公共关系人员来说十分重要。优秀的公共关系工作者始终把国家利益、公众利益、组织利益放在首位，他们时刻牢记：权力是人民给的，个人不仅代表自己，更是代表着组织的形象。那种利用职权营私舞弊、贪污受贿、欺诈勒索，是不道德的。

4. 公道正直，耐心团结。公共关系事业是高尚的事业，献身于这一事业的公共关系人员应该有高尚的品德。因此，每一个公共关系人员都应做到为人正直、处事公道、不拿原则做交易。那些公私不分、争功夺利、妒贤嫉能的行为，都是背离公共关系职业道德的思想行为。公共关系工作是一种群体工作。合作、互助、友爱、互相信任和互相尊重，是工作顺利、事业成功的可靠保证。公共关系人员在待人接物上，应表现出耐心、尊重、举止、言谈、衣着都应得体有分寸，应作风民主、平等待人、气度宽宏、容人之短、闻过则喜、知错必改。这些都是做好公共关系工作的重要条件。

二、公共关系人员的培养

随着社会的不断进步和发展完善，经济体制改革正推动着行政和组织职能的分离。组织走向市场，组织之间的各种形式的联合、协作和竞争，使公共关系活动得以广泛开展，并逐步走向成熟，在社会活动中显示出越来越重要的作用。作为公共关系活动的核心因素之一，公共关系人员的出色工作将是推动经济发展和经济体制改革的重要因素。因此，开展公共关系人才培养已成为当前公共关系工作的重要课题。

对于公共关系人员的培养途径有很多，总结下来主要有以下几点：

1.通过学校的学习相关课程，可以在大学、中等专科院校建立公共关系专业，同时开设公共关系课程来增加大学生获取公共关系相关理论知识。国内外不少大中专院校在新闻、管理、商业、外贸、旅游等系开设公共关系课程，也有很多大学可设公共关系专业，公共关系专业主要培养从事公共关系工作的专门人才，课程设置要有很强的科学性和系统性，可以使学生拥有合理的知识结构，同时要培养学生的实践能力。对学生进行公共关系理论和实务知识的教育，有助于完善不同专业学生的知识结构。有志于公共关系事业的学员，在在获取公共关系理论和实务知识后，通过适当的实践锻炼后，就可以担任某些项目的公共关系工作。

2.通过参加社会实践来增加公共关系的实践经验。有些公共关系人员，没有学习过相关的公共关系理论知识，他们在工作中，有机会参加公共关系实务活动，经过切实的参与公共关系多次实务活动后，获取了丰富公共关系实务知识，再在业余时间自学补充相关的公共关系理论知识，这样也会担任其从事公共关系工作。

3.举办公共关系培训班和函授教育。近几年来，全国各地公共关系组织举办了不少中短期公共关系培训班，向社会在职人员介绍公共关系的基本理论，交流公共关系的经验。一些高等院校举办了公共关公共关系基础系函授教育。接受公共关系培训和函授教育的人一般具有一定的社会工作经历，能够理论联系实际。所以，面向在职人员进行公共关系培训教育，对迅速充实公共关系队伍，提高公共关系人员的素质，增强能力，有着不可低估的作用。当然，这种培训方式还需要进一步提高质量。

第三章
公共关系的工作程序

公共关系工作有四个工作程序,即公共关系调查、公共关系策划、公共关系实施和公共关系评估。其中公共关系调查是确定问题,是工作的前提;公共关系策划是工作的重点;公共关系实施是工作的关键;公共关系评估是工作的保证。

第一节 公共关系调查

公共关系调查是公共关系工作程序的第一步,公共关系调查是指公共关系部门或者公共关系人员运用定量分析和定性分析相结合的方法,科学地、准确地调查研究组织的公共关系历史和现状,分析预测内外部公共关系发展趋势,检验公共关系活动效果的一系列公共关系实务活动。公共关系的调查应该善于运用科学的方法,有步骤地考察组织的公共关系状况,了解公共关系活动的条件,为公共关系活动的策划和实施提供科学的依据。

一、公共关系调查目的和意义

1. 为组织的形象定位与塑造服务。组织的社会形象是由公众的评价来决定的。通过公共关系调查,组织可以准确地了解其在公众中的形象地位,了解公众对组织的知晓程度以及对组织的看法,从而可以找出组织自我期望形成的公共关系活动的策划工作,有利于提升公共关系活动的实效性。

2. 强化组织与公众的联系,及时把握公众舆论。公共关系调查的结论是在统计分析具体、真实的数据基础上得出的,具有很强的权威性;而且,这些数据的取得需要公共关系调查人员同调查对象进行多种形式的交流。因此，公共关系调查的过程实际上也是组织与公众沟通的过程，借此可以进一步强化彼此间的联系。更重要的是，公共关系调查能够准确、及时地监测与把握公众的意见和看法，这就是公众舆论。众所周知，在现代社会，公众舆论具有巨大的社会影响力。积极的公众舆论有利于组织的发展，消极的公众舆论有损于组织的形象，甚至会造成组织的危机。通过公共关系调查，监测公众舆论，组织可以及时采取适当措施来扩散积极舆论、减少负面舆论，这对于组织的形象塑造来说意义重大。

3. 为组织的科学决策提供重要依据。没有调查就没有发言权，没有调查也就没有决策。公共关系调查的主要任务，是为了获得全面、真实、准确的组织形象和公众意愿方面的相关数据，避免公众不感兴趣的公共关系项目，预防组织把时间、人力、物力和财力资源浪费在不重要或者并不存在的事情上。在调查中获取的资料可以为组织管理层进行相关决策时做参考，并能让决策的正确与否得到有效检验。公共关系调查的数据越周密，组织的决策就越符合公众意愿，产生的效果就会越理想，组织的良好形象也能得到很快提升。

4. 提高公共关系活动的有效性和成功率。组织的公共关系活动如果是建立在全面、真实、准确的调查研究基础之上，再加上相关对策的谋划科学，公共关系工作策划就会有很强的针对性，并切实可行，实施的效果必然会相当理想。

二、公共关系调查的内容

（一）组织自身状况调查

公共关系调查中组织自身调查是基础，主要包括以下几方面的内容：

1.组织基本情况调查

组织基本情况调查主要包括：

（1）组织的历史、公共关系状况、组织的性质、任务、类型与规模，组织的管理体制、机构设置、主管部门等；

（2）组织的经营情况，包括组织的经营发展目标、组织的企业精神、组织的经营方针、经营战略、组织的产品及特色、组织的市场占有率等；

（3）组织的荣誉情况，如组织所获得的荣誉、奖励，组织对社会做过哪些贡献、做过哪些慈善活动等。

（4）组织的文化情况。包括组织的物质文化、行为文化、精神文化和制度文化，例如企业文化、企业精神、经营理念、文化活动等。

2.组织实力情况调查：

组织实力情况调查的主要内容包括：

（1）组织的物质基础，如组织的占地面积、生产设备、试验设施、办公环境和手段等；

（2）组织的技术实力情况，如组织拥有的技术人员的数量和知识构成情况，组织拥有的科研器材和实验手段、组织技术的领先程度等；

（3）组织的经济实力情况，如组织的固定资产总额、流动资金总额、组织在同行中的竞争力、组织的上市情况、人均利润等；

（4）组织成员的待遇情况，如组织成员的住房面积、工资水平、劳动保障情况等。

（二）相关公众调查

1.公众构成情况调查：

每个组织都有多方面的公众，这些公众关乎着组织的生存和发展，所以对公众调查至关重要，主要包括以下内容：

（1）内部公众构成情况，如人员数量、专业构成、年龄构成、性别构成、能力构成、文化程度构成、职务职称构成等；

（2）外部公众构成情况，如外部公众的数量、构成、特征、需求，以及与组织的联系状态、对组织的重要性、对组织的依赖性等。

2.公众需求调查：

公众需求调查主要包括：公众对组织的期望值、公众对组织的态度、公众对组织有哪些需求等。

公共关系调查是社会调查的一种形式，但与其他的社会调查的关注点有所不同。它根据公共关系管理的需要，通过收集相关信息、分析各种问题及其相互关系，考察组织的公共关系状态尤其是公众对于组织形象的评价，确立公共关系目标，或者检验某一项公共关系活动的实际运作效果。公共关系调查是一项专门的技术，它不仅可以有效管理组织的相关信息，同时也是组织开展公共关系活动的必要前提。

（三）传媒调查

主要包括组织利用的传媒分布在哪些地区、有类型分布、覆盖范围有多大、传播内容如何、有哪些传播特色、传播重点是什么、传播动向在哪里、传播效果如何、社会影响怎么样等方面的调查。

（四）社会环境调查

调查范围包括政治环境、经济环境、社会环境、科技环境、竞争环境等。

政治环境调查包括所在国家和地区的政治结构、政治气氛和变化趋势，国家和政府有关部门近期已颁布或有可能颁布的各项政策和法令以及这些政策与法令对组织的发展有可能产生的影响。

经济环境调查包括世界经济发展现状和走向、国家经济发展战略、经济发展趋势、资源和能源的储量和开发情况、当前国民经济发展的整体水平。国民收入的现状和发展趋势、社会购买力的特点以及居民消费结构的变化特点和发展趋势。

社会环境调查包括社会观念和行为规范的变迁、社会流行思潮及其对公众行为的可能影响、人们的价值观念、行为方式、消费倾向、宗教信仰、文化素质、道德规范等方面的变化以及上述因素对组织发展的制约和影响。

科技环境调查包括目标市场的技术水平、技术特征、技术要求、技术标准、技术类型以及国际市场创新的趋势和值得关注的问题。

竞争环境调查包括组织所在的行业情况、组织在竞争中所处的地位、竞争对手的现状和动向以及竞争对手的公共关系活动情况。

三、公共关系调查的原则

调查工作是一项复杂的系统工程，对数据的真实性要求很高。因此相关的准备工作要充分，参与人员要精干，实施程序要科学合理。考虑到调查对象的数目巨大，为了保证数据的可靠性，公共关系调查要求所选调查对象必须具有较高的代表性、能反映总体现象的全面情况，因此抽样调查的方法被广泛采用。

公共关系调查的基本原则是：

（一）提前规划的原则

第一，公共关系调查是一项重要而复杂的经常性工作，必须体现在组织的季度、年度工作计划中,并有一套科学、规范的工作程序。

第二,在开始一项具体的公共关系调查之前,应该制定周全的调查策划,对任务指标、人员安排、工作进度以及可能出现的问题和对策做一个详细的方案。

调查策划在实施前需要进行可行性评估和优劣评估。可行性评估方法通常有逻辑分析法、经验判断法和试点调查法,检查调查策划是否符合逻辑和实际情况,存在哪些问题,是否切实可行。优劣评估有三个角度:一是策划是否准确体现了调查的目的和要求;二是策划的科学性、操作性如何;三是策划可否使调查的质量明显高于以往类似调查的质量。

(二)以事实为依据的原则

公共关系调查的目的就需要全面真实的数据。由于条件有限,公共关系调查中运用普查比例不大,经常采用的方式是抽样调查、问卷调查、新闻调查和重点访谈等方法。因此,在确定调查对象时首先要注意其代表性,这些代表必须能真实反映出其所代表的公众的整体态度和全面情况,既有全面性,又有代表性。其次,在调查过程中要准确把握公众对于组织的客观态度,不能把公众的主观臆想当作客观态度,使数据失真。最后,调查数据必须尽可能地全面,各个方面公众的各种意见都要真实、客观地反映出来。

此外,以事实为依据的原则也要求公共关系调查人员立场要客观,不能因为自己是组织的员工就对公众对于组织的某些看法有所偏重,既要如实宣传组织的成就,对组织存在的问题也要实事求是,不掩盖不回避。

总之一句话,公共关系调查所取得的数据要真实反映出目标公众的真实态度。

(三)尊重公众原则

公共关系调查是组织的常规性工作,公共关系人员在此过程中的表现也代表着组织的形象。因此,在整个调查工作中,调查人员都要举止文雅、态度谦和、细致耐心,尊重公众的生活习惯、宗教信仰、生活方式等,以此获得公众的积极配合,从而获得真实可靠的信息。否则,既损害组织的形象,也会妨碍调查工作的顺利进行。

(四)讲求效益原则

这里的效益原则包含两个意思。第一是讲求经济效益,第二是要使调查有时效性。公共关系调查是一项费时费力的重大工作，费用一般不会小。只有科学规划、统筹安排、勤俭节约才能取得"花小钱办大事"的效果。此外，要注意调查工作的时效性。公共关系调查都是在一定的时间内进行的，公众的态度随时会因各种因素发生改变。既要做到公共关系调查实施的全面准确，又要做到对公共关系调查数据处理的迅猛快捷。只有这样，才能够把调查报告及时提供给组织决策层，便于组织及时采取相应的对策。

四、公共关系调查的方法

公共关系调查要采取一定的方法，调查方法是实现调查目标的途径，科学的方法是获得科学结论的重要前提。在公共关系调查工作中，常用的方法有：

（一）抽样调查法

抽样调查又称为样本调查，是根据部分实际调查结果来推断总体调查对象情况的一种方法。其原理是，按照一定的科学程序、方法、步骤从若干单位组成的事物总体中，抽取部分样本单位进行试验、观察，用所得到的调查数据来代表样本总体，推断总体情况。科学地抽取样本是公共关系调查中的关键环节，如果调查样本抽取不科学、不具有代表性，调查结果就会失真。

抽样调查一般分为随机抽样或者概率抽样、非随机抽样也叫重点调查两大类。随机抽样又可以分为简单随机抽样、系统抽样（等距抽样）、分层抽样、聚类抽样（整群抽样）等；非随机抽样又分为判断抽样、定额抽样、典样、聚类抽样（整群抽样）等；非随机抽样又分为判断抽样、定额抽样、典型调查、个案调查等。抽样法是在公共关系调查中最为常用的方法。

（二）普查法

普查法也称为全面调查法。指的是在规定的时间内，按照一定的方法，统一的项目、统一的调查表和统一的标准时点，对全体样本普遍进行无遗漏的、一次性的调查登记的方法。如我国的人口普查采用的就是此法。除非特需，这种调查法仅适合于调查对象总体数目不大、调查成本不高的情形。

普查法能够获得全面、准确、完整的信息资料，其结论具有相当的权威性，便于调查者从宏观上、整体上掌握情况。在调查对象数目较小时，是获取调查对象全面信息的最佳选择。但这个调查法的缺点也很明显，主要就是当调查对象数目较多时，不仅需要投入的成本太高，而且很难获得更深入的资料。所以这种调查法不常被采用。

（三）媒介调查法

媒介调查包括两种具体操作法，一种是新闻调查法，一种是网络调查法。

新闻调查法，就是调查人员根据各类新闻媒介上出现的新闻报道，了解并研究调查公众的意见和态度的方法。

网络调查法，指的是调查人员通过网络获取调查公众信息的方法。公共关系调查人员可以通过点击访问、传递电子邮件和在线发放问卷等方式同公众交流。由于网络具有传播范围广、传播速度快、亲和度高等特点，不仅可以使得公共关系调查的数据来源广泛，且能够及时获取直接信息，获取相对真实的信息。

（四）重点访谈法

此法是通过人际交往的方式进行调查的一种方法。选择关键人群或重点人物（政府官员、社会名流或舆论领袖）做访谈，直接向他们提出问题让其直接回答，以调查和了解他们的意见和态度，然后分析这些态度和意见的形成原因，探究改变这些意见和态度的途径的一种方法。之所以选择这些重点人物，主要是考虑到他们有一定的知名度和社会号召力，能左右公众意见和态度。

重点访谈法可分为三种形式：面对面访谈法、网络访谈、电话访谈。这种方法对调查人员的综合素质特别是社会交往能力的要求比较高。此外，如何确定合适的重点人物也是一个挑战性很强的工作。

（五）问卷调查法

问卷调查法，是指调查人员向特定调查对象发放事先设计调查问卷，问卷里含有公共关系调查人员希望获取的相关信息的问题。在调查对象填写完并由调查人员收回做统计分析的一种调查方法。凡是属于第一手资料收集的公共关系调查，都要经过问卷调查这一环节。这种调查法要求调查人员科学、严谨设计问卷，如此才有可能让调查获得成功。

由于调查是一项目的性很强的工作，因此在开始之前，公共关系人员首先要明确调查的目的，并把它用前提假设和理论框架表述出来。前提假设是调查问卷的基础，如果调查结果与之相吻合，那么调查得出的数据结果就是为前提假设提供的证据。理论框架由被调查者基本情况、动力因素、态度和行为所构成，建立理论框架的目的是为了采用相应的理论将调查的内容加以深化。

一般来说,问卷调查法成本较低,获取的数据较为客观。但是因为调查对象自身素质和配合度等情况,回收率难以保证。而且,由于公共关系本身是一门科学与艺术,调查问卷中常常会出现相对高级、复杂的问题,这对调查对象的文化素质提出了较高的要求,因而选择恰当的调查对象也比较费精力。

在问卷调查中,根据对问题和答案设计的不同,问卷可分为封闭式问卷和开放式问卷。开放式问卷实质上是一个没有提供答案的调查提纲,提问的答题者可以自由选择答案。此种问卷适合于素质较高的被调查者,多用于探索性研究,适合讨论一些比较复杂、有一定深度的问题,调查人员可能会因此得到颇有见地的看法和其他有价值的信息。但这种调查方法也有缺点,主要是答案多种多样、很难得到调查人员事先预想的结果,另外回收率难以保证,且不方便对回收的答卷进行统计。

封闭式问卷要求答题者只能在调查人员提供的多项答案中选择一种或多种答案。在实践中,封闭式问卷因其具有答案规范统一、便于调查人员统计分析的优势而广受欢迎。其不足之处就是可能会遗漏一些尚未被调查人员认识到的重要问题和答案,如果这类答案的比例偏大,势必影响调查的整体质量。

上述两种问卷在实际操作过程中各有利弊,调查人员要根据调查对象的客观情况和工作的实际需要灵活选用。通常的做法是将两种问卷综合使用,能获得比较客观、真实、全面的数据,调查效果比较好。

一般调查问卷包括三部分内容:引言或导语、调查项目以及相关信息。

引言或导语主要用于简要说明调查意义和目的,以及有关事项的说明,如调查者是谁,调查结果如何使用,有哪些保密措施(个人隐私和涉及敏感问题时)等,还包括解释某些项目的意思,提示如何填写问卷等内容;调查项目也就是具体的问题及其回答方式,一般分为开放式、封闭式两类;相关信息包括问卷编号、调查对象基本情况、问卷使用日期、问卷各部分序号等,这些主要用于统计资料时用。

（六）观察法

观察法指的是安排有敏锐观察能力和分析判断能力的调查人员到现场,以公开或隐蔽的身份,利用现代影像器材来观察调查对象的态度与行为,并形成记录资料的一种方法。这种方法效果直接，被经常采用。但对环境的要求较高。

（七）实验法

这是由调查人员在事先设置的环境里，现场观察被调查人员的态度与行为，进而获得相关信息资料的一种方法。此法在西方传播学研究中被广泛使用，有一定的效果。不少公共关系调查活动也采用此法。

（八）文献法

文献法指的是通过查询别人的调查研究文献来了解和分析情况的一种方法。这些文献包括出版物、档案（政府相关文件、各类统计材料、相关会议记录、大型活动的记录等、个人资料（日记、信函、回忆录、合同等）。文献调查法的实施步骤是，第一步，建立索引，即根据调查对象开列文献清单；第二步，根据索引查阅和记录文献资料；第三步，核实文献并分类登录。核实文献就是去伪存真、避轻就重的过程，目的是获取有价值的文献。经过鉴别的文献，要根据调查任务和提纲的要求进行分类，然后把分类后的每一份文献都标上编号并保存备用。

（九）个案调查

个案调查与通常所说的典型调查有一定的相通之处，都是去深入地"解剖麻雀"，即对某个特定的对象做深入细致的了解。

五、公共关系调查的程序

（一）调查准备阶段

首先，明确调查任务。就是确定公共关系调查活动的课题，即研究要解决什么问题，达到什么目的。一般来说，组织所能选择的调查课题很多，这主要取决于组织的现实或长远需要。调查课题一般分为两类，即描述性课题和解释性课题。前者通过具体数据来描述对象的轮廓和细节，后者则解释某些现象之间的因果关系并提出解决方案。

其次，制定调查方案。调查人员根据组织形象的现状和目标要求，分析现有条件，设计出最佳行动方案。具体包括设计调查指标、选择调查对象和规划调查活动等部分。再次，准备调查条件。主要是人员分配、物资器械、交通食宿等方面的准备。

（二）资料收集阶段

在此阶段最主要的工作就是搜集公共关系活动需要的资料，包括之前的公共关系活动情况、组织的相关文件资料等。要运用科学合理的手段，尽可能地保证资料的真实性和高水平的问卷的回收率。

（三）整理分析阶段

首先，整理调查资料。即对调查中所取得的全部资料进行检验、归类、统计。

其次，分析调查结果。即对所收集的资料进行科学的统计和分析摒弃不真实不必要的数据。

（四）报告完成阶段

撰写调查报告是公共关系调查活动的最后一个环节，也是最重要的一个环节。它可以准确反映组织的公共关系状态特别是公众舆论情况，检验公共关系活动的完成情况及其社会影响，总结公共关系工作经验与教训，便于今后进一步开展工作。

调查报告包括的内容一般有：

调查主题、导言包括调查委托人、调查主持人、调查日期、调查原因和目标、调查的内容、调查对象、调查方法等、调查结果和数据、结论、建议、署名包括调查单位和报告完成时间，以及附件包括公共关系活动中的相关调查表、统计数据及表格、背景资料等。

调查报告应按照标准格式写作，在写作时注意以下问题：

第一，使用通用的普及词汇，尽可能地避免出现行话和专门术语；

第二，要考虑读者的立场、观点、阅历和阅读习惯；

第三，尽可能用简单直观的方式表述例如统计图、统计表来显示材料；

第四，注意合理安排各部分之间的篇幅比例，重要的项目可以适度深入展开。

一份合格的调查报告应做到内容简明，体例系统，数据准确，分析严谨，重点突出，结论可靠。

（五）总结评估阶段

调查报告形成后，还必须对调查过程与调查结果进行总结评价，重点说明调查中的资料收集情况、技术手段的运用、调查程序等，以便组织相关人员更清楚地了解调查的完成情况，准确地掌握调查成果，总结过去公共关系工作中的经验教训，为以后的公共关系调查活动提供借鉴。

第二节　公共关系策划

策划的含义是谋划，是一种智慧创造活动。公共关系策划指的是组织的策划人员围绕公共关系活动的整体目标，根据组织的现有条件，依据组织形象现状，分析内外公众环境和约束条件，事先对公共关系活动方案进行的科学构思和设计，从而制定最佳活动方案的过程。它以客观的公众分析为基础，以最佳活动效果为目标，是公共关系工作程序的一个重要环节。

公共关系策划提高了信息传播的科学性，有利于推动组织的目标管理，它是公共关系价值的集中体现。正因为如此，有学者认为，作为一种较高层次的工作，策划在公共关系中的地位应该是最重要的，它不仅是一切公共关系活动的先导，同时也应当是公共关系活动的核心。应该说这种观点不无道理，但有点偏激。事实上公共关系活动有一整套科学严谨的运作程序，每一个环节都非常重要，不可或缺。那种不考虑客观环境因素、脱离组织和公众实际的所谓超级"点子"并不适用于公共关系活动。

一、公共关系策划的意义与特征

科学的策划是社会组织制定有效的公共关系行动方案的保证。

（一）公共关系策划的意义

公共关系策划在公共关系"四步工作法"中有着极其重要的作用，因为公共关系调查是以策划为目的，公共关系实施和评估要以策划为依据。同时，公共关系策划对社会组织形象管理具有十分重要的作用和意义，具体表现在以下几方面：

（1）公共关系策划是公共关系工作取得成功的保证。通过公共关系策划，社会组织制订出周密、科学的公共关系活动策划是公共关系活动取得成功的重要保证。首先，周密、科学的策划有助于进一步澄清问题；其次，周密、科学的策划能使公共关系活动有序地开展；再次，周密、科学的策划可以为公共关系活动获得组织内部各部门的支持与协作；最后，周密、科学的策划可使公共关系工作人员胸有成竹，对成功充满信心。

（2）公共关系策划可以强化组织形象目标。通过公共关系策划，可以帮助组织分析现有形势，发挥组织特长，设计一系列有效的公共关系活动，能把组织形象的完善和形象地位的提高具体化、数量化。同时，能使组织摆脱困境，巩固和发扬现有成绩，开拓新的发展途径，达到实现组织的发展目标，进一步完善组织形象的目的。如上海公交公司为改善组织形象，策划出以"优质服务、满意效果"为目标的系列公共关系活动，并以"公交职工为上海大变样做贡献"为主题，成立路访小组，开展评选"百名文明安全驾驶员、百名优质文明乘务员、车辆规范服务车组"等活动，使广大市民由埋怨公交到理解公交，圆满实现了改善组织形象的目标。

（3）公共关系策划是组织在竞争中取胜的法宝。随着市场经济的建立和发展，社会组织之间在加强协作的同时，竞争也日趋激烈。竞争从根本上说是人才的竞争，智慧的较量。而公共关系策划正是公共关系人员智慧的结晶，里面蕴藏着许许多多竞争取胜的奇谋妙计。公共关系策划的公共关系活动是社会组织在竞争中取胜的法宝。

（4）公共关系策划是公共关系运作的飞跃。大量的公共关系调查和一些基础工作，只有通过策划才能得以提炼和升华，组织形象的树立，只有经过精心策划，才会在公众中留下深刻的记忆和印象。只有策划，才能使公共关系运作上一个新的台阶，产生一种巨大的飞跃。所以说公共关系策划统率了公共关系运作。

（二）公共关系策划的特征

1. 目标性。公共关系策划具有明确的目的，所有的公共关系策划都是围绕公共关系目标展开的。公共关系目标既是公共关系策划的起点，同时也是归宿。

2. 计划性。公共关系活动要按照组织自身发展的特点和公众接受信息的客观规律，有计划、有步骤地展开。

3. 科学性。公共关系策划是一项专业化程度很高的技术工作，它拥有丰富的专业技能和手段，因此必须立足于组织的现实，立足于公众的意愿，立足于所处的环境，要符合客观规律，按照严格规范的科学程序与方法来进行。不能随心所欲，异想天开。

4. 整体性。策划是对组织整体公共关系活动的规划，涉及面广，社会利益、组织利益都要考虑，要纵观全局，结合组织的长远目标、近期目标来统筹考虑。

5. 创新性。公共关系策划必须突破常规，依靠创造性和表现力所形成的"亮点"，吸引公众的兴趣，引起公众的共鸣。创新是公共关系策划的灵魂。

6. 灵活性。组织赖以生存的环境随时都可能在变化，组织本身也在不断的变化发展过程中，相应地，公共关系目标及其公共关系活动也要随之变化。

当代策划已经发展到了多学科、多方人力共同合作、完成的群体策划阶段，从经验决策变为了科学决策，这是一个里程碑式的进步。

二、公共关系策划的原则

（一）以事实为依据原则

任何策划都要以客观事实为依据，尊重客观事实和客观规律。塑造组织形象必须做到真实、全面和公正。此外，还要根据客观环境、组织目标、组织资源的变化，随时调整公共关系策划方案

（二）创新创意的原则

独创性是组织形象竞争的需要，公共关系策划应该包含独特新颖的因素，有一定的创意，才能令人耳目一新，从而吸引公众的注意力。

（三）适应公众的原则

在现代社会，公众的态度与行为对于组织的发展生死攸关，组织要想获得良好的生存发展环境，必须适应公众的要求，处处为公众利益考虑，与公众保持密切的关系。要吸引公众，当然是"攻心为上"，适应公众需求，进而以产品、服务和观念去引导公众，在此过程中巧妙地传递组织的良好形象。

（四）公众利益优先的原则

在进行公共关系策划时，社会组织和个人应自觉地把公众利益放在首位，肯

在公众身上搞感情投资，这样才能赢得公众的信赖和支持。特别是当组织利益与公众利益发生矛盾时，组织更应不犹豫地优先满足公众的利益，这并不是完全要组织牺牲自身的利益，而是要求组织在考虑自身利益和公众利益的关系时，始终坚持把公众利益放在首位。要求组织不仅要圆满完成自身的任务，为社会做出贡献，同时还要重视其行为所引起的公众反映并关心整个社会的进步和发展，以此获得自身利益的满足。组织只有时时、处处为公众着想，坚持公众利益至上，才能得到公众的好评，才能使自身获得更大的、长远的利益。

（五）与整体策划相一致的原则

公共关系工作是组织整体工作的一个分支和组成部分，策划是在组织整体策划的约束下进行的，所策划的行动方案应纳入组织的整体策划，并与组织的整体策划相一致，服从并服务于组织的整体目标。否则，与组织的整体策划相悖，再好的行动方案，也只能是一种空想，再好的策划也是劳而无功，所以公共关系人员在进行策划时，应遵循所策划的行动方案与组织的整体策划相一致的原则。

（六）创新性与持续性相统一的原则

公共关系策划是一种创造性活动，它推崇的是标新立异、独辟蹊径、大胆创新、奇中取胜。因为社会环境总是处在不断的变化中，特别是现在，世界进入了信息社会，信息的激增使社会环境变得越来越复杂，人们对信息的选择范围也越来越大。如果方案没有新意，就不能引起公众的注意，公共关系部门发出的信息就会淹没在信息的汪洋大海里。所以一个成功的公共关系策划必须根据社会条件的变化，制定出与以往不同的新内容，不仅要比自己组织过的策划有所创新，更重要的是要比自己的竞争对手有所创新，使组织策划的活动能够先声夺人。在强调公共关系策划的创新时，还必须考虑到公共关系效果的积累性，坚持公共关系策划承上启下的连续性，良好的组织形象不是一次就能建立的，它需要长期不懈的努力，通过一次次的活动，为组织建立一个完整的形象。因此应根据组织的总体目标，制定一个较为长久的公共关系策划，并在落实公共关系策划时，尽量出新，同时要注意形象目标的相对稳定性，紧紧围绕着现代公共关系活动的重要职责、塑造组织形象、维护组织形象、提升组织形象来进行策划。

（七）社会效益与经济效益相统一的原则

一个好的公共关系策划不仅应做到公众利益与组织利益的统一，也应做到社会效益与经济效益的统一，公共关系策划应与组织机构的整体运行策划和社会发展条件相吻合。首先，公共关系活动必须重视经济效益，公共关系活动不是孤立进行的，它应与组织的整体营运策划或销售策划密切配合，在设计方案之前，应先与组织机构的其他部门进行沟通，在掌握准确资料的基础上，使推销组织形象的策划与推销产品、技术和服务的策划相协调，使公共关系工作的社会效益与能够产生的经济效益统一起来。其次，公共关系活动的目的之一是使组织与其公众相互了解与适应，而这种了解与适应的最佳共同基础就是社会效益。公共关系在满足本组织经济效益的同时也必须注意社会效益，并获得社会的认可和赞赏。再次，应处理好经济效益与社会效益的辩证关系。社会效益主要指与人民大众生活有关的公益活动，公共关系策划为这些活动投资，从长远观点看，是为了争取公众舆论的支持，扩大组织的影响，提高经济效益，树立组织的美好形象。而组织自身的效益，包括在社会效益之内，创造组织自身的经济效益是创造社会效益的基础和经济保障。当然，不能把经济效益同社会效益完全等同起来，应努力做到两者的和谐统一。

三、公共关系策划的方法

前面提到公共关系策划追求新奇独特，讲究的是具有创意，没有新奇性也就无所谓公共关系策划。公共关系策划是公共关系原则与创造性思维的碰撞结合，这种碰撞结合形成了一些相对稳定的思路和轨迹。公共关系策划的方法很多，这里着重介绍以下几种方法：

（一）制造新闻

制造新闻是社会组织或个人在尊重事实、不损害公众利益的前提下，有目的地策划、组织、举办具有新闻价值的事件，制造新闻热点，争取报道机会，通过新闻媒介向社会传播，以达到吸引公众注意，扩大组织知名度和影响力的目的。

1.制造新闻的原则

（1）以事实为依据。说真话是公共关系的信条，对于组织制造新闻活动具有指导意义。制造新闻中的新闻事件不是自发产生的，而是社会组织或个人在具备确凿事实的前提下，有目的的精心策划安排，目的是在真实可信的前提下，使策划出来的新闻事件更富有戏剧性和吸引力。

（2）有较高新闻价值。新闻界流传着一句话叫"狗咬人不算新闻，而人咬狗就成新闻了"。社会组织或个人策划的新闻事件要具有较高的新闻价值，能够明显引起公众注意和兴趣。也就是说策划制造的新闻，越具有新闻性，越容易吸引新闻界的报道。

（3）抓住公众心理。组织或个人策划的新闻事件要具有新奇性、普遍性、趣味性，这样才能吸引公众广泛关注，才能产生轰动效应。

2.制造新闻的类型

根据切入点的不同，制造新闻可分为四类：

（1）传播媒介新闻。传播媒介新闻是社会组织通过与新闻媒介联合举办智力竞赛、社会活动等形式，引发新闻媒介的报道，借以传播组织影响的一种方式。这种活动形式由于与新闻媒介联系在一起，被报道的机会大，容易收到预期的效果。

（2）名人新闻。社会组织与知名人士建立某种能引发社会关注的联系，借以吸引新闻界报道，引发公众注意。诸如请名人参观、发表见解，对名人表示关注、慰问、感谢、奖励等。

（3）公众新闻。公众新闻就是社会组织通过与公众建立新联系来显示自己的价值观和经营观念，从而赢得公众的注目和好感。

（4）制造新闻。抓住某些初露端倪的事物，巧加点化，制造出轰动性新闻。

（二）攀龙附凤法

攀龙附凤指社会组织在策划公共关系活动时，将组织及其产品与声望高、权威性强的名人、知名组织、有影响的事物事件联系起来，借助他们的名望、声望及权威来扩大组织的影响及知名度，从而达到事半功倍的效果。

1.攀龙附凤的原则

（1）采用这种方法的公共关系人员必须具有较高的信誉度。公共关系专家卡特利普和森特在《有效公共关系》一书中指出：沟通者的信誉度取决于他的动机、信用历史和专业水平，因为这些品质标准为目标公众所掌握。沟通者较高的信誉度增加了公众态度向有利于组织一面转化的可能性；相反，较低的信誉度则缩减了这种可能性。沟通者的知名度越高，他的目标公众就愈有可能倾向于将自己的信仰朝沟通者所倡导的方向转化。

（2）权威应具有较强的影响力和说服力。常言道：人微言轻，人贵言重。一个人或组织的权威性直接关系着它的影响力和说服力。

四、公共关系策划的程序

公共关系策划的制定和行动方案的设计，关系到组织形象的树立和完善，关系到组织的生存和发展。因此，公共关系人员在进行公共关系策划时，应按照一定的程序开展工作。

公共关系策划的程序是指在调查研究的前提下，通过对组织形象现状及原因的分析，确定公共关系目标、设计活动主题、分析公众以及选择媒介、预算经费和审定方案等一系列活动。

（1）确定公共关系目标。公共关系目标，实际上就是组织通过公共关系策划和实施所希望达到的形象状态和标准。确定目标是公共关系策划的前提，没明确的公共关系目标，公共关系策划也就无从谈起。目标一经确定，全部工作都应以目标为中心，策划活动方案、活动策划的实施以及活动效果的评估都应以目标为依据。

公共关系工作的具体目标是同调查分析中所确认的问题密切相关的。一般来说，所要解决的问题也就成了公共关系工作的具体目标。公共关系工作的具体目标与公共关系的总目标乃至组织的总目标是不同的，具体目标应是总目标的一部分并客观存在，而且受总目标的制约。公共关系策划所依据的目标是组织公共关系工作的具体目标。如：当一个组织在其形象差距分析中，出现了自我期望形象与公众形象差距大、美誉度和知名度都很低的不良状况时，公共关系任务虽然很重很艰巨，但在策略上，应有轻重、缓急、先后的顺序。应先考虑如何提高美誉度的问题，主要先在提高业务水平、工作效率、服务态度等方面的公共关系策划上下功夫。公共关系目标是一个目标体系，有两类，即长期目标和短期目标，它包含着各种不同类型的目标。一般分为一般目标和特殊目标。

长期目标。这类目标是指和组织长远发展战略相一致、塑造社会组织在公众中应有的总体形象、推动社会组织的发展、通过社会组织长时间努力才能达到的目标。

短期目标。这类目标是长期目标的具体化。它内容具体，方向明确，一般在短期内可以完成，是长期目标的积累过程。

一般目标。这类目标是依据各类或同类公众的要求、意图、观念和行为的同一性制定的。比如：增加某产品的销售量是组织员工、股东、政府、顾客等公认权益要求中的一个共同点，所以，"促进产品销售量的增加"就成为公共关系工作的一般目标。

特殊目标。特殊目标是针对那些与组织目标、信念、发展以及利益相同或相近的公众的特殊要求制定的。这类目标具有特殊的指向性。比如，某酒店为了提高住房率并增加营业额，决定改变住房结构，把组织家和商人作为主要的服务对象，制定了"中外通商之途，殷勤款客之道"的特殊目标，成功地塑造了组织的特殊形象。

美国有一家生产瓷器的公司，在其老板娘从故世的丈夫手中接过来之前，只是一个规模很小、名气不大的专门生产花鸟禽兽造型的瓷雕艺术品的小公司。老板娘接管之后，决定策划一系列的公共关系目标，从根本上改变公司形象。她给公司确定了两项长远的宏伟目标：一是本公司要以艺术家形象著称于世，其产品要跻身于美国国家博物馆的珍品之中，以此抬高身价；二是本公司要以慈善家形象著称于世，其产品象征人类保护的野生动物，并向保护自然生态环境的世界组织捐款，以此提高声誉。为了实现这两个长远目标，她又制定了近期目标，将公司的产品生产分为两条线：一条生产高中档艺术品盈利，并拿出部分利润捐助一些慈善机构，逐步扩大影响；另一条是生产低档产品，目的是培养人才，各种产品均以手工操作，以显示其艺术价值。由于该公司树立起与众不同的形象，很快引起公众瞩目。1972年，尼克松总统访华，该公司抓住良机，迅速向尼克松献上该公司生产的一尊天鹅瓷器珍品。因为该瓷器的英文正是China，尼克松非常惊喜，于是把这尊具有双重意义的艺术品带到中国。小小的瓷器公司也因此而声名大振，营业额急速上升。

公共关系目标还有其他一些分类方法。比如，按公共关系活动的类型分为：传播信息、联络感情、改变态度、引起行为；按公共关系活动的作用分为进攻型目标、防守型目标等。这样一些分类方法都有利于确定具体的工作目标。

（2）设计活动主题。公共关系活动主题是对公共关系活动内容的高度概括，是公共关系活动的直观体现，对整个公共关系活动起着指导作用。主题设计是否精彩、恰当，对公共关系活动的成效影响很大。

公共关系活动主题的表现方式是多种多样的。它可以是一个口号，也可以是一句陈述或一个表白。比如，日本精工计时公司，为使精工表走向世界，利用在东京举办奥运会的机会，进行了以"让全世界的人都了解：精工计时是世界第一流技术与产品"为目标的公共关系活动，活动的主题是"世界的计时——精工表"，结果一鸣惊人。

（3）分析公众。任何一个组织都有其特定的公众，公共关系工作是以不同的方式针对不同的公众展开的，确定与组织有关的公众是公共关系策划的基本任务。因为，首先，只有确定了公众，才能选定需要哪些公共关系人员来实施公共关系方案。如果仅是维系一般顾客关系，那么，可以由一般公共关系人员来完成。如果是开拓国际市场，会见、接待外方重要人物，则要求中方相应的人物出席参与。其次，只有确定了公众，才可确定如何使用有限的经费和资源，确定工作的重点和程序，科学地分配力量。再次，只有确定了公众，其文化素质等也就确定，不同的公众对媒介有不同的选择与适用范围。最后，只有确定了公众，才有利于搜集准备那些既能被公众接受，又有实效的信息。一个组织每天收到的信息是大量的、千差万别的，这些信息并非都适合于所有的公众。确定公众之后，就可以有意识地筛选和利用有关信息，对特定公众进行有目的的传播，而不是漫无边际的传播，造成不必要的浪费。确定公众一般分为三个步骤：首先，是鉴别公众的权利要求。公共关系在本质上是一种互利关系，一个成功的策划必须考虑到互利的要求。要想做到这一点，就必须明确公众的权利要求，将其作为策划的依据之一。其次，对公众对象的各种权利要求进行概括和分析，先找出各类公众权利要求中的共同点和共性问题，把满足各类公众的共同权利要求作为设计组织总体形象的基础。进行概括和分析时，应注意不要简单地按照公众的法律地位或表面的一致性来考察，而应从各种公众的意图、权利要求、观念和行为的一致性来加以考察。最后，分析各类公众的特殊要求。那些带个性的问题，是制定组织特殊形象的基础。这时要注意将不同的权利要求分出轻重缓急来，一般应选择同组织的信念和发展利益相同、相近或利益关系特别紧密的公众,作为工作的主要对象。

（4）选择媒介。根据公众类别和要求的不同,考虑选择适合他们的传播媒介,一般来说,可供选择的媒介有以下几种:①个体传播媒介。这是个人对个人所进行的传播,这种方法对象最明确,能深入、细致地解决一些特殊问题,但传播面较窄,适用于针对某些特殊公众或关键公众。②群体传播媒介。个别人对一群人所进行的传播,可针对一群人的特殊要求或特殊问题进行传播,如报告会、演讲会等。③大众传播媒介。传统的大众传播主流媒介主要是以广播、电视为主的电子媒介和以报纸、杂志为主的印刷媒介。20世纪末,电脑和国际互联网的广泛使用,使人类社会全面进入"电子时代"。互联网络重塑了一个全新的经济形式——网络经济。电子革命大大丰富了公共关系传播手段,如:电子邮件、因特网、网上报纸、网上杂志、网上数据库、线上信息服务、互联电视、数字频道、微信、QQ等新兴的传播手段都可以用来开展公共关系活动。按发展趋势,这种网络传播和电子报刊取代传统的主流媒介的传播方式,使信息有更强的时效性,传播更迅速,辐射面更广,影响力更大。网络已经改变人们的生存和生活方式,冲击和影响人们周围的一切。互联网络是人类最庞大的信息库,组织可以在电脑网络上建立一个窗口,通过这个开放的窗口,进行网络传播、网络攻关,策划多种多样的信息内容,向全世界传播充分的组织信息,借以树立自己的美好形象,有利于解决共性问题。

（5）预算经费。公共关系具有经营管理职能,每种管理职能都应该有正常预算。预算对于公共关系工作来说是必需的:它可以从财力物力上保证公共关系正常开展;可将公共关系的策划具体化;便于监督管理,堵塞漏洞;便于事后核算成本和考查绩效。编制公共关系预算的方法有两种:①按销售量抽成法。即按组织总产值或销售量,抽取一定的百分比作为公共关系预算费用。这种方法的优点在于能够很快决定预算。其主要缺点在于预算缺乏弹性和策划性,不一定适合实际需要。②目标作业法。即先制定出公共关系期望达到的目标和工作策划,然后将完成任务所需的各项费用详细列举出来,核定各单项活动和全年活动预算。这种方法的优点在于:策划性强,弹性较好。但需要事先的审慎策划和预测,如预测不准确,就可能超支、短缺或浪费,且主观性较强,容易影响预算。公共关系预算的基本构成包括以下方面：劳务工时报酬、行政办公经费、专业器材和成品制作费、宣传经费、实际活动费、赞助费。

（6）审定方案。在制定公共关系行动策划时，往往会面临多种可供选择的行动方案，因此，公共关系人员在众多的可行方案中应考虑各方面的因素，权衡优劣，选择出一个最有利于目标实现、经济效益最佳的方案。为此公共关系人员必须做以下两个方面的工作：①优化方案。在选择方案时考虑方案的目的性、可行性，花费最少的人力、物力、财力、时间而获取最佳的效益，这就是选择最优方案的原则。在遵循这一原则的前提下，可采取以下几种方法选择最优方案：优化法，即在选择方案时，趋利避害，权衡利弊，从众方案中选择利大于弊的方案。优点综合法，即博采众长，综合众方案的优点和长处，或借用某一方案的优点，重新制定并形成一个最优方案。集体决策法，即充分发动领导、专家及有关专业人员参与选择，发挥集体智慧，保证方案的科学、正确。列举法，即分析和列举各方案的问题或条件，逐个进行研究、分析，并用数值的方式把各方案的效果或花费表示出来，使用收益"小中取大法"和费用"大中取小法"进行比较和选择，保留一个花费最小、收效最大的方案。②方案论证。方案论证就是在行动方案订好以后所进行的可行性论证。一般由有关领导、专家和实际工作者对策划的可行性提出问题，由策划人员答辩论证。方案论证包括如下几个方面：一是对目标进行分析，即分析目标是否明确以及实现程度如何。二是对限制性因素进行分析。因为任何一项公共关系活动都是在一定条件下进行的，都要受到资金、时间、人力、转播渠道以及其他有关条件的限制。这就必须分析，公共关系策划在哪些条件下可以实行，在哪些条件下不可以实行。三是对潜在问题进行分析。即预测公共关系活动策划实施时可能发生的潜在问题和障碍，分析防止和补救的可能性。四是对预期结果进行综合效益评价，判断该策划是否付诸实施。

五、公共关系策划的方法

公共关系策划是一种创造性的思维过程，这种创造性思维需要借助很多方法和技术予以配合，才能创造出切实可行的方案来。

（一）德尔菲法。

德尔菲（Delphi）是古希腊城市名，据传希腊神在此降服妖龙而闻名。后人用"德尔菲"比喻神的高超的预见力。德尔菲法始于美国兰德公司,用于市场预测领域。公共关系策划借用这种方法,目的在于借助专家们的经验、知识和综合分析问题的能力,保证策划方案的质量,并以此获得最佳的效果。

1. 德尔菲法的实施步骤。德尔菲法的主要过程是组织者把公共关系调查材料、策划主题内容、目标、要求等,交给策划者,请其独立完成一项策划,并做好时间限制,如期收回,再由专人对这些反馈的策划意见进行整理,以不公布姓名的方式将归纳后的结果寄回给专家,继续征询意见。如此经过几轮的反复,直到意见趋于集中为止。具体实施有以下四个步骤:①经各位专家发函,提出所要调查或决策的问题。问题的提出不应带有任何倾向性,由专家自由地发表意见和看法。②将回函所得的专家意见进行统计、归纳、综合,了解在此问题上共有几种看法,并将这些意见制成第二轮表格,再寄给专家,由其进一步做出评价,并阐明理由。③决策分析小组在收到第二轮专家意见后,再进行归纳整理,将意见进一步集中,然后制成第三轮表格,再一次请专家进行分析判断,专家既可以坚持原来意见并使他们充分阐述其理由,也可以改变意见而选取另一种意见。④按领导小组的要求,对某些提出独特见解的专家,有针对性地进行征询意见调查,使他们做更进一步的论证。

经过以上四个步骤的调查、分析、综合之后,所得出的结论往往比较准确。

(二)头脑风暴法。

此法是由美国创造学家奥斯本在1939年发明的一种创造技法。这一方法在我国又被称为"智力激荡法""脑力激荡法"等。又称自由思考法,简称BS法。原意是精神病人的胡言乱语,引申为无拘无束地思考问题。其核心是高度自由的联想。这种方法一般通过一种特殊的小型会议,使与会者毫无顾忌地提出各种想法,彼此面对面地激励、相互诱发、引起联想,从而导致创造性设想的连锁反应,产生众多的创造性设想。

1. 头脑风暴法会议的组织方法:(1)确定会议人选。一般以5~12人为宜,并提前几天将会议的主题通知与会人员,使其有所准备。(2)确定1名会议主持者和1~2名记录人员。主持者在会议开始时就要说明会议目的,要解决的问题或目标,宣布会议的要求和注意事项,鼓励发言,并鼓励提出新的构想,注意把握会议的主题方向,发言要简明。记录员要记下会议中提出的所有方案设想。

（3）会议一般不超过1个小时，最多不超过两个小时。（4）由专家小组对所有设想进行比较，综合选择。对评出的好想法，要进一步提升、改进、完善，形成几个具有实用价值的方案或设想，供决策部门采用。

2. 头脑风暴法会议的要求：①在会议中绝对禁止批评或评判别人的想法。因为创造性设想有一个诱发深化、发展完善的过程，一些即使看似杂乱无章、不合逻辑，甚至是比较幼稚、荒诞的设想，说不定能引出许多有价值的设想，因此不应轻易加以批评，更不能加以否定。②提倡与会者自由思考。因为与会者只有不受已有概念、传统逻辑、固有方法、常规思想的约束，才能敞开思路，打破常规，运用自由联想等方法，激发创造想像，进行创造性思考，才能构建新奇的方案。③会议参加者都必须充分利用别人的设想启迪自己的思维和智慧。只有用获得的新知识弥补自己的不足，才能活跃思维，开阔思路。也只有对别人提出的设想进行改善、发展、综合、重组、提高，才能产生新的设想。④主持者，尤其是高级领导不要在会议上发表意见，以免影响会议的自由气氛。要学会在不怀偏见中倾听各种意见，并有目的地吸取决策所需要的东西。

（三）专家会议法

是根据公共关系的目的与要求，邀请有关专家，通过会议的形式，就组织或组织公共关系中存在的具体问题及所要实现的公共关系目标等情况展开讨论、分析，并做出判断，最后综合专家的意见，制定具体的行动方案。

第三节 公共关系实施

公共关系实施是在公共关系方案被采纳之后，将方案所确定的内容变为现实的过程。公共关系方案的制定属于理论形态阶段，而方案实施则是一种行动的过程。理论是否符合客观实际，只有经过实施，才能显示出它的合理性、科学性。好的策划方案是公共关系工作取得成功的基础，但仅有好的策划方案是远远不够的，公共关系工作取得成功还有赖于对策划方案实施的全面、准确、到位。

一、公共关系实施的意义

公共关系方案在实施过程中，实施者不仅要运用各种传播手段，把组织信息传达给公众，把公众的信息反馈给组织，改变组织或公众的态度和行为，从而塑造良好的组织形象，而且要正确认识公共关系实施的重要意义。

1. 公共关系实施是解决问题的关键。公共关系工作的终极目的不是研究问题，而是解决问题。公共关系的策划还只是研究问题，只是设想，只有将策划方案付诸实施，才是直接地、实际地、具体地解决问题的过程。一个完美无缺的公共关系策划，如果不去实施，那么它无论对社会组织还是对公众都是毫无意义的。公共关系实施是把公关策划方案按策划转化为现实的公关活动，使之接受广大公众和实践的检验，充分展示公关人员的实际操作能力和专业水平。

2. 公共关系实施是反映策划正确与否的试金石。策划还只是理论的东西，理论与实际并不是一回事。公共关系实施是一种实践活动，策划是否符合社会现实，是否可行，是否符合公众的需要等，只在实施过程中才能最终得到验证。在实施过程中按预定策划向公众集中地传播某些方面的信息，引起目标公众的关注，使他们加深对该组织的了解，形成组织所期望的态度与行为。

3. 公共关系实施影响着策划的效果。公共关系策划方案成功实施可以圆满地完成策划中确定的任务，实现组织的策划目标。实施人员在实施的过程中可通过创造性的努力弥补策划的不足，可以采用多种传播途径和技巧，在公众中树立本组织的良好形象。如果实施不当，不仅不能实现策划目标，反而会使关系恶化，与策划的目的背道而驰。从这个意义上说，实施这一环节不仅决定了策划方案能否实现，而且也影响了策划实施的效果。因此公共关系实施是解决组织公共关系方面存在的具体问题，实现公共关系工作既定目标的重要手段。

4. 公共关系实施的结果是以后工作方案制定的重要依据。一项公共关系策划方案成功与否，都会在社会上造成影响。社会组织过去开展的公共关系工作所形成的结果，又是继续制定公共关系策划方案的重要依据。因为前一项策划实施效果反馈的信息，就是组织重新研究新问题的直接材料，所以公共关系策划实施的情况，对组织以后制定方案有重要的意义。实施阶段的公众反馈的信息、取得的成效、出现的问题，既可以用来检测、评估公共关系活动的效果以及组织的公关系状态、环境变化和无形资产的质量，同时也为开展后续的公关工作创造了新的条件，提出了新的任务和奋斗目标。

二、公共关系实施的原则与方法

公共关系实施过程中的动态性、创造性及影响的广泛性构成了实施活动的复杂性。为了确保实施活动不偏离既定的公共关系战略目标，公共关系实施人员必须遵循一定的实施原则，并掌握正确的方法。公共关系实施主要有以下原则与方法：

1. 把目标作为导向的原则与方法。目标导向的原则是指公共关系策划实施过程中，公共关系实施活动不能偏离策划方案中制定的目标。执行目标导向实际上是加强控制的一种手段。这里的目标导向有三个方面的内容：一是在实施过程中不得任意改变或超出范围；二是在实施过程中要按照策划方案的发展进程进行；三是公共关系实施人员利用目标对整个实施活动进行引导、制约和促进，以使整个实施能按策划方案如期完成。在实施策划方案的过程中，把目标作为导向的原则是十分重要的。现代组织的管理方法大都采用目标管理原则，并且把目标编入程序，利用网络进行管理。

2. 线性排列的原则和方法。线性排列法是将所有公共关系行动、措施按先后顺序逐一排列起来，一步一步向目标迈进的方法。

例如美国农业部想把一种新型的杂交水稻推广到农村去，所以在实施的过程中采用线性方法，一步一步地让农民们接受这种新型的水稻，采用四个阶段让农民接受新型水稻。第一步，认识，实行宣传措施让农民头脑中有这种新型水稻的概念。第二步，感兴趣，通过媒体让农民在知道这种水稻存在的基础上，对这种新型水稻感兴趣，并且知道去搜寻更多的材料来了解这种新型水稻。第三步，接受，继续实行实地展示的方法，让农民就收这种新型水稻，并决定亲自播种。第四步，试验，农民开始在自己家的农场里小范围的播种这种新型水稻。

通过一系列线性的公共关系实施活动、美国农业部成功地把新型的水稻推广到农村中。

3. 控制进度的原则与方法。控制进度的原则是指根据公共关系策划方案中目标的需要，按照一定的程序掌握工作的进度，以避免出现顾此失彼的现象。控是着重于对一个组织的策划方案在实施过程中与策划有差异或背离策划的行动进行纠正或克服的行为。例如，现在企业竞争激烈，很多服务部门为了提高自己的服务质量，不顾自身的情况，盲目效仿知名同行的做法，结果耗时耗力，收获甚微。因此，在公共关系实施过程中，需要经常检查各方面工作的实施进度，及时发现超前或滞后的情况并加以调整，以求在公共关系目标指导下，使各方面工作达到同步和平衡发展。贯彻控制进度的原则必须具备两个条件：一是要有明确的控制目标；二是要重视反馈信息。

4. "整体协调的原则与方法。整体协调原则是在策划实施过程中使工作涉及的方方面面达到和谐统一、合理互补的状态的原则。协调和强调实施过程中的各个环节之间、部门之间及实施主体与其公众之间相互配合。协调的目的，是要使全体实施人员在认识和行动上取得一致，保证实施计划和谐顺利地进行。最普遍、最常见的协调有两类：一类是纵向协调；一类是横向协调。纵向协调指上下级之间的协调。横向协调是同级部门或实施人员之间的协调。因为公共关系工作不是一个部门能独立完成的，需要全体实施人员共同努力，因此消除组织内耗，保证实施活动的同步和谐，才能提高工作效率，取得良好的实施效果。

5. 信息反馈的原则和方法。反馈是信息论的一个专业术语，意为受传者对传播者发出信息的反应。在公共关系活动过程中的反馈，就是要求公共关系人员在实施活动方案的过程中，随时接受公众的反馈信息，并根据组织环境的变化、社会公众的意见等因素，随时调整和修正方案，弥补计划的不足，增强活动的效应。无论确定的公共关系活动方案如何客观和科学，在未付诸实施前，都可以说它是主观活动的产物，是一种预测行为和计划行为，即使最科学的方案也不可能完全等同于现实。另外，随着时代的发展，社会环境复杂多变、众多的不可控因素使人们很难预料和把握、制订策划方案时遗漏的方面和实施方案过程中出现的新问题，都要求在实施方案时，及时注意和收集环境及公众的反馈信息。一方面检验公共关系活动方案是否适应变化着的形势要求，另一方面根据反馈的实际情况，及时对公共关系活动方案进行调整。只有这样，才能顺利实现公共关系活动的目标。如某化妆品公司在进行公共关系实施活动中，碰见一位女士因为使用该公司化妆品而出现过敏现象，实施公共关系工作的人员，及时做出反应，带着这位过敏的女士来到医院，确定了女士的皮肤不适合使用她之前选择的该公司的化妆品，但是却适合使用这次活动推出的另一款化妆品。于是推荐给了这位女士，女士得到了专业医生对自己皮肤的检测，又得到了公共关系实施人员认真的推荐，于是心理得到了极大的满足，成为该公司忠实的公众。同时，公共关系实施人员马上调整之前的策划方案，增加一种现场测皮肤的项目，吸引力很多女性公众，增加了这次公共关系实施的效果。

6.抓住时机的原则与方法。在公共关系计划实施的过程中，必须考虑一个关键的因素——时机因素。抓住时机是促使公共关系策划方案在实施过程中取得成功的必要条件。公共关系实施的时机是否适当，直接地影响到实施的总体效果。抓住适当的实施时机，也就是在最能强化公共关系效果的时间内，把所要传播的信息适时地传播出去。最佳传播时机对公共关系人员来说，实属一种不可控制因素，必须在长期实践中不断摸索经验。

在实施公共关系策划方案时，究竟应怎样抓准正确的时机呢？第一，注意避开或利用重大节日。凡是同重大节日没有任何联系的活动都应该避开节日，以免被节日活动冲淡；凡是同重大节日有直接或间接联系的公共关系策划则可以考虑利用节日烘托气氛，扩大公共关系活动的影响。第二，注意避开或利用国内外重大事件。凡是需要广为宣传且与重大事件无关的公共关系活动都应避开国内外重大事件，以免被重大事件所冲淡；凡是需要为大众所知，又希望减少影响且与重大事件有关的活动，则可选择在重大事件发生期间，这样可借助重大事件的影响减少舆论的压力和关注。第三，不宜在同一天或同一段时间里同时开展两项重大的公共关系活动，以免其效果互相抵消。

三、公共关系实施的障碍

在实施公共关系计划的过程中，不可避免地会遇到各种障碍，从而影响公共关系计划的有效实施。因此，公共关系人员要尽可能地找出障碍因素，进行正确分析，并加以排除，才能实现公共关系计划实施的最佳效果。影响公共关系计划实施的因素是多方面的，一般来看主要有以下三方面的障碍：

1.目标障碍。指在公共关系人员在制定公共关系策划方案时，因为制定的公共关系目标模糊、不具体给实施带来的障碍。在公共关系实施过程中，无论有什么特殊情况，实施过程都基本上要根据策划方案所规定的内容进行，否则，它就不是公共关系实施了。因此，公共关系策实施必然要受到策划方案的影响。如果策划方案中目标模糊、不具体，尽管实施人员尽心尽力，也得不到预期效果。例如：公共关系策划目标如果出现了不符合公众利益的问题，那么，在实施过程中必然会受到目标公众的抵制；如果出现了公共关系策划目标过低的问题，往往不能唤起目标公众的合作热情，目标过高，则会使实施人员望而却步。因此，要想有效地开展实施活动，就必须排除各种目标障碍。排除目标障碍的根本途径是要求策划方案的制定者尽量使策划目标正确、明确和具体。实施人员在开展工作之前应该从以下五个方面检查一下公共关系策划方案中的目标是否正确、明确和具体：①检查策划目标是否切实可行；②检查策划目标是否可以进行比较和衡量；③检查策划目标是否指出了所期望的结果；④检查策划目标是否是策划实施者的职权范围所能完成的；⑤检查策划目标是否规定了完成的期限。如果这五个方面有疏漏，实施人员应主动与策划方案制定者取得联系并促使其重新修订。策划目标模糊或用宣传口号式的语言来表达策划目标，都会使实施工作无法有效地开展。实施人员可能因不明确策划目标的具体要求，或所得到的指令笼统含糊，从而引起误解，产生错误的行动，这就是实施人员排除目标障碍的意义所在。清晰的、具体的策划目标是实施人员行动的依据，也是对策划方案实施完成后进行评估的基础。

2.沟通障碍。公共关系策实施过程实际上主要是进行传播沟通的过程。公共关系实施中的沟通障碍是指公共关系实施过程中由于传播沟通的媒介运用不当、方式方法不妥、渠道不畅等所造成的障碍。现代社会，每个人不断地受到各种各样大量信息的冲击和影响，同时，自己也以书面的、口头的、动作形式，向外传递自己的知识、经验、观点等信息，向外施加影响。这种相互影响交织在一起，一方面促进了沟通，另一方面对沟通又形成了干扰，使沟通出现障碍。所以，实施过程中的传播沟通并不是一帆风顺的，它常常会因传播沟通工具运用不当、方式方法不妥、渠道不畅等而使实施工作不能如愿以偿。在实施过程中，常见的沟通障碍主要有下面几种：

（1）语言障碍。语言障碍主要有由于语言差异造成的隔阂、语义不明造成的理解上的困惑和失误、一词多义造成理解歧义等。语言是人们表达感情、交流思想、协调关系的工具，沟通离不开语言。不同国家、不同民族有不同的语言，造成了语言障碍。在同一国家、同一民族中,由于地区的不同,有着各种不同的方言,也会造成语言障碍。由于语言方面的原因很容易引起沟通麻烦,甚至会引起纠葛。所以,我们在实施公共关系策划时首先要排除语言障碍,一次成功的公共关系活动也意味着不同的语言文化的相互交流和相互接受。

(2)习俗障碍。习俗即风俗习惯,是在一定文化历史背景下形成的具有固定特点的调整人际关系的社会因素,如道德习惯、礼仪礼节、审美传统等。习俗世代相传,是经过长期重复出现而约定俗成的习惯。虽然习俗不具有法律的强制力,但通过家族、邻里、亲朋的舆论监督,往往迫使人们入乡随俗,在公共关系策划实施的沟通中如果忽视习俗因素,就会导致沟通失败。不同的礼节习俗常常造成沟通中的误解,以致使沟通受挫。

(3)观念障碍。观念属于思想范畴,是由一定的知识和经验积累而成的,是一定社会条件下人们接受、信奉并用以指导自己行动的理论和观点。有的观念是促进沟通的强大动力,有的观念则会阻碍沟通,形成观念障碍。常见的观念障碍及其影响有两种:一种是封闭观念排斥沟通。封闭观念源于人们的成长经历和受教育的程度以及社会环境的影响。另一种是极端观念破坏沟通。在公共关系活动中我们常常见到这样的情况,公共关系人员与社会公众双方只是抓住沟通过程的某一环节,根据自己的思维和价值观去理解问题,彼此否定,谁也不服谁,其结果双方不欢而散。观念的障碍还有其他类型,比如理解障碍、思维障碍、认知障碍等,在此我们仅举两种说明观念障碍是影响沟通的不可忽视的一个因素。

(4)心理障碍。心理障碍是指人的认知、情感、态度等心理因素对沟通造成的障碍。如在谈判过程中,由于认知方面的障碍因素常常出现一方误解了另一方的意图,或没弄清事情真相而导致谈判无法进行下去或失败。所以,在沟通过程中,应时时注意检查自己的认知,努力去理解对方的正确意图。总之,研究沟通过程中的心理障碍,目的是为了了解它、掌握它、利用它或排除它。公共关系人员要注意在认知、情感、态度等各种层次上的沟通,因势利导,消除公众的心理障碍,进而实现公共关系的沟通目标。

(5)组织障碍。"组织"这一概念在这里指由若干"系统"所组成的、开放的社会技术系统。合理的组织机构能够有效地进行内外沟通。反之,不合理的组织机构则会沟通不畅。沟通过程中的组织障碍主要表现在以下三个方面:第一，传递层次过多造成信息失真。信息在传递过程中，中间环节越多，保真率越低，甚至有时最后的信息与原来的信息相比已面目全非。因此，在组织机构上减少层次，减少信息传递环节，尽量做到上线级直接沟通，建立一个快捷有效的沟通传播渠道，是保证沟通准确无误的有效措施。第二，条块分割造成沟通"断路"。条块分割的组织机构，使信息很难畅通无阻，有时，只要一关通不过，就不能实现沟通。第三，渠道单一造成信息量不足。这种沟通中的组织障碍主要是指信息的传递基本上是单向的——上情下达。忽略了信息从下层传达到上层的重要性，组织结构的安排不大考虑便于从下往上传递信息的渠道，因而送达到决策层的信息量明显不足。

（6）政治障碍。不同的国家有不同的政治制度，社会制度，存在着不同国家中的沟通障碍，各国政府从自身的政治需要出发，会对某些信息的输入或输出进行限制，阻碍了沟通的进行。

（7）经济障碍。由于经济状况的差异会影响公众接受和采用信息的渠道、手段和方式、方法。经济水平不同，人们的需求也不同，从而使他们对信息的取舍也不同，没有网络的农村，人们自然会对智能手机兴趣不大。因此在公共关系实施中，不同经济水平的地区，要采用不同的大众化传播媒介方法。尤其是随着知识经济的到来，使得商品中科技含量日益提高，许多商品具有"高、精、尖"的特性，然而许多消费者对它是陌生的，在认识上存在许多盲点，因此，在知识经济条件下的市场营销的策划与实施，不能停留于过去的形式单纯的广告等，而要以认知教育为先导，对消费者进行知识的灌输，使消费者从无知走向有知，达到以教育培育市场的目的。

（8）年龄障碍。不同年龄的人思维方法不同，经历不同，存在着"代沟"，在沟通中就要采取不同的方法，公共关系活动必须适合不同年龄的特点开展，才能取得理想的效果。

第四节　公共关系评估

公共关系评估就是根据与提升组织的知名度、美誉度和和谐度相关的特定标准，按照一定的程序与方法，对公共关系策划、实施及效果进行检查和评价，以判断其优劣并提出修改意见的过程。

1.公共关系评估的目的和意义

公共关系评估的目的是根据组织所开展的公共关系活动的不同需要、不同的侧重点，提供相应的信息。其意义是：

（1）公共关系评估是改进公共关系工作不可或缺的重要环节，对公共关系工作具有"效果导向"的特殊作用。

（2）公共关系评估能有效强化内部沟通，鼓舞士气。公共关系是一种开放的、需要员工积极支持、主动配合的工作。评估不仅可以让组织的管理层看到开展公共关系的诸多益处，也能让员工看到本组织的利益和实现途径，从而激发他们的工作热情，增强对组织的凝聚力。

（3）公共关系评估是开展后续公共关系工作的必要前提。公共关系工作是为塑造和维系组织形象服务的，它具有连续性的特点。一般来说，一项公共关系活动计划的制订与实施，总是以原来的公共关系活动及其效果为背景的。没有对原有公共关系工作的评估，新的公共关系工作策划就没有决策依据，因而也就不可能把它制订好。

2.公共关系评估的主要内容

公共关系评估虽然从程序上来讲，是公共关系工作的最后一个环节。但从其发挥的作用来看，公共关系评估贯穿于公共关系工作整个过程，每一个环节都要进行评估。其主要内容包括：

（1）公共关系调查工作评估。包括背景材料是否充分、信息内容是否充实，以及公共关系调研的方案设计、调研方法、信息表达方式、调研结论等方面的方案涉及是否合理以及合理程度如何。

（2）公共关系活动策划工作评估。包括是否合乎社会的法律道德要求、策划的公共关系目标设置是否合理、实施的方法与程序是否需要调整，实施公共关系计划所需资金是否恰当、是否留有余地等，尤其是要进行项目的可行性评价，这个最为关键。

（3）公共关系策划实施的过程与效果评估。包括准备工作的情况、既定目标的实现程度、传播范围和效果如何。具体有公众的态度变化情况、组织的社会形象改善情况、传播的具体效果（信息发送数量的多少、媒体采用的信息数量的多少、公众接收、注意到的信息量的多少、改变观念态度行为的公众数量、达到的目的和解决的问题、对社会文化的影响等）。简单来说，就是评价公共关系策划实施是否达到了预期目标。以上从公共关系活动过程的角度概述了公共关系评估的基本内容。从其他角度也可以进行评估。这些常见的角度有公共关系状态（分为内部公共关系状态与外部公共关系状态两方面）、传播沟通情况、专项公共关系活动、公共关系人员工作绩效等。

3. 公共关系评估的依据

（1）媒体报道情况。包括参与报道的媒体的权威性及其社会影响力、媒体对组织及其活动的报道频率及其总数量、报道的质量。一般来说，权威性媒体的正面报道越多，影响力越大，公众对组织的好感增加的就越多，越有利于塑造和维系组织的良好形象；否则，效果就相反。

（2）组织内部的相关材料。包括组织的决策管理层、股东和一般员工对组织开展的公共关系活动成效的评估材料，以及组织经营管理方面的资料，如统计报表、财务报表、公众来信、会议记录等。

（3）组织外部的相关材料。主要包括客户反馈信息、相关机构（主要是合作者、竞争者）的反馈信息、社区公众对组织的态度与评价、政府对组织行为的态度等。

4. 公共关系评估的方法

公共关系评估的方法很多，分类方法也很庞杂。为了获得准确的结论，在实践中往往会利用不同的评估主体，不同的具体操作方式来进行评估。但一般都要求定量评估和定性评估相结合。

常见的评估主体有公众、专家、组织以及公共关系人员自评等。

公众评估指的是依据公众的反应（有关材料须通过调查取得）来评价公共关系活动的效果。这是所有公共关系评估中最重要的一种途径。

专家评估指的是聘请组织外部的公共关系专家评价组织的公共关系工作。由于专家立场中立、经验丰富，所做的评估往往很有参考价值。

组织评估指的是有组织的负责人安排专人（非公共关系活动的参与者）对组织的公共关系工作做出评估。

公共关系人员自评也称为自我评估。具体的评估操作方法有比较法、实验法等。比较法指的是选择若干影响公共关系活动的重要因素，将其小范围地改变，观察能否得到预期的效果，然后决定是否推广的一种方法。该法要求实验范围必须很小，实验对象必须要有代表性。

上述诸种方法各有优势与不足，如何采用要依据实际需要来选择。一般来说，由于公共关系活动涉及的方面很多，相关的数据和其他信息很庞杂，如果仅仅依靠一种评估方法，往往不容易获得准确的结论。要想获得比较真实的结果，需要综合运用其他方法。

5.公共关系评估的一般程序

（1）设立评估目标。

统一的评估目标是进行检验公共关系工作效果的参照物，只须将两者进行比较就可以知道结果。

（2）选择评估标准。

适度的评估标准有利于对公共关系活动进行恰如其分的评价分析。

（3）广泛收集资料。

对公共关系活动进行评估，其主要依据就是公共关系活动开展以来组织内外公众发生各种变化的信息。在收集资料的过程中，要注意选择最佳途径。

（4）评估分析资料。

运用合理的评估方法（评估方法的选择取决于评估的目的和评估标准），将上述信息进行比较分析，就可以了解公共关系活动所带来的变化情况。特别是检验活动的那些项目达到了预期目标，并分析部分项目未能达到预期目标的原因。

（5）汇报评估结果。

完成评估后，要以书面形式如实向组织的决策层反映或汇报，以备下次开展公共关系活动之际组织领导决策时参考。这样做，不仅可以保证决策层能及时掌握情况，协调工作，同时也可以进一步发挥公共关系活动在实现组织目标过程中的重要作用。因此，及时向决策层汇报评估结果应该成为开展公共关系活动的一项固定的制度。

撰写评估报告应注意：第一，要做到定量与定性相结合；第二，所提建议与策略要具有可操作性；第三，语言准确、精练；第四，结论要客观和具体。

（6）应用评估结果。

公共关系活动的评估结果对于整个公共关系工作有极大的应用价值，它能够承前启后，使公共关系工作得以高效合理的开展，使组织步入良好的公共关系环境。在公共关系的实践中，人们常常发现，公共关系活动的每一个周期都要比前一个周期表现出更大的影响力。其原因就在于，通过评估结果的运用，对相关方面的走势的确定和形势的分析将会比以前更加准确，更加符合组织的长远发展要求。

具体来说，公共关系评估结果的运用包括以下几个方面：第一，用于调整公共关系工作策划；第二，对策划新的公共关系目标方案有直接帮助；第三，用于改进组织的决策；第四，用于改进组织全面的公共关系工作。此外，公共关系活动的评估结果可以经过理论概括，成为下一步公共关系活动的指导原则与操作方法。既可以把它运用于以后的公共关系活动，也可以把它提供给社会供各界人士特别是公共关业从业人员学习借鉴。

第四章

组织形象塑造

第一节 组织形象概述

组织形象是指社会公众对一个组织综合认识后形成的印象和评价。组织形象对社会组织来说具有重要作用。

一、组织形象的界定与构成

组织的形象是一个有机整体，每一个要素都会对组织形象产生效应。要树立良好的组织形象，必须使每一个要素都发挥作用。组织形象包括的内容很多，如组织精神、价值观念、行为规范、道德准则、经营作风、管理水平、人才实力、经济效益、福利待遇等，组织形象是这些要素的综合反映。

（一）组织形象的界定

组织成员与组织在多大程度上保持认同，因人而异。但一个成员与组织之间的认知上的联系与他感受到的组织形象密切相关。

1.整体性。组织形象是整体发展的结果。以一个企业为例，企业形象包括：

（1）企业历史、社会地位、经济效益、社会贡献等综合性因素；

（2）员工的思想、文化、技术素质及服务方式、服务态度、服务质量等人员素质因素；

（3）产品质量、产品结构、经营方针、经营特色、基础管理、专业管理、综合管理等经营管理因素；

（4）技术实力、物资设备、地理位置等其他因素。

2. 客观性。公众心目中的组织形象不是从天上掉下来的，也不是公众头脑中固有的，它是公众在对组织各方面有了具体的感知和认识之后才形成的印象，是组织各方面活动和所有外在表现在一系列客观状况和公众心目中的反映。因此，组织形象具有鲜明的客观性。社会组织应全面重视自己的各项活动，力求把每件小事做好，以便使自己在公众心目中留下良好的印象。

3. 相对性。组织形象的好坏既受同一定的参照物相比所表现出来的优劣的影响，又受主观因素的影响，任何一种要素的变化都会对组织形象产生作用。因此，组织形象具有相对性特征。

4. 稳定性。组织形象是组织综合行为的结果。组织形象一旦形成，不论其内在理念还是外在形象，都会在一定时空条件下，在一定的公众心目中形成一种心理定势，它不会随着组织行为的某些变化而马上变化。

（二）组织形象的构成

组织的总体形象的建立是受众多具体要素影响的。以组织为例，其构成组织总体形象的要素有以下几点：

1. 实力形象。它是组织形象存在的物质基础。富有强大的经济实力，便使形象的其他因素具有了富丽的落脚点。实力形象主要包括组织固定资产、总资产、流动资金、产品销售与生产规模、员工人数、装备先进性等。

2. 文化形象。它是组织形象的精髓所在。它以组织的价值观念为基础，以组织系统和物质系统为依托，以组织员工的群体意识和行为为表现，形成具有特色的生产经营管理的思想作风和风格。文化现象主要包括组织使命、组织精神、组织价值观和组织目标。

3. 人才形象。它是组织现有人才状况对组织形象的影响。一个人才济济、阵容整齐的组织，会使组织的形象倍增光彩。人才形象主要包括人才阵容、科技水平、管理水平等。

4. 品牌形象。即组织的产品质量和服务、组织的标志等给公众的总体印象。品牌形象是组织形象的生命线。如果在其他要素上存在缺陷仅会影响其局部形象的话，品牌形象的低劣则会使组织形象毁坏殆尽，从而直接威胁到组织的生存。

5. 信誉形象。即组织在长期的业务往来和商品交换中形成的消费者或顾客对商品生产者和经营者的一种崇高的信任感。包括组织：①在经营活动中是否重合同、守信用。②是否勇于承担社会责任。③是否努力为公众办实事。

6.竞争形象。即组织在与同行竞争中表现出来的遵循竞争规则、注意相互协作、相互理解、平等竞争的形象。主要表现为：①能否把握竞争中的摩擦点。②是否能正确处理竞争矛盾。③能否寻找合作机会。

二、组织形象的特征与意义

（一）组织形象的特征

1.客观性

组织形象是客观存在的。因为形象形成的基础是组织自身状况及其行为的表现，脱离了组织的客观表现，就无法评价一个组织的形象。而且组织形象的优劣，不该由该组织对于自身的评价来决定，而应由组织的产品或服务体现出来，并在公众的心目中产生某种影响和印象，从而客观地反映出来。

2.相对稳定性

组织形象一旦形成，当影响形象的因素不发生变化时，不论是它的理念还是外在形象，都会在一定时空条件下，在一定的公众心目中形成一种心理定势，因而组织形象具有一定的稳定性。但这种相对的稳定性，并不是绝对的不变性。反之，若影响形象的某一因素发生变化或开展某项公共关系活动后，组织形象也会发生某些变化，甚至发生根本变化。所以对组织而言，塑造良好的组织形象就应设法使公众对组织持认可和赞许的态度，使组织形象在某种程度上保持相对的稳定。

3. 主观性

组织形象是公众对组织的意见或看法，因而是一种主观性的东西。因为社会公众本身具有差异性，他们的社会地位、价值观念、思维方式、认识能力、审美标准、生活经历等各不相同，他们观察组织的角度、审视组织的时事维度也不相同，这样社会公众对同一组织及其行为的认识和评价就必定有所不同，"公说公有理，婆说婆有理"就是这个道理。此外，在形象塑造和传播过程中，必然要发挥组织员工的主观能动性，渗透组织员工的思想、观念和心理色彩，因此，组织形象是主观的。

4.传播性

组织形象的塑造离不开传播。传播是连接组织与公众的桥梁。组织要在公众中树立良好的形象，必须借助于传播这一渠道和手段。群众对组织形象的了解，主要是通过各种渠道的信息得来的。组织形象的塑造得到公众的认同时，说明组织在塑造形象的过程中的传播是成功的。如果组织的实际形象与公众心目中的形象不一致，甚至相反，说明传播是不成功的。由于信息量的巨大和信息渠道的多元化，公众在接受信息的时候往往具有极强的选择性，所以，充分重视并成功地利用大众传媒和其他传播方式，是在公众中建立良好的组织形象的一个极为重要的问题。

5.整体性

组织形象是一个有机整体，本身是由复杂的因素组成的。有社会公众容易了解的产品的质量、功能、包装、品牌等外在组织形象；还有一些看不见的、公众不容易感知的组织文化、宗旨和精神等要素，这些要素相互依存，相互联系，共同构成了组织形象的有机整体。当然，对于有些组织而言，可以会因某一方面的形象比较突出，进而掩盖其他方面的宣传，导致组织形象不完整。这是因为组织的宣传有侧重点，公众不可能全面了解组织的所有情况。这就要求组织认真地对待每一个方面，从而形成在公众心目中良好的组织形象。

（二）塑造组织形象的意义

市场经济的基本特征是竞争。竞争的最高层次就是组织形象的竞争。谁拥有了良好的组织形象，谁就能赢得公众的支持，谁就拥有了市场，并获得源源不断的利润，而且能使产品和组织在激烈的市场竞争中立于不败之地。塑造组织形象具有以下几个意义。

1.组织形象是无形资产的重要组成部分

无形资产是组织资产的重要组成部分，它是不具有实物形态而以知识形态存在的重要经济资源。世界知识产权组织总干事弗朗西斯·高锐在《2017年世界知识产权报告》发布会上说："当今全球价值链中的无形资本将逐渐决定企业的命运和财富。它隐藏在我们所购买产品的外观、感受、功能和整体吸引力中，决定了产品在市场上的成功率，知识产权则是企业维持无形资本竞争优势的手段。"美国可口可乐公司的老板曾说过，如果公司在一夜之间被大火烧为灰烬，第二天各大银行就会主动上门来向公司贷款。因为公司还有360亿美元的无形资产。可见，无形资产的作用和价值远远超过有形资产。自然灾害可以损毁有形资产，但却不能减少无形资产的价值。世界上许多著名的组织，其无形资产都具有很高的价值。苹果公司每售出一部约810美元的iPhone 7，就有42%的销售收入归属苹果公司，显示出该行业无形资本的高回报率。无形资产具有如此大的魅力是因为它代表组织在公众心目中的良好形象，组织形象的好坏决定了无形资产价值的高低。无形资产主要是靠组织形象来作为表现形式的。组织形象的认知度越高，美誉度越好，和谐度越佳，定位越准，无形资产的价值就越大，增值率就越高。

日本丰田汽车公司就是依靠其组织形象的不断完善来维系、保护它的无形资产的。一般的汽车公司厂家维修中心都是顾客把汽车开到汽车维修中心进行维修，而丰田汽车维修中心接到电话后，会安排人开辆好车到用户家中，开走需要维修的汽车，留下一辆好车供用户日常使用。汽车修好后，维修中心会在汽车中加满汽油再开回用户家中，开走上次留下的汽车。这种处处为用户着想的服务思想，为丰田汽车公司树立了良好的组织形象。这种深入用户心目中的组织形象使丰田汽车公司的无形资产倍增。因此，一个组织要不断的发展、维系自己的无形资产，就必须充分重视组织形象。

第二节　组织形象塑造

一、组织形象的分类

组织形象是多层次、多维度的，因此我们也应该从不同角度来把握组织形象。

1.按组织形象的内容可分为特殊形象和总体形象

特殊形象是指某一个方面或少数几个方面给公众留下的印象，或者组织在某些特殊公众心中形成的形象。如组织的良好服务使某些顾客形成了组织"优质服务组织"的形象，组织的某一慈善捐款给公众留下了乐善好施、热心公益事业的形象。特殊形象对组织很重要，因为公众是不可能全方位、全面地了解组织的。

组织在他们心中留下的往往就是这种特殊形象，而且某些公众就是为组织在某些方面的独特形象而支持组织的，如歌迷之于演唱会、球迷之于球星等。因此，特殊形象是组织改善形象的突破口。总体形象是组织各种形象因素所形成的形象的总和，也是各种特殊形象的总和。

2.按照组织形象的真实程度可分为真实形象和虚假形象

真实形象是指组织留给公众的符合组织实际情况的形象，虚假形象则是组织留给公众的不符合组织实际情况的形象。虚假形象形成的原因是多方面的，既有传播过程中的失真，也可能有公众评价的主观性、片面性原因。需要说明的是，真实形象不一定就是好形象，而虚假形象也未必等于坏形象，如组织经营伪劣商品被曝光在公众中形成的一个不好形象是真实形象，而一个骗子在被揭穿之前的公众楷模形象往往是虚假形象。一些组织也通过虚假统计数据而在上级部门那里形成了一种好形象，但这肯定是虚假的。对组织来说，当然应追求真实的良好形象，而避免虚假的、不好的形象。真实形象有助于组织取得公众的理解和信任。增强组织塑造良好形象的内驱力。

3.按照组织形象的可见性可分为有形形象和无形形象

有形形象是指那些可以通过公众的感觉器官直接感觉到的组织形象，包括产品形象，如产品质量、性能、外观、包装、商标、价格等、建筑物形象、员工精神面貌、实体形象、如市场形象、技术形象、社会形象等，它是通过组织的经营作风、经营成果、经济效益和社会贡献等形象因素体现出来的。无形形象则是通过公众的抽象思维和逻辑思维中形成的观念形象，这些形象虽然看不见，但可能更接近组织形象的本质，是组织形象的最高层次。对组织而言，这种无形形象包括组织经营宗旨、经营方针、经营哲学、价值观、组织精神、组织信誉、组织风格、组织文化等。这些无形形象往往比有形形象有价值，如对麦当劳、可口可乐、奔驰、苹果公司、华为公司等组织而言，他们的组织信誉等无形资产比那些机器设备和厂房更重要得多。

4.按照组织形象的现实性可分为实际形象和虚拟形象

组织实际形象是公众对组织所持有的认识和评价，它是为公众所普遍认同的形象。组织的历史、创始人、现任领导、员工素质、机构制度、组织文化、管理水平、经济实力、经营水平均是影响组织实际形象的要素。组织形象可以通过形象调查，了解社会各类公众对组织的普遍看法，然后有的放矢地开展组织形象塑造工作。实际形象不仅是形象塑造过程的起点，而且是影响组织生存发展的最现实的因素。因此塑造组织的良好形象就要保持和完善组织受欢迎的形象，改变不受欢迎的形象。虚拟形象是指组织期望在公众心目中树立的形象，又称组织的理想形象。它是一个组织为自己设计的目标和努力方向。任何一个组织要改善自己的形象，都要设计自己的期望形象。形象定位，就是确定一个理想形象。

5.按照组织形象形成的过程可分为组织内部形象和组织外部形象

组织内部形象是组织内部员工对组织的看法和评价。组织通过自己的经营活动使所属员工对该组织产生认同感、归属感、自豪感和荣誉感，愿意做其中一员并为之而献身，这就是该组织所追求的内部形象。外部形象是指组织的外部公众对组织的看法和评价。组织通过自己卓越的经营管理活动，为公众及整个社会做出的贡献，结外部公众留下长期可以信赖的印象，并为全社会所肯定，这就是组织所追求的外部形象。一般来说，组织内部形象是外部形象的基础。如果组织内部公众对本组织都没有良好的认识和评价，那么外部公众也不会形成对组织的良好印象。因此，组织要首先注意处理同内部公众的关系，增强组织的凝聚力和向心力，树立良好的内部形象，这是建立良好组织形象的关键。

二、组织形象塑造的原则与方法

（一）组织形象塑造的原则

组织形象塑造的原则是组织制定、实施组织形象战略必须遵循和贯彻的指导思想，是塑造组织形象的行为准则。

1.以质量取胜的原则

组织的产品形象是树立组织良好形象的关键。除了形象独特的产品商标外，还必须靠产品过硬的质量、合理的价格、周到的服务取信于公众。当代组织之间的竞争是产品质量、价格、服务和信誉的全方位竞争。组织如果不注重产品开发，不注重产品的质量管理，不注重优质服务，即使是名牌、老牌子也会倒掉。经营者永恒的主题就是以质量取胜，以质量悦人。质量不仅表现在产品上，在服务行业，服务质量就是树立组织形象的关键。例如，新加坡航空公司为了在同行竞争中脱颖而出，制定了一系列服务标准并且要求所有人员严格执行：（1）

对所有乘客一视同仁地施以关心和礼貌，在一切微小的服务细节上给乘客留下难忘的印象。（2）修改其他航空公司乘客在订票时是不能拿到座位号，登机前才能在机场领得印有座位号的登机卡这样的做法。利用在全球各地的电脑订票系统，使乘客在任何国家预订任何班次的机票时，能够同时得到飞机上的座位号。（3）每个航空服务员事先记住自己所负责的那一舱位所有乘客的姓名，乘客上机时只需将座位号贴在登机卡上，乘务员在机舱门口，引导乘客对号入座，并对每个乘客称呼直接以姓氏，使乘客被尊重被重视，加深了对该公司的印象，提升了组织的形象。（4）洲际飞行时，为了减少乘客的疲劳感，飞机服务人员给每位乘客送上一双尼龙软鞋套和遮光眼镜，供乘客休息时用。还送来一份印刷精美的菜单，上面以英、法、德三种文字印有全程每餐饭的菜名，改其他细节服务更是周到全面。（5）在旅客结束愉快的旅行时，公司为每个旅客准备一包包装精美的盥洗用具，包括：牙刷、牙膏、肥皂、梳子和两小瓶化妆品，上面都印有新加坡航空公司的标识。乘客如需写信，均可由新航免费邮寄至世界各地，乘客如果填写一张表格，便可将自己的姓名地址存入公司的计算机，并取得一个编号，日后公司会寄给这旅客一二十张优待券，一年之内可凭优待券优先购买机票，行李超重可不付费，有时候也会寄给旅客一些新加坡百货商店的优惠券。通过一系列充满活力的公共关系服务措施，使新加坡航空公司在国际航线上赢得了声誉，赢得了顾客，在激烈的国际竞争中遥遥领先。

2. 视信誉为生命的原则

良好组织形象的核心指标是信誉，欲塑造良好形象的组织必须视信誉为生命。人留名，树留影，信誉比金子还宝贵。信誉好的组织和名牌商品在消费者心目中树立了牢固的形象基础。真正注重形象的组织可承受经济上的损失，也不会失去信誉。

英国航空公司所属波音747客机008航班，准备从伦敦飞往日本东京时，因故障推迟起飞20小时。为了不使在东京候此班机回伦敦的乘客耽误行程，英国航空公司及时帮助这些乘客换乘其他公司的飞机。190名乘客欣然接受了英航公司的安排，分别改乘其他公司的飞机飞往伦敦。但其中有一位日本老太太叫大竹秀子，说什么也不肯换乘其他班机，坚决要乘008号班机。出于信誉，原拟另有飞行安排的008号只好照旧到达东京后再飞回伦敦。这样东京至伦敦008号航班只载一名乘客，航程达13 000千米。大竹秀子一人独享该机的353个座位以及6位机组人员和15名服务员的周到服务。有人估计说，这次飞行使英航至少损失约10万美元。从表面看英航的确是不小的损失，但从深层来看，英航却换取了一个用金钱也难以买到的良好组织形象。

信誉，是组织的生命，是无可替代的财富。组织及一切组织塑造形象，首先要坚持"信誉高于一切"的原则。

3. 注重全局发展的原则

对于一个组织来说，建立良好的组织形象是一项全方位的工作，这是由组织形象整体性特点决定的。它主要包括四个方面：一是组织形象的目标具有全面性的特点；二是组织形象涉及各方面；三是组织形象的塑造需要全体人员共同努力；四是塑造良好形象应运用多种方法。正因为塑造良好的组织形象涉及组织的许多方面，所以要求组织必须注重全局，切忌各自为政，一定要从全局出发，制订统一的公共关系政策来协调组织内部的公共关系活动；若需要对外开展公共关系活动，组织公共关系部门应事先争取各有关部门的支持、配合，求得协调一致，以防止出现相互重复，甚至自相矛盾的做法，导致不良后果，甚至毁坏组织的整体形象。

4. 注重传播的原则

一个良好的组织形象，首先来源于这个组织的行为，来源它的实力和努力。但是，仅靠这一点是不够的。良好的公共关系活动必须注重有效的传播。这就是说，必须通过适当的渠道宣传自己，使本组织尽可能在更多的公众心目中留下好的形象。因此，可借助于必要的传播渠道，把真实、美好的组织形象介绍给公众。只有注重传播的组织公共关系发展得会越来越好，组织形象会更鲜明。

（二）组织形象塑造的方法

1. 策划组织形象

对于一个组织而言，其形象的策划一般包括组织现有形象的调查、组织形象框架的设定以及组织形象方案的论证三个阶段。组织现有形象的调查中需要在明确组织的核心产品或服务、基本市场、主要技术以及组织性质的基础上确定组织的目标以及理念，同时考察组织所处的市场环境的情况设想组织未来发展的条件，从长远考虑，从组织理念、行为规范、识别系统三个方面制定组织形象的框架。最后，必须经过多次反复的论证，请组织内外不同领域部门的专家对于确定的组织形象进行可行性研究，这才完成组织形象设计的主要过程。

2. 分析组织形象的要素

社会组织不同，满足社会需要的方面和程度也不同，公众对组织的印象和评价也不一样。所以，不同社会组织之间、构成组织形象整体的要素和方面员有复杂多样性。因此组织要注重分析自己形象要素，注重形象要素内容的塑造。这里仅以组织为例，主要介绍以下几种构成要素：

（1）产品形象。

产品形象是指组织的产品或提供的服务所反映出来的组织形象。它是构成组织形象的基本要素。公众直接通过产品了解一个组织，组织通过产品来争取公众。

产品形象是整个组织形象的物质基础。产品形象分为有形商品形象和无形服务形象两个方面。有形形象义包括质量、性能、外观、包装、色彩、商标以及制作水平等，无形服务形象包括服务行业的服务项目、质量，商品的售前、售中、售后服务等。其中，产品质量是用户评价组织的最高标准，是影响组织形象的实质性要素，从这个意义上讲，可以说"质量是组织的生命"。良好的产品形象最容易形成名优产品。组织取得成功的基础，也是组织塑造整体形象的重要途径。

（2）经营形象。

经营形象是通过组织的经营管理活动展现出来的形象。它体现在组织一系列经营管理活动中，如组织的企业文化、经营作风、管理效率、履行合同的信用、技术开发和市场拓展的业绩、人事制度、就业条件、市场占有率、同行竞争情况、职工福利、价格策略、销售服务等。

（3）员工形象。

员工是组织的主体。员工形象是通过组织成员的言谈举止、素质、能力、态度所展现出来的形象，体现出组织拥有的人才阵容、人数、专业人员的比例等方面。它主要包括组织领导管理者的形象、公共关系人员的形象、组织内部典型人物的形象和组织群众的形象等，都是组织形象的化身。因此，建设一支高素质的组织领导人和员工队伍，实行规范化服务，展示一流的组织风貌，提供一流的购物环境，是组织形象工程的重要方面。

（4）环境形象。

环境形象是通过组织及相关的环境实施所展现的形象。它对组织起着烘托和装饰的作用，是构成组织形象的硬件部分。环境形象包括地理位置、建筑风格、园林小品、点缀装饰、门面招牌、厂容店貌、橱窗布置、产品陈列以及展览室、会客室、办公室的摆设等，构成了现代办公文明、生产文明、商业文明的一部分。

（5）文化形象。

文化形象是组织通过一系列文化要素展现出来的形象，是构成组织形象的软件部分。组织的企业文化体现出组织形象的特点与风格。它包括组织的价值观念、管理风格、历史传统、精神风貌、道德规范以及组织标识、口号、训诫、歌曲、旗帜、服装及各种宣传品。这些要素都共同体现着一个组织的形象特色，其中，价值观念和管理哲学是文化形象的核心，在诸要素中起着导向和决定的作用。

（6）标识形象。

标识形象是组织通过标志和识别系统所展现的形象，它能够帮助公众识别、记忆组织的形象。它包括组织名称、产品品牌、商标、徽记、广告、主题词、典型音乐、字体、颜色等。此外还有一些构成要素，如组织实力、管理水平、办事效率、财产情况、信誉记录、经营方针、税收状况、同行竞争、接受监督、社区关系等内容。可见组织形象的构成是多方面的，是综合性的有机整体。

3. 塑造组织形象

（1）员工形象的塑造。

员工形象是组织员工在职业道德、专业训练、文化素养、精神风貌、言谈举止、服务态度和仪容仪表等方面的集体表现。员工形象是组织形象的代表和展示者，是组织形象人格化的体现。塑造员工形象的目标是使员工成为优秀的组织人和工作者。

塑造员工形象的主要途径，一是要提高员工的整体素质，让员工认识形象塑造的重要性和方法，自觉成为组织形象的塑造者和代表者；二是培养员工的敬业精神，要求员工对事业执着追求，对工作一丝不苟，将自己的前途与组织的发展紧密联系起来，以主人翁的态度工作，树立同舟共济、荣辱与共的思想，人人关心组织的经营，人人重视组织的效益，人人珍惜组织的荣誉；三是力求让最好的员工享受最好的待遇，即将员工的贡献与待遇联系在一起，激励员工不断努力工作，发挥员工的生产积极性和主动性，把实现员工的自身价值当作实现组织价值的主要途径和目的；四是鼓励员工建立高尚的情操、进取的精神和健康的价值观，让组织具有蓬勃向上的活力。

（2）领导形象的塑造。

领导者的形象是指组织领导者的思想政治水平、知识结构、工作经验、组织指挥决策能力、开拓创业精神和气质风度等给外部公众和内部职工留下的印象。

塑造领导形象的目标是使领导者成为有奉献精神和服务意识的高素质的决策者和精明的管理者。

塑造领导形象的主要途径，一是配备合理的领导结构，即领导者的知识结构多元化，年龄结构合理化、年轻化，让领导这个群体具备开拓、实干和朝气蓬勃的精神。二是实行唯才是举的方针，不拘一格地提拔有能力、有前途的年轻干部。三是及时反馈工作成绩，考核领导者的政绩和作为，表彰优秀领导者。四是培养领导者的服务意识，让领导者正确认识自己承担的角色，严于律己，率先垂范。

（3）产品形象的塑造。

塑造产品形象的目标是将产品塑造成一个内在质量和外观质量相一致的、使消费者满意称心的形象。塑造产品形象的途径如下：

a. 重视产品的基础设计，采用新思路、新技术、新工艺和新材料，开发富有特色的产品。

b. 认真实行全面质量管理，即将生产、经营或者管理过程中的各工序、各岗位、各部门直至各员工，都规定明确的质量标准和目标，保证产品质量最优。

c. 注重产品的外观形象塑造，产品的外形、颜色、包装都应该符合审美要求。

d. 要充分利用传播手段，扩大产品的知名度。让更多的公众了解产品，使用产品，提升产品的美誉度，为品牌战略打好基础。

（4）品牌形象的塑造。

品牌是整体产品的一部分，是组织为自己的产品所设置的有别于其他同类产品名称、图案、标记及其组合。经过注册的品牌即为商标,它不仅具有经济价值,而且具有信誉价值,是组织的无形财富。

品牌形象的塑造指为本组织产品建立"名牌"形象,也就是知名度高、美誉度也高的优秀产品形象。它是产品的内在本体价值和外在效用价值的统一。

名牌形象塑造的主要途径如下:

a. 要树立名牌意识,更新重质量、轻牌子的旧观念。

b. 要实施重点战略,集中组织的人财物力打名牌攻坚战。

c. 要坚持长期不懈的努力,一个名牌产品的培育、产生、成长、成熟及维护需经长期的努力,绝非一日之功而能成就的。

d. 要实施名牌系统工程,既要注重外在的品牌形象,做好产品的名称、包装、广告等策划工作,也要重视品牌的内在形象的塑造,在产品的质量、包装、服务、价格等方面独具特色,优于其他产品。

(5)服务形象塑造。

服务形象就是指组织的员工在经营活动过程中所表现出的服务态度、服务方式、服务质量、服务水准及由此引起的消费者和社会公众对组织的综合、客观评价后形成的印象。随着社会的发展,人们在享受产品的同时,越来越注重享受服务。服务形象塑造的目标是树立一种服务态度诚恳、热情,服务技能娴熟、高超,服务过程及时、快捷,服务项目完善、细致,服务方式新颖、别致的形象。

服务形象塑造的主要途径如下:

a. 树立优质服务意识,它要求组织全体员工牢固地树立"顾客至上"的服务理念,随时随地准备为公众提供优质的服务。

b. 要配置完善的服务设施和条件,即满足优质服务在物质上的要求,配备一流设施、一流环境、一流服务态度,没有物质基础的服务是不可能达到高水平的。

c. 要设置周到的服务项目和内容。服务项目主要根据顾客的需求来考虑,如供应配件、免费提供安装、调试、维修、上门服务,培训、包退、包换、建立用户档案、处理好顾客投诉等,一经承诺,就要切实履行,切不可开空头支票。

(6)竞争形象塑造。

在市场经济条件下,敢于竞争、善于竞争的组织才能得到生存和发展。塑造组织竞争形象的目标，是要将组织塑造成遵循竞争规则、注意相互合作、相互理解和平等竞争的形象。

塑造组织竞争形象的重要途径如下：

a. 要把握竞争的焦点。在目前生产力条件下，我国组织竞争的焦点集中在价格、合作、广告、商标和技术等方面。组织产品定价要考虑顾客需要和成本，以及竞争的要求；组织之间既有竞争，也不乏合作机会；广告商标一定要遵纪守法，不搞欺骗、造假等损人利己的手段；在技术上，一方面要注重开发新的技术，另一方面也要重视技术成果的保密和有偿使用。

b. 要正确处理竞争矛盾。竞争中与同行、与对手产生矛盾是正常的事情，关键要在矛盾出现后，保持冷静的头脑，谨慎处理，不要因小失大，更不能利用非法手段"摆平"对方，让组织形象陷入灭顶之灾。

c. 在竞争的同时，寻求合作的机会。因为组织不可能有一成不变的竞争对手和合作伙伴，在这个问题上双方可能是竞争对手，在另一个问题上双方又可能成为合作伙伴。

（7）信誉形象的塑造。

组织的信誉形象是公众对组织的工作效益、产品质量、技术水平、服务态度、人员素质和总体实力等方面的信任和评价，它主要来自组织的社会责任感。对于公众而言，组织的信誉可以让其在荣誉、感情、性格、爱好等精神需求方面得到满足；对于组织而言，信誉则是重要的无形资产，能够为商务组织带来高于正常投资回报的利润。信誉形象塑造的目标是让组织在公众心目中树立一种恪守信用，对公众负责，勇于承担社会责任的良好形象。

塑造信誉形象的主要途径如下：

a. 在生产经营活动中重合同，守信用，讲究职业道德，不搞假冒伪劣；不以牺牲公众的利益来获取不法利益；不做违法犯罪的事。

b. 要勇于承担社会责任。要通过自身优良的产品和服务为社会做贡献；要关心由于自身行为引出的社会问题的解决；要对由于自己的过错造成的社会损失负责。

c. 努力为公众办实事，即用实际行动维护消费者的合法权益，为公众提供物质上和精神上的帮助，为社会解决诸如就业、污染治理等实际问题。

（8）环境形象塑造。

环境形象是指组织机构的生活、生产、工作及对外营业等各种环境的总和。对组织外部公众而言，组织环境是他们认识和识别该商务组织形象的窗口；对于组织员工而言，组织环境是他们工作的岗位环境和居住的生活环境；对于组织本身而言，环境代表了组织的精神风貌和管理水平。优美舒适的组织环境，会使人奋发向上，力求进取，使组织员工产生一种热爱本组织、为组织而工作的信念；良好的对外服务与营业环境，会使更多的公众对组织产生好感，愿意接纳它的产品和服务。尤其是组织，每天都要接待成千上万的顾客，经营环境的好坏，是给顾客第一印象的最主要标志。因此，组织环境形象的好坏对员工的精神状态、行为模式、工作态度、人际关系、工作质量和数量都将产生极大的影响。

环境形象塑造的目标，是为商务组织塑造一种优美高雅、整洁有序、个性鲜明的环境形象。

塑造环境形象的途径，一是要注重环境的全方位美化，即要搞好五个方面的工作：①院落和厂区的美化与绿化；②办公和生产场所的整洁有序；③庭院中的雕塑、装饰及点缀设计合理；④建筑群落的艺术风格和特征设计协调精美；⑤废气、废水、废渣治理有成效。

二是强调环境的个性特征。也就是说，商务组织的环境应当具有鲜明的特色。不管是建筑物、绿化带，还是车间、办公室、庭院的装饰和布置，均应别具一格，独树一帜，具有独特的个性差异，充分体现商务组织的形象特征。

第五章
公共关系礼仪

第一节 公共关系礼仪概论

一、公共关系礼仪概论

礼仪，是指人们在生活和工作中应遵守的行为规范和行为准则，体现个人的文化教养，是人们在交际中约定俗成的礼节和仪式。公共关系礼仪，则是公共关系人员在工作场合所必须遵循的礼节和规则，通过仪容、仪表、仪态表现出对公众必需的尊重。公共关系礼仪作为一种传播和沟通的技巧，是公共关系人员在公共关系活动中必须遵循的礼节和仪式。

（一）礼仪在公共关系中的重要作用

在公共关系中遵循礼仪，不仅有利于组织与公众沟通，也有利于树立良好的组织形象，它可以充当以下三个角色。

1. 工作中的"通行证"。一般来说，了解并遵循礼仪的组织代表和公共关系人员可以受到公众的欢迎，因此礼仪可以作为工作中的"通行证"，有利于与公众进行交流和顺畅地完成公众关系任务。

2. "润滑剂"。礼仪可以作为美丽的语言、服饰和姿态，在组织和公众之间建立友谊桥梁，并有利于进一步的交流。

3. 工作"基石"。公共关系人员的礼仪不仅可以反映个人的素质，还能反映组织的整体形象，使公众乐于与组织接触，为以后的工作打好基础。

（二）礼仪原则

礼仪不仅反映个人的自尊、道德和教育。同时也表现在交流沟通中尊重合作伙伴。

礼仪有四个原则：尊重的原则、适中的原则、真诚的原则和自律的原则，尊重原则是最重要、最基本的原则。

1. 尊重的原则（也称尊重公众的原则）。首先是尊重对方的个性、地位和职位。只有当你站在对方立场上考虑和解决问题时，你才能很容易地得到公众的理解和支持。其次，尊重公众意味着尊重对方的观点和要求，努力使对方满意。即使你有不同的观点。你应该试着真诚地解释并请求他的理解。

尊重公众意味着平等对待，互惠互利和要求相互礼貌。

2. 适度原则。这意味着双方应遵循一定的规范和习俗，在社会活动中展示礼仪，尽量做到自然和适度。在公共关系活动中，我们应该根据具体情况展示我们的礼仪。

3 真诚原则。它的意思是在公共关系的社会活动中，要把注意力集中在组织团体上，并且从对方的立场考虑问题。

4. 自律原则。这意味着公共关系中的交往双方应该对自己严格要求，宽容地对待同行。

二、公共关系中的一些常见礼仪

礼仪是指尊重、问候和社交的意思。这是礼貌的具体规定，在言语、行为举止和礼仪上反映了一个人的内在美。它的本质是尊重他人。以下是一些在公共关系中的礼仪。

（一）称谓礼仪

称谓是公共关系社会活动过程中的第一道礼仪。我们要注意三点：第一，词语要适合对方的性别、年龄、身份、地位、国籍、文化等背景。第二，说话的语气要谦虚。第三，声音应该是美丽的。第四，我们应该互相尊重，穿着谦虚得体。如果彼此关系比较亲密，我们可以叫昵称。

（二）介绍礼仪

介绍是公共关系中相互了解的基本途径，包括自我介绍和介绍他人。

1. 自我介绍。这里有三点需要注意：第一，用词应该礼貌、适度、谦虚和舒适。第二，我们应简要介绍我们的个人资料，并适当地使用肢体语言和辅助语言。第三，展现你的尊重，谦虚地结束自我介绍。

2. 介绍他人。这里有四个基本的礼仪：第一，注重介绍个人资料，并按顺序介绍（主人在客人后，男性在女性后，自己在他人后。）。第二，我们要有礼貌地适当使用肢体语言和辅助语言。第三。我们应该选择适度的信息引入话题。第四，在介绍时要注意避免个人隐私。

（三）致意礼仪

见面时的另一个重要礼节是致意。表达致意的方式有很多种，如点头、微笑、挥手等。我们要注意以下两点：

1. 适当。在公共场合向朋友示意或点头是适当的，而不应大声喊他们的名字。男士应该举止绅士，在女士面前要体贴。

2. 遵循当地风俗。各国风俗习惯各不相同。无论你在哪里，你都应该遵守当地的风俗习惯。所以你应该了解不同地方的风俗习惯。

（四）会话礼仪

1. 集中。你应该仔细倾听，保持目光接触，集中注意力在谈话上，并说一些简单的话来保持谈话的顺利进行。

2. 举止文明。你不能在谈话中四处张望。你应该在谈话中和蔼可亲和真诚。

3. 不打断别人。在谈话中打断别人是不礼貌的，因此，你应该先表达歉意并请求允许，然后在必要时插话。

4. 避免重复。你不应该在公共关系交谈中重复同样的话题。你应该试着寻找共同感兴趣的话题来保持谈话进行下去。

5. 内容选择。会话内容广泛，但应以主题为中心。如果对方说了什么不恰当的话，你应该试着巧妙地换个话题，认真处理你的事情。

6. 礼貌。如果你想参与别人的谈话，你应该打招呼并请求允许。如果有人想参与你的谈话，你应该打招呼问候。无论你和谁谈话，你都应该在公共关系社会化中表现得有礼貌。

7. 时间管理。第一次会议的谈话时间不宜太长。当有人忙于他的工作时，你应该长话短说。如果你晚上拜访某人，你应该尊重他的习惯和私人时间，并尽量简短交谈。

8. 保持距离。这包括心理距离和空间距离。公共关系社会活动中的双方代表特定的组织，各自有自己的利益。他们保持距离对有一个互利的对话和促进相互发展至关重要。

（五）宴会中的礼仪

宴会是为了欢迎、感谢、祝贺和联络的精心组织的一种常见的公共关系活动。宴会上的礼仪不仅是常规的习惯，而且体现个人素质和自我修养。

1. 主人的礼仪。宴会期间主要的礼仪如下：（1）安排客人有序的入座；（2）接待客人然后开始晚宴；（3）敬酒；（4）认真接待客人，介绍菜肴，劝说客人适当饮酒等；（5）请客人在餐后休息，饭后喝茶或吃点水果。

2. 客人的礼仪。（1）准时赴宴；（2）注意自己的着装；（3）优雅地问候主人；（4）按主人的意愿去做。

3. 就餐的礼仪

（1）从椅子的左侧入座或离开；请不要用你的手支撑下巴或把手臂放在桌上；请不要用餐巾擦餐具或玩弄餐具。

（2）当主人敬酒的时候，客人应停止进食和说话，适时地鼓掌。

（3）汤是热的时候请稍等片刻；吃东西的时候请不要发出任何声音，嘴里有食物的时候请不要和其他人说话；请咳嗽或吐痰时候请离开座位或用手帕遮住嘴，并且把身体朝向外侧。

（4）吃饭时你不应该松腰带或领带，或卷起袖子，或脱衣服。

（5）不应该只吃自己喜欢的菜，并且面对其他菜不感兴趣。

（6）喝酒或者喝饮料的时候，应该慢慢品尝，并且只喝到你酒量的三分之一；喝酒或者喝饮料的时候不应该吸烟；当敬酒的时候你的杯子应该低于主人。

（7）保持冷静，妥善处理在吃饭的时候发生意想不到的事情。

（8）如果中途离去，应该把餐巾放在你的椅子上，用餐结束时，把餐巾折叠起来放在你的盘子的右边。

（9）在客厅，吃水果或饮用茶时，你应该首先问各位长辈和女士。

（10）当道别的时候客人应该真诚地感谢主人的热情好客，主人应该感谢客人的到来。当主人送客人离开的时候，客人应该要求主人留步然后挥手说再见。

（六）拜访的礼仪

除了会议、晚宴，拜访是组织和所有人联系的一种常见的方便的方式。拜访最主要的礼仪是展示你的礼貌和尊重。

1. 要礼貌和体贴。在你去拜访前你应该征得主人的同意，确定清晰的合适的时间，通知去拜访的人；拜访一定要准时；礼貌地和主人以及他的家人打招呼。

（1）着装得体，在进屋后首先摘掉眼镜、帽子、手套、围巾等。

（2）注意你坐的位置。

（3）在抽烟前询问主人和女士的允许，然后请他们先抽。

（4）没有允许不要参观主人的院子和卧室；在被带领参观的时候不要碰主人的书和陈设。

（5）你不应该踢主人的猫、狗和其他宠物。

2. 在拜访中不应该安排太多的内容。不应该拖延时间来解决谈判中未解决的问题。因为这只是一次礼貌式的拜访。

3. 你在访问时应该在主人方便之时。最佳时间是上午十点到下午四点前。

（七）接待礼仪

招待会在公共关系中是非常重要的活动。它决定了公众的第一印象，进一步影响该组织的声誉以及形象是否温暖待人、礼貌和周到。以下是一些接待的建议：

1. 仔细准备。公共关系从业者自身应该在主观意识、外表、衣着和行为上做好准备；美化环境从而友好、热情地接待客人。

2. 真诚欢迎。你首先应该热情地问候拜访者，请他们坐下，喝茶，然后详细询问他们的姓名、身份、目的和要求等信息。然后你应该快速地决定和调整接待标准，程序和方式。不同的访客需要不同的方式来接待。每天的接待工作都要做到真诚有序。

3. 热情周道地招待。意思是为拜访者提供方便。特别是对来自远方的拜访者或代表，应该为他们提供住宿和食物，安排参观和讲习班，帮助他们买回票等。目的是帮助他们完成任务，让他们感到宾至如归。

三、对外事务中的公共关系礼仪

（一）在外交事务中的会见和送别中的礼仪

1. 在国际公众到达之前，你应该周全准备。试着了解情况，准备好，这样你就不会感到遗憾了。

2. 在国际会议之前确认接待标准和问候顺序。根据习俗，人们遵循互惠原则。在多国家的联系中，人们按照每个国家的英文名的第一个字母顺序排列，或者是他们到达的优先顺序。国际公共关系活动的重大场合通常会悬挂国旗。

3. 在开会的时候，上级的接待者应该首先和客人握手，并逐一介绍他的团队成员；迎宾员应与客人打招呼、点头、微笑、握手以示敬意。

4. 接待者应安排向客人献花，如果客人是高级贵宾，则由一个可爱的孩子或一个活力四射的女孩去上前献花。在送花前，你应该把不同国家的风俗禁忌和花卉语言考虑进去。

5. 接待人员，尤其是他们的领导，应该把客人带到他们的休息场所。如果有陪同人员，在他们短暂休息后，则由领导向客人介绍陪同团的人员。介绍日程和生活环境，帮助客人解决暂时的问题。

6. 在国际公共关系活动之后，接待者应该为客人购买他们的回程机票，并送他们离开。

（二）宴会上关于外交事务的礼仪

1. 中餐的礼仪（指上文提到在宴会的礼仪）

（1）避免禁忌。例如，当你邀请西方人共进晚餐时，要避免数字"13"；当你在斋月期间邀请伊斯兰教的客人享用晚餐时应该安排在日落之后。（2）把你的注意力放在社交活动上。（3）接待者应适应客人的方便。只介绍菜肴的名称和特点，而不是说服他们多吃或多喝。

2. 西餐的基本礼仪

（1）座位顺序。在两个人的情况下女性应该坐在男性的右边，在三个人的情况下，女性应该坐在两个男性的中间；有两个男性或女性的情况下，座位附近的墙壁应该留给老年人，并且安排在男性和女性的中间。男客人应该坐在主人的右边，而他的妻子在主人的右边。跟随主人的行动展开餐巾，然后折2/3放在你的大腿上；在你离开的时候把餐巾放在椅子上。

（2）如何使用餐具。餐具应从外到内，用右手拿刀。如果你想休息的话，把你的刀叉摆成"八"的图案，或者在你的盘子上摆成3:40的时钟的样式，用餐完毕，应将刀叉摆成"四点钟"的时针方向放在盘子里，并同时将餐巾折叠成小块放在盘子的右边。一般来说，只有在喝汤的时候，你可以用勺子和勺子来帮助你吃面条，而你说话时不应该玩弄刀叉。

（3）商务餐可以参考上述礼仪用餐规则和原则。

首先，穿着得体。西装和鞋子要整洁干净，男人在正式场合打领带。女士们应该穿裙子和高跟鞋。便服不适合任何正式场合。其次，女士优先。女士应先入座，先品尝。第三，坐得优雅。你应该从左边坐下，身体和桌子保持10厘米的间距，坐直，后背靠在椅子背来显示你已经适应并且坐着很舒服。男性膝盖略分开，手自信地放在腿上或椅子的扶手上。女士膝盖并拢，手放在大腿上，或交叉双腿，双手放在腰和大腿之间，或放在椅子的把手上。第四，当主人敬酒时，客人应停止进食并以掌声回应。第五，饮酒规则。不宜饮酒，饮酒量应控制在每日饮酒量的1/3，饮酒时请勿吸烟或摇晃酒杯。用拇指、食指、中指握住杯子，底部的小指握住杯子的脚。

人们通常喝红酒吃冷菜，喝白葡萄酒时吃鱼、蛋和烤肉。一般来说，主人会按宾客的重要性顺序敬酒，年轻的或者辈分小的应该向长者弯腰，杯子应该低于长者以示礼貌和尊重。

（三）涉外礼仪中的赠送礼仪

公共关系活动中送礼是社会活动中的常见现象。在公共关系中送礼是为了表示你的友好，如祝福、祝贺、怀念、关心、鼓励、欣赏等。以下是赠送礼物的小窍门。

1. 仔细选择。请根据收件人的兴趣和对方在公共关系关系交往中的主题来选择礼物。不同民族、不同地域的人对动物、植物、花卉、色彩等有不同的认识，有不同的禁忌，尽量避免受国籍和习俗的限制。

2. 创新务实。送礼要美观、新颖、实用。更重要的是礼物的意义，而不是它的成本。

3. 礼貌回应。收件人应该在送礼人面前打开礼物，说"好""漂亮""很好","这是我最喜欢的礼物。非常感谢"无论是什么样的礼物,都要表现出你的礼貌和真诚的感激。

第二节 公共关系中的社交技巧

一、人际交往概述

（一）人际交往在公共关系活动中的意义

交往也被称为"交流"或"信息交流",它指的是人们在社交活动中相互联系、交流信息和交流思想的过程。这是把信息从一个人传递到另一个人的过程。人际交往在公共关系中的意义如下：

1. 传播信息。公共关系最重要的功能之一是传播和交流。良好的人际关系将培养公共关系人员和组织的声誉和形象,有利于双方的自然沟通。

2. 铺路搭桥。随着组织的公共关系人员与公众之间进行进一步的互动,双方将更好地了解彼此,提高公众对组织的信赖感,这将为组织未来的个人交往和进一步发展铺路搭桥。

3. 树立形象。组织的良好形象,是无形财富。公共关系从业人员的态度、口才、外表、知识、道德和专业水平等都会给公共关系活动中的个人和组织之间的交往中留下深刻的印象,影响到整个组织本身的形象。

4. 增加凝聚力。"内求团结,外求发展"是公共关系活动的目标。如果一个组织有内部和外部的和谐的人际关系,都是一个思想,那么任何事情都是很容易处理的。

（二）影响人际交往的因素

人与人之间总会有某种关系,影响人际交往的因素很多。

1. 选择性。

（1）个体的主体性、需求性和利益性是影响他们在人际交往中选择性的重要因素。根据这些"标准",他们会根据标准来选择同类的事物。"物以类聚,人以群分。人们会选择和自己同想法的人属于同一个群体。"此外，公共关系从业者的情绪也会影响他们的选择。

（2）从对应的角度看，人们之间是否具有吸引力也是一个问题，是影响人际交往选择性的重要因素。如果一个人具有良好的职业技能和道德品质，就很容易满足同行对人际交往的需求；如果一个人风度翩翩、举止优雅，他很容易成为别人交往的对象。

2. 有效性。

（1）"首因效应"，即"第一印象"，是影响人际交往的一种典型现象。人们接触之初得到的有关对方的信息越具体、越真实，就越愿意和对方交往下去。

（2）"近因效应"，即"同类项"现象，是指交往双方在时空上的接近或相同，对交往的深入影响。例如，亲戚、朋友、同学、同事、同文化层次、同兴趣爱好，在人际关系中特别容易达成共识，就是这种效应的表现。

3. 先入为主性。

先入为主性是指人们根据自己以往的人际关系经验，判断对方，处理事情。

4. 整体性。

这是人们相互了解的过程，从第一印象的整体认识，从肤浅的外表、服饰和行为，再到对内在的资格和专业技能。因此，公共关系从业者不应草率评判别人，尽量避免把一部分当作整体。

（三）人际交往中应该遵循的规则和原则

1. 尊重他人。正如老话所说："你尊敬我一尺，我敬你一丈。"人们不仅希望而且需要受到尊重。任何人都喜欢与尊重他人的人交流。

2. 遵纪守法。在人际交往中，你必须遵守纪律，遵守法律。你的言论和行为不应触犯法律或违反社会道德。

3. 待人诚恳。你应该善待别人，无论贫穷或富有、美丽或丑陋，他都是同样真诚的。你不应该从外表、衣着或社会地位来判断一个人。

4. 履行承诺。正如俗话说"精诚所至，金石为开"。机会通常不会降临一个违背诺言的人或组织身上。因此，你应该遵守你的诺言，在人际交往中努力满足别人的要求。如果你对某事不确定，你应该要求以后进一步讨论，如果你不能胜任某事，你应该说对不起并婉言拒绝其他人。

（四）人际交往中的病态心理

1. 自卑心理。这种人会看不起自己，缺乏信心，所以不能发挥自己的优点和长处。自卑的人不会有自己的想法，只听别人说话。

2. 胆小心理。这种人性格内向，通常缺乏经验。懦夫很难实现自己的目标，而怯懦的心理则是束缚他思想和行为的绳索。

3. 猜疑嫉妒心理。这类人往往会怀疑别人，认为别人不可靠。当他看到别人谈话时，他很可能认为他们在说自己的坏话，所以他通常会惹上麻烦。这样的心理也很容易伤害别人。

4. 消极心态。这类人通常会在谈话后表现出他异常的一面。不管别人怎么说，他都会为争论而争吵。他往往混淆了什么是对或错，真或假，因此很容让别人感到厌恶。

5. 独占心理。这种人喜欢在自己的范围内做些事情，拒绝扩大自己的思想范围。

6. 游戏心态。这样的人喜欢游戏人生，把交朋友当作一场游戏，对任何人都不能真诚交往，所以很难交到真诚的朋友。

7. 贪婪的心态。这种人结交朋友只是为了"有用才交朋友"，所以他通常会结交一些对他有用的朋友，以及能给他带来好处的朋友。像这样的人通常"过河拆桥"，喜欢用不公平的手段获得额外的好处，所以他很容易为自身带来伤害。

8. 漠不关心的心态。这种人对任何与自己无关的事都漠不关心。他通常用严厉的语言说话，带着高傲和冷漠的态度。这会使他人疏远他，失去更多的朋友。

（五）克服人际交往中病态心理的方法

1. 请克服自卑心理，正确认识和评价自己。

2. 保持积极的心态，"敢于尝试，不要害怕失败。"

3. 调整心情，摒弃沮丧情绪。

4. 给自己些时间，慢慢来。

5. 选择一个熟悉的时间、地点和内容来谈论。

6. 抛弃"自我保护"的心态，积极参加社会活动。

7. 敞开你的心灵，消除你的偏见，与他人自由交往。

8. 及时回应别人的话，表扬他们的成就。

9. 多做少说，在关键时刻直接切入问题的核心。

10. 保持谦虚，并且充满希望。

11. 工作踏实，在幕后扮演一个快乐的角色。

12. 适当打扮自己，提高你的声音。

（六）公共关系的基本社交技能

1. 保持稳定。公共关系从业人员应该在他的言谈举止中保持稳定，言行一致。在公共关系场合，他不应该有许多"面孔"，应该和他的话保持一致。

2. 和组织在一起。公共关系人员代表一个组织，所以他应该在他的言谈举止中，对组织有信心，与组织"同舟共济"。

3. 寻求相同。你应该寻找与对方的共同点，拉近彼此之间的距离。

4. 自我训练。公共关系从业者应该从各个方面提高自己的社交技巧，并在适当的时候展示自己，以吸引公众。

第六章
大学生公共关系形象塑造与求职艺术

第一节 大学生公共关系形象塑造

一、公共关系形象塑造的含义

（一）形象

形象就其本义而言是指形状相貌。是指人们在交往过程中留给别人印象。形象不仅仅指外在形象，还包括性格等内在特征。人作为一个能动的主体，除了相貌、体态、举止等外在形象外，还有丰富的内涵形象，如一个人的谈吐、修养、气质、风度、性格等都是构成一个人整体形象的组成部分。我们所论及的"形象"就是指外在形象和内在形象相统一的总体形象。

目前，随着公共关系学在国内广泛传播，"形象"一词的应用已被大大地扩充了，已不仅仅指个人、群体形象了。诸如：组织形象、政府形象、名牌形象、商标形象、城市形象等等纷纷见诸各种传播媒介。"形象"一词和"公共关系"一词一样，已成为人们津津乐道的热门话题。大学生作为一个具有高文化素质的知识群体，作为祖国的栋梁之材，其形象如何，备受社会关注。良好的形象需要努力去塑造。那么，什么是形象塑造呢？

（二）大学生形象塑造

人的形象除了外在形象中的长相、身材、肤色等是与生俱来的外，其他内涵的东西如言谈、举止、气质、态度、修养、性格、情绪、才能等则是后天习得和修炼的。人通过学习、训练、修养可以改变自己的总体形象。通过接受教育和自身努力改变形象的过程就是形象塑造。这个过程是潜移默化的，但又是可以明显感知的。教育和自身努力可以改变一个人的形象。

随着社会的发展，人类不断地在美化生活。而美化生活首先是美化自身形象。学习公共关系礼仪的目的，正是为了塑造大学生良好的形象。树立良好形象有助于增强人际吸引，赢得他人的好感，受人欢迎，易被社会接纳，因而有助于使自己走向成功。这对大学生来说具有十分重要的现实意义。

（三）公共关系形象塑造

公共关系形象是指个人、群体或组织等在公开场合下、在社交中或在公共关系活动中给社会公众留下的总体印象；或者说，是社会公众对某个人、群体或组织在公众中或在开展的公共关系活动中的行为表现的总体评价、看法和态度。大学生公共关系形象则是指大学生个体或群体在公开场合、社交中或公共关系活动中给社会公众留下的总体印象。大学生作为具有高素质的知识群体，作为社会的佼佼者，其形象好坏自然会成为社会公众评价的焦点。

作为大学生，无论是个体还是群体都会因自身的外在表现和行为等客观状况形成实际形象。而在社会公众心目中，对大学生总体有一个理想形象，即有知识、有文化、爱学习、有正义感、穿着朴素、富有朝气、举止言谈符合大学生身份角色、能赢得社会广泛赞誉、受社会公众欢迎的形象。由实际形象努力向理想形象转变的过程就是形象塑造的过程。

二、大学生要注重公共关系形象塑造

当代的大学生是跨世纪的人才。21世纪是个继往开来、竞争激烈、更加开放、知识经济高速发展的新世纪。新世纪将赋予大学生新的使命。

（一）大学生公共关系形象塑的意义

第一，大学生面对的是21世纪新的竞争、新的挑战、新的考验和新的机遇。以什么样的素质、什么样的姿态、什么样的形象迎接挑战，参与竞争，经受考验，抓住机遇，推销自我，是每一位大学生都不得不认真思考的严肃问题。因此，21世纪大学生形象问题已成为高等学校校园里竞相议论的热门话题。大学生如何塑造良好的公共关系形象已提到高等学校教育的议事日程上。从北京大学学子开展的"修身"教育活动,到上海大学、湖北民族学院等高校开展的大学生形象问题大讨论,足以说明大学生注重公共关系形象塑造已刻不容缓。

第二,大学生是一个特殊群体。他们的言行举止都会被社会人士标注上形象的标签,影响到社会对大学生的评价。

第三,对大学生集体而言,良好的大学生形象是无形的财富,是无形的召唤,可以形成强大的凝聚力把他们吸引到一起,形成集体荣誉感,为塑造最佳形象而共同努力。良好的大学生形象是一种潜在的无穷的力量。

第四,对大学生个体而言,良好的形象就是良好的人生、良好的形象就是光明前程。塑造形象,就是塑造人生、设计前程。个人在社会中的形象是一个人生活的一部分,个人形象本身就是其人生与前程的缩影与反映。

(二)公共关系素质培养与公共关系形象塑造

良好的公共关系形象的塑造有赖于良好的公共关系素质的培养。一个人公共关系素质的高低决定其公共关系形象的好坏。大学生要使自己具有较高的公共关系素质,需要在以下几个方面努力:

1. 行为一定要端正。不需要像古人那样"行如风,立如松,坐如钟,卧如弓",但至少要站有站样,坐有坐样。

2. 要遵守公共文明。譬如在公共场所不要高声喧哗,不要随地吐东西,不要带给人不便,如乘坐扶手电梯要左行右站,坐车坐地铁的时候不要把整个身子靠在扶杆上等等。

3. 对人要有礼。所谓"礼多人不怪",中国是一个礼仪之邦,作为大学生,要懂礼、学仪、用礼,对长者有敬,对幼者有爱,对友者有义,对仇者有容,这才是真正的礼。

4. 多做运动。大学生平常的生活比较懒散,成天对着电脑一动不动,这不仅直接损害视力,更影响了大学生们的身体健康。如果大学生拥有足够的知识却没有健康的身体来支持他们行动,他们怎么可能把想要做的事做好?任何组织都不会喜欢没有健康体魄的人,所以大学生要多做运动,拥有健康的身体。

5. 加强品德修养。要使自己通过刻苦修炼做到为人真诚忠实,办事公道正派,工作讲求信誉,待人谦恭有礼,不卑不亢。爱祖国、爱人民、爱科学,具有勤奋努力、团结协作、开拓进取的精神。

6. 培养良好性格。人的性格既不是与生俱来的，也不是一成不变的。虽然性格会受到先天遗传因素的影响，但后天教育和磨炼，是形成和改变性格的重要因素。大学生在接受文化教育的同时，也要不断优化自己的性格，培养热情、开朗、大方、自信、乐观、活泼的性格。待人处事文明、礼貌，富于幽默感。

7. 提高社交能力。具不具备社交能力，是衡量一个现代人是否适应现代开放社会的标志之一。随着科技的发展，各国之间往来频繁，整个世界已经成了"地球村"。作为当代大学生应善于社交，善于与人交往、沟通，善于与不同地区、不同民族、不同国家、不同层次、不同性格的人进行交往沟通，广结良缘，建立良好的人际关系网络。

8. 改进情商。大学生的智商应该说相对比较高，但大学生的情商就不一定了。智商高表明头脑聪明，具有认识客观事物，获得知识，并用来改造客观世界的能力，智商一个人成功的因素之一。成功的另一个因素是情商，据心理学家研究表明，成功的两个因素中，情商是一个人成功的决定因素。情商主要指人的个性心理品质，包括动机、兴趣、情绪、信念、意志、性格等。情商更多地体现一个人的综合素质。情商高的人，其情绪特质表现出稳定、平和，心理承受能力强，既能认知自身情绪，也能认知他人的情绪，并能妥善管理情绪。遇到挫折、失败时，能很快摆脱低落的情绪，重新集中精力于工作。而情商低的人，常常处于情绪低落状态，即使他有很高的智商，也无法让自己很快排除低落的情绪，获得成功。大学生要想自己能获得成功，必须提高情商，并遵循这样一条成功规律，即：树立正确的理想目标，充满自信心，以极强的克制力和恒心为达到目标而付诸行动，养成良好习惯，不断修正不良行为和习惯，培养良好的个性心理品质，以坚强的意志力和百折不挠的努力去赢得成功。

9. 调整和完善知识结构。随着全球科学技术的综合化趋势日益加强，单一的"专门化"人才已不适应新世纪的要求。大学生择业取向不断多元化，用人单位对"复合型"人才的需求不断提升，大学生的知识结构亟待调整和完善。对大学生除了要强调基础知识、专业知识外，还应加强综合知识的学习。大学教育必须提高大学的文化品位；必须提高大学生的文化素质。大学生只有综合知识，全面提高整体素质，才能塑造出良好的公共关系形象。

10. 强化公共关系意识。注重公共关系形象塑造必须强化公共关系意识。公共关系意识是公共关系规范与行为准则的内化。公共关系意识是公共关系实践在人们思维中的反映，是一种现代社会的文明观念。公共关系意识与公共关系形象塑造呈正相关关系。公共关系意识愈强，其公共关系形象则塑造得愈好，反之则愈差。公共关系学界知名学者余明阳教授曾经说过："公共关系的竞争必然是公共关系人员素质的竞争，而公共关系素质的核心就是公共关系意识。"作为一种意识，它以许多符合公共关系精神的现代观念为基础，像追求卓越、适度表现、和睦悦人、注重信誉、善解人意、富有分寸感和责任心等。大学生只有强化了公共关系意识才可能在社会上、在自我推销过程中、在公众面前主动地塑造一个良好的公共关系形象。

三、塑造公共关系形象从校园生活开始

高校的校园生活除了学习之外，文艺、体育、社交、协会团体、剧团、联谊会、沙龙、社会实践、社会公益等活动丰富多彩，其中许多活动属校园公共关系活动。积极参与这些活动，有利于锻炼和提高自身素质，也有利于公共关系形象塑造。例如，校园内经常开展的演讲赛、辩论赛、文艺汇演、公共关系礼仪大赛、主持人选拔赛、卡拉OK赛、时装表演、诗歌朗诵，创文明班级、文明寝室、文明校园等活动都是极富挑战性、竞争性的活动，也是大学生展示风采和自我推销的极好机会。校园外的各种适合大学生参与的社会公益活动，如青年志愿者活动、为社会献爱心活动、捐助希望工程和敬老爱幼活动、校际联谊活动、社会调查活动等亦属公共关系活动。大学生与这些活动的过程中，不仅为个人，也为大学生群体塑造了良好的公共关系形象。

大学生在参与校内外各种公共关系活动中，不仅锻炼了性格、磨炼了意志，而且还扩大了社交、陶冶了性情、提高了素质，更重要的是塑造了良好的形象。

用人单位也往往会按照社会主导价值观的标准来评价一个大学生的好坏并进而决定录用与否。因此，大学生应充分利用四年大好时光来努力塑造自身良好形象，逐步向社会认同的理想形象靠拢。

迈出校门的第一步，面临的第一个考验是接受社会的挑选，过求职应聘关。在求职应聘过程中，树立良好的公共关系形象将有助于求职的成功。

第二节　大学生求职应聘与公共关系形象塑造

由于人才竞争日益激烈，社会和用人单位严格、审慎、挑剔的眼光，大学生不仅知识结构、专业基础、能力水平等要符合用人单位的要求，而且公共关系形象如何也成了用人单位录用与否的重要条件。在其他条件基本合乎要求的情况下，具有良好的公共关系形象就会受到用人单位的青睐；而公共关系形象不理想则难免被用人单位拒之门外。

一个人求职应聘的过程实际上就是自我推销的过程。推销是现代社会中一种重要的生活技能。公共关系形象塑造是自我推销中的前提条件和最有效的手段、方式之一。

一、求职应聘的外在公共关系形象塑造

外在公共关系形象主要指一个人的仪容、仪表、仪态、言谈举止的综合反映。集中体现在相貌、形体、服饰、体态、气质和表情上。

（一）相貌、形体和服饰

一个人的相貌、形体是受遗传因素影响的，是与生俱来的、先天的、难以改变的。尽管现代医学技术可以通过整形、美容来修正容貌，但毕竟是大多数人所不愿尝试的，况且还有风险。以自己自然的形象和身材，加上适当的化妆打扮，展示自己的本色，同样能赢得他人的好感。适时的装扮是必要的。求职应聘时，打扮要得体，要符合所求职业的要求。

女生可借助化淡妆来修饰、美化自己，大学生在求职中适当突显出化淡妆，不但能体现出大学生的修养，也能表示大学生对求职的重视，对考官和求职单位的尊重。化妆要遵循自然、协调、美观、大方为原则，切忌浓妆艳抹、珠光宝气、香味刺鼻。脸部化妆要注意与发型、服装、饰物等相配，形成协调一致的整体美，充分体现出大学生的热情、活泼、质朴、清纯、聪慧等个性特征。恰如其分的化妆不仅能使自己显得更美、更具魅力，而且，也能振奋精神，表达一种热爱生活的积极心态，同时也是尊人敬业的表现。

男生要注重面部清洁、个人卫生。蓬头垢面、衣着不整的形象只会引起招聘单位的反感。如果应试者在求职时都不能以得体的装束来迎接面试，公司怎能寄

希望于他受聘后会变得更赏心悦目呢？

服饰是不容被忽视的，它往往折射出一个人的文化修养和品位。服装一般分为便装、正两种装等。女生在求职应聘时最好穿裙装，体现出知识女性的独特魅力，突显出端庄稳重、大方成熟。在颜色的选择上要注意选择单色、装饰和花纹少的颜色，根据自己的身材配合自己的发型，选择适合自己的裙装。可以选择套裙，也可以选择连衣裙。注重仪表，穿着整洁、合体、庄重不一定保证能找到工作，但有助于求职的成功。而不注重仪表，不修边幅的人很难找到理想的工作。服饰对于现代人来说，它的功能早已不局限于御寒、遮羞了，而是大大地扩充了，如展现体形、显示性格、反映心情、区别职业、区分性别和年龄、烘托气氛等等。通过服饰可以传递诸如经济状况、审美水平、个性特征、兴趣爱好、文化品位等种种信息。从这个意义上说，服饰是一种文化、一种文明。我们应根据求职应聘的需要及自己的身份、性别、年龄、形体美感需要选择合适的衣着。

（二）体态、表情、风度

体态、表情、风度均为后天习得和养成的，是可以改变的。在求职应聘时，体态、表情、风度都会不同程度地向招聘者传递各种信息，这些信息或多或少地会成为影响录用与否的因素。

求职应聘要讲究仪态，站有站相，坐有坐相，举止稳重大方，神情亲切自然，风度潇洒自如才能给招聘者或主考官留下好印象。对于面试而言，仪表仪态、语言表达可说是测试重点了。

面试时，首先神态要显得轻松自然，过于紧张就会出现体态变形、手足无措、语无伦次的状况，最终难免失败。神情要大方，走进面试场所前可先深深吸一口气，慢慢呼出，使紧张的心情平静、放松一些。如面试场所的门是关着的，则应先轻轻敲门，待对方允许进去后再进去，不要贸然闯进去。进门后要面对房间里的人，侧手把门关好，任何时候不能把自己的背部面对房间里的人。门要轻开轻关，然后大方、自然、从容地站到主考人面前，视当时具体情况，或微笑致意问好，或握手问好。经对方让座后再落座。落座时声音要轻，动作要缓，坐姿要正确。上身正直，稍向前倾，不要贴靠在椅背上。双手自然地放在大腿上。表情要自然，神情专注，目光注视着考官而不要左顾右盼、东张西望。要显出谦恭倾听的样子。回答考官提问时，切忌挠腮抓耳、抠头吐舌头或抠鼻子、掏耳朵等，这样既不雅观，也不礼貌。

遇到难以对答的问题时，要冷静思考，既不要唯唯诺诺、结结巴巴，也不要显出浮躁不安或趾高气扬、不屑一顾的样子。应始终保持沉着稳重、机灵坦诚、不卑不亢的神态和风度。

应聘面试过程中，表情要真诚自然，不要矫揉造作。要保持微笑。"微笑"是一种良好心情的表露，是乐观开朗的表现。微笑向对方传达一种友好、亲和、热情、尊重的信息；微笑对自己则透露一种自信、善良、积极、敬业的个性。

二、内在气质与修养

与外在形象相对应的，是内在的气质与修养。一个人内在的气质与修养虽不像外在形象那么直观，那么一目了然，但仍然是可感知的。许多招聘广告中有一条常见的要求：应聘者要有修养，形象、气质俱佳……气质与修养并不是看不见的，它通过人的举止言谈、态度、情绪、脾气等明显地反映出来。大学生在学校应努力培养良好的气质，不断提高文化修养。在求职应聘中尽量显现出脱俗不凡的气质和良好的修养，这将极有利于求职的成功。

求职应聘时，大学生的行为修养显得格外重要，因为其他修养如政治、思想、道德、文化、知识等修养，招聘者是通过简历、推荐表、求职信等文字资料来了解的，而行为修养则可直接观察到。大学生求职应聘时的一举一动、一言一行都会映入招聘者的眼帘，从而产生第一印象。从心理学的角度分析，由于"首因效应"的影响，第一印象往往会左右人们对一个人的总体判断和评价。

有这样一则例子：

一位先生登报招聘一名办公室勤杂工。约有50多人前来应招，但这位先生只挑中了一个男孩。他的一位朋友问他：你为何喜欢那个男孩？他既没带一封介绍信，也没有任何人推荐。"你错了。"这位先生说，"他带来许多介绍信。他在门口蹭掉了脚下带的土，进门后随手关上了门，说明他做事小心仔细。当他看到那位残疾老人时，就立即起身让座，表明他心地善良、体贴别人。进了办公室他先脱去帽子，回答我提问时干脆果断，证明他既懂礼貌又有教养，其他所有人都从我故意放在地板上的那本书上迈过去，而这个男孩却俯身拣起它并放回桌子上。他衣着整洁，头发梳得整整齐齐，指甲修得干干净净。难道你不认为这些就是最好的介绍信吗?"

这一事例充分说明了行为修养在求职应聘中的重要性。

三、求职应聘公共关系语言的运用

求职应聘中交谈、询问、对话或面试是招聘和应聘双方心理沟通的过程。对应聘者来说,这是一次自我推销的机会,应紧紧把握这次机会,利用语言交流来加深对方对你的良好印象,吸引对方对你的注意和兴趣。在交流沟通的过程中,公共关系语言的运用不仅能为自己树立良好的公共关系形象,而且能促成求职目的的达成。

所谓公共关系语言,是指当你传递语言信息时,会产生这样的效果:(1)引起对方的兴趣;(2)使对方产生愉悦感和认同感;(3)给对方留下良好印象;(4)语言具有感染力,能打动对方;(5)能出奇制胜。

国外曾有这样一个故事:一位盲人在路旁向人们乞讨,在他面前放着一张纸条,上面写着:"我的眼瞎了,请给我几个钱吧!"路上来来往往的行人从他身边走过,很少有人施舍。有一位诗人路过这里,盲人向他乞讨,诗人说:"我今天没有带钱,但可以为您写两句诗。"诗人在盲人的纸上写道:"阳光多么美好,可惜我看不见!"匆匆过往的行人看到这简短的两句诗非常感动,纷纷为盲人解囊。前一张纸条要钱却得不到钱,而后一张纸条没有提钱却让行人主动施舍。这后一种语言就是打动人心的公共关系语言。这个故事给我们许多启示。

求职应聘中要注重公共关系语言的运用。

(一)礼貌用语贯穿求职应聘始终

求职应聘要注重礼貌用语。礼貌用语不仅反映了应聘者对对方的尊重,也体现了应聘者本人的修养。不论自己是否被录用,礼貌用语都要贯穿始终。以"您好"开场,以"谢谢!再见"收场,要显现出大学生彬彬有礼的风度。在整个交谈过程中忌说粗话、脏话等。因为说粗话、脏话不仅不能表现出一个人的爽直、坦诚、随和,反而恰恰暴露出这个人粗俗、素质低下、修养差。

(二)以真诚为原则

真诚是公共关系的最重要原则,同样真诚又是公共关系语言的最基本的原则。谈话是否真诚,这不仅能被谈话的任何一方真切地感知,而且也是双方都十分看重的。美国心理学家诺尔曼·安德森于1968年曾对信息传播者的个性品质进行了专门研究。他列出了555个描写人的个性品质的形容词，然后让大学生们挑选出他们最喜欢的形容词。研究的结果表明：大学生们评价最高的个性品质是真诚。说话的态度要真诚，这是语言传播沟通的一个基本原则，也是获得对方信任的前提。

（三）恰当使用赞美语

在应聘的面谈或面试时，选择适当时机，对招聘单位、招聘者、考官等表达自己对对方的欣赏、赞美之情，不仅会使对方有一个好心情，而且还会给招聘者留下好印象。但赞美一定要发自内心，出自真诚，不要有阿谀奉承之嫌。

（四）说话谦恭有礼，讲究艺术性

在求职过程中，不论对方提出何种问题，都要谦恭有礼，要把握分寸，讲究艺术性。有的大学生到用人单位自我介绍：我是××大学毕业的高才生，我是要来当经理的。这种话会使对方觉得你既不识时务，也不知天高地厚，其结果是可想而知的。

（五）树立自信，把握应答技巧

面谈、面试时一定要充满自信。自信是肯定自己。"高傲之气不可有，自信之心不可无。"如能充满自信地回答考官的提问，意味着在自我推销中迈出了成功的第一步。如面对考官的提问，羞怯害怕、唯唯诺诺、谨小慎微、生怕答错，则说明自己本身有自卑感。自卑是一种不健康的心理现象，是一种认为自己不可能成功的心理状态。自卑感往往会挫败一个人的勇气，夺去自信心，面试时难免要失败。

（六）善于倾听，提高面试效果

面试时还要善于倾听，集中精力，准确理解考官提问的核心、要点和实质，以便有针对性地做出积极的反应。善于倾听就要做到神情专注，听得认真；积极思考，答得中肯、坦率、巧妙，这将极有利于提高面试效果。

（七）实事求是，不能不懂装懂

在面谈或面试时，一定要以实事求是的态度对待。当遇到自己不知、不懂、不会的问题时，采取回避不答，或牵强附会，或不懂装懂的做法都是不可取的。应该诚恳坦率地承认自己的不知或不足，反而会赢得考官的信任与好感。

（八）语言精练，口齿清楚

在与用人单位交谈，或接受主考官面试时，由于时间有限，应该突出重点，言简意赅，吐字清晰。一定要用普通话。语言要透出坦诚、机智、聪慧、幽默。语言节奏适中，语速、语气、语调都要适宜，以引起对方对你的兴趣、重视和信任，以期获得求职应试的成功。

第三节　大学生就业技能

一、大学生找工作的基本要求

一般来说，只有当三个因素——政策、能力和机遇起到综合作用时，才能在社会上取得成功。对大学生来说，充分利用"公平竞争""自主择业""双向选择"等政策优势，在人力资源市场上销售自己是非常重要的。

（一）做好准备，抓住机会

"机会留给有准备的人。"要做好准备，抓住机会成功推销自己。

1. 了解自己。只有了解了自己，才能自信并成功。一个大学生应该了解他的现状，并在特定的环境系统中明确自己的位置，比如你的专业是"长线"还是"短线"，是"受欢迎的还是不受欢迎的"；你的学习成绩好还是坏；你比别人有什么优点等等，然后才可以确定在求职方面的目标、水平和范围。

2. 了解别人。大学生应了解就业政策和大学生情况以及自身情况，如经济发展对大学生的要求、雇主的要求以及竞争对手的情况等。否则，可能失去就业机会。

3. 展示你自己。大学生应该抓住机会展示自己的才能和技能在面试中推销自己。应该表现出良好的修养、风度和形象来吸引雇主的青睐。

（二）表达自己

处在公共关系中的人都要依靠自己的才能和利用可能的机会来表达自己，给相关的公众留下好印象并被他们接受。如何通过表达自己的情感、经历、观点和成果来树立良好形象，建立良好的人际关系呢？这里有一些小贴士可供参考。

1. 坚持实事求是的原则。大学生正处于人生的最佳时期，前途光明。作为一名大学生，应该坚持实事求是的原则，不仅要介绍自己的知识水平、技能水平、道德等等，而且包括他的发展潜力、短期和长期目标，使雇主可以有一个全面的了解。

2. 利用好前几分钟介绍自己，像俗话说得好："机不可失，时不再来。"对大学生来说抓住机会并且利用好前几分钟做一个好的自我介绍很重要，会给雇主留下良好的持久的第一印象。

3. 为自己树立良好的形象。好的形象在面试中很重要。除了能力和天赋之外，还得穿着得体，注意非言语性的语言，为了在面试中表现突出，精神要处在最佳状态。

4. 口齿清晰富有活力。从某种程度上说，一个人的言谈可以代表性格和修养。在面试中，大学生要注重自己的速度，说话时的语调，表现出自信和活力。

5. 言谈精巧。大学生应遵循"适度原则"，在面试中有序地表达自己的观点。这意味着应该提供适量的个人资料和自我评价。既不应该自吹自擂也不妄自菲薄。要遵循以下原则：

（1）选择合适的词有序地表达自己，使自己能清楚地被理解。

（2）注意其他人的回应，努力调整语言，满足其他人要求。

（3）尽量避免不必要的语言例如"哼"和"嗯"，这样影响语言的连贯性和逻辑性，并且使人厌烦。

（4）避免使用"但是""也许""可能""似乎"，等这样的不确定的词的使用，也不能低着头，这样的肢体语言削弱你的可信度。

（5）尽量避免使用一些模糊的术语和令人不快的称谓，并且不要用开玩笑的语气说一件正事，这将让你留下不好的印象。

二、求职技巧

（一）求职面试的基本要求

大学生应注意以下几点：

要有充分的准备，俗话说得好，"机会总会光顾有准备的人。"大学生要在面试前培养自己各方面的良好形象。应该在校园里参加不同的模拟面试：参加面试前检查他的衣着、表情、眼神接触和举止等,记录演讲来检查自己的声音和语调。只有这样,才能在面试前取得好的经验,减轻紧张情绪。

2. 注意开头。正如一句老话所说,好的开端是成功的一半,抓住第一次见面的机会,留下良好的"第一印象"是很重要的。首先,应该在面试中有礼貌地对待考官,说"你好""微笑"和"握手",接下来,做一个简短的自我介绍和引导谈话;最后,注意你走路姿势、站姿和坐姿,等等。

3. 做一个好的倾听者。应该用心倾听考官,并跟他有目光交流和微笑,用"正确""合理"和"是"来回应,显示你的注意力和礼貌。

4. 不要打断别人。不应该打断考官的话。即使有什么要补充解释的,也应该请求允许,并乞求原谅。例如:"请原谅,李先生。我可以在这里插句话吗?"

5. 要有耐心。应该保持耐心,回答问题有条不紊,在面试时做到详细、如实回答。

6. 展望未来。在回答问题的时候,要审视自己的职位和事业的未来,表现出对这份工作的热爱、热情和创造力。

7. 礼貌地告辞。应该对面试的机会表示感谢,在面试结束时感谢考官,然后礼貌地告辞。例如:"谢谢你,先生。今天给我一个自我介绍的机会。我真的很感激。""谢谢您的关心,李经理,我现在可以走了吗?再见。"

(二)如何面对面试官的挑战

性格、兴趣和风格因人而异,所以面试和如何回答面试官的问题变得复杂。求职者应尽量了解面试官的思考和说话的风格和态度,在一开始,合理应对他的挑战。

1. 在一个"谦逊有礼"的面试官面前。有些面试官看起来很谦虚,很平易近人,但实际上很严格,很有见地。应该有足够的警惕和足够的诚实来表达你的观点,不应该在这些面试官面前盛气凌人。

2. 在形式主义的面试官面前。有些面试官不灵活,对局势的变化似乎漠不关心。这样的面试官在原则上通常是内向、固执的。他的行为有一定的框架。你应该试着说些有吸引力的话来激发他,激发他的兴趣去多说。然后你耐心地听他讲话,假装是他的老朋友。

3. 在一位经验丰富的面试官面前。一个有经验的面试官会礼貌和体贴,但你能感觉到他的礼貌的距离。他们似乎很热情，但有时漠不关心。你应该少说话，多加小心，特别是当你谈论你的能力、愿望、要求和感受时。在自我介绍后，你可以询问他的想法，问他："您是怎么看的？"

虽然他不会表达他的态度，但他希望如此得到尊重。一旦他做出了决定，就很难改变。因此留下良好的第一印象非常重要，要给对方一种坚定、聪明、高效、负责、值得信赖的印象。

4. 在一个高傲的面试官面前，通常像这样的面试官他的眼神里充满了傲慢的表情，使自己与众不同。你应该足够勇敢，不应该顾及他的态度。你应该有礼貌地和他进行愉快的谈话。记住要简明扼要。

5. 在一个安静的面试官面前。这种面试官通常坐在那里静静地，观察你，等待你的行动。有时，即使你说了很多话，他还是保持沉默，就像一个哑巴。你不应该被他吓到，相反，你应该勇敢地表达自己，充分发挥你的优势。

（三）准备推荐信的技能

一封自我推荐信不像直接面对面的面试。面试人不可能通过读申请人的自荐信而深刻了解他，但是自荐信（包括在网上发布自己的个人资料信息）也有不可替代的优点。首先，你可以准确地、彻底地、有序地在自荐信里进行自我介绍，通过文字、图表、图片、特殊的措辞和设计。

此外，你可以腾出大量的时间和精力与更多的公司联系，以收集就业数据作为你的参考来做决定。因此，选择信件或在网上上传你的个人资料是求职的好方法。

这里有一些建议供你参考：

1. 了解不同雇主对申请人的要求，不同的雇主对申请人的性别、年龄、身体、视力、地址、学校记录等有不同的要求。只有当你知道这些要求，并认为你符合他们的要求时，你才能发送你的自我推荐信，等待你的进一步机会。

2. 仔细准备你的材料。你应该仔细地准备你的材料，分析哪些是客观的，哪些是主观的。例如，你在学校的成绩、社会地位、奖项和荣誉都是客观的；你的特点、兴趣爱好、才能和潜力是主观的。如果雇主对你提任何强有力的观点，你可以强调它们并凸现自己。

3. 向你的老师或学院请求推荐。如果你有一封来自你的老师或就业指导中心的推荐信，带有个人签名或办公室印章，"情况属实，同意推荐"。在这种情况下，雇主会认为你是值得信任的，并且对你有很好的印象。许多大学已经开设了自己的网站，上传大学生的个人资料，这可以增加数据的可信度。

4. 写一封简短的求职信。你应该写一封简短的求职信，然后用几百个词来清楚、礼貌地申请一个职位，用附件的个人资料或图片来说明。最后，写下你的地址和联系电话，然后你就可以发送自荐信了。

（四）填报申请表的技巧

大学生要填写很多种表格，范围从"求才表""问卷调查"、到"摸底表"等不同形式。这里有一些建议，供您参考。

1. 整理不同的表格以确定表单样式和侧重点。

2. 注意选择材料，注意措辞和内容剪裁。

3. 用漂亮书法精心、有技巧地填写表格。

4. 简明扼要。在填写内容较多的表格时，要使用时间顺序，使内容清晰易读。在填写求职申请表时，大学生应该谨慎小心，实事求是。更重要的是，你要简明扼要。那样你才是一个成功的申请人。

第七章

公共关系危机的管理

当一个组织陷入危机时,它对公共关系来说是非常具有挑战性的。由于危机是破坏性的和偶然发生的,所以很少有人愿意关注它并准备好应对它。对于组织领导和合格的公关人员来说,为危机发生的可能性采取预防措施是明智的。一旦陷入危机,他们可以根据灵活的计划来应对挑战。危机管理是公共关系工作中一个重要的现实任务。

第一节 公共关系危机概论

一、危机的概念、分类和危机的特征

(一)危机的概念

危机是指严重影响组织生存和发展的恶性事件,即对组织的生存和发展产生重大影响的突发事件。

突发事件指狭义上的恶性事件,这对一个组织是不利的。突发事件在狭义上分为两种,即常见的突发事件和严重的突发事件。常见的突发事件是指企业的商业活动中的公共关系纠纷,包括企业内部的纠纷、与消费者的纠纷以及不同组织之间的纠纷。严重事故是指在生产和经营中发生的重大事故(如严重工伤事故和环境污染事故),生产和经营决策失误,自然灾害严重损失,等等。

(二)危机的分类和特征

1. 危机的分类

究其原因,危机可以分为以下类别:

（1）主观因素造成的危机，如巨大的质量事故、环境污染、建筑物倒塌、食物中毒等。

（2）地震、火灾、洪水和不可预料的自然灾害等客观因素造成的危机。

（3）公众误解造成的危机，如公众舆论中的严重危机、媒体批评、行为冲突等。

2.危机的特点

任何一种危机都有四个特点：

（1）突发性。任何突发事件都是不可预料的，因此它们所造成的危机使人们难以处理，会给一个组织造成严重的损失和麻烦。

（2）迅猛性。任何危机都是迅猛的，迅速蔓延并具有严重的影响。

（3）严重性。危机不仅危害组织的生存也危害社会。它们会破坏组织形象以及影响生产，造成形象危机和企业巨大的经济损失。

（4）敏感性。人们往往对危机很敏感，因此，危机很容易成为新闻媒体的焦点和公众关注的热点，它会引发负面的社会舆论，使危机更加难以解决。

二、公共关系危机的概念和分类

（一）公共关系危机的概念

公共关系危机是指社会公众或组织之间明显不利的意见之间的严重冲突。公共关系危机虽然不同于组织的严重事故危机，但它们之间有着密切的联系。公共关系危机虽然不是突发性恶性事件，但其造成的损失难以计量和弥补，无形损失会造成有形损失，甚至危及组织的生存和发展。

公共关系危机的原因是：

（1）未能解决突发性恶性危机的组织有负面舆论不利于本组织。

（2）忽视公共关系的作用，就会导致组织与公众之间日益严重的冲突。

（3）公众对不了解真相，并存在误解，就会导致不良舆论和行为。

（4）沟通不良造成组织信息错误未能顺畅传达或与事实不符的信息等造成沟通危机。

（5）社会舆论领袖导致的信任危机。

（二）公共关系危机的分类

按性质公共关系危机可分为以下几类。

1. 自然灾害引起的公共关系危机

公共关系危机是指由自然灾害或不可抗拒的社会灾害如山洪灾害危机、发生雷击、地震造成的组织危机，等等。灾难危机发生突然，独立于人的意志。他们通常会破坏生产和组织的运作，并造成巨大损害的组织的公共关系和形象，从而导致公共关系危机。

公关人员的重要职责是号召员工团结起来克服困难，鼓励他们为维护组织形象而奋斗。

2. 声誉危机

声誉危机是指严重损害企业信誉和形象的危机。这种危机通常是由于企业未能履行合同或产品或服务的劣势而造成的，从而损害了消费者的利益。

声誉危机在公共关系中表现为损害一个组织存在的公众信任和支持。

3. 管理危机

这种危机通常是由管理失误或组织管理不善引起的。许多企业之所以在财务中遭受很大的损失，是由于其管理和决策中长期存在的缺陷。这个问题必须马上解决，否则企业的生产经营就会恶化，甚至破产。

4. 信用危机

信用危机意味着企业失去了金融组织的信任，无法获得必要的周转资金，企业无法顺利运转，最终陷入危机。所谓"企业间债务链"是一种信用危机，是继管理危机和声誉危机之后的第二次危机。

5. 质量危机

质量危机是指组织在工作人员、设备和管理上的劣势，没有竞争力，许多质量危机的企业不能引进创新技术或开发新产品，因而在竞争中处于被动地位，或面临被兼并或破产。

6. 形象危机

形象危机是指因组织丑闻而引发的危机，如被指控受贿、偷税漏税等违法行为，形象危机是一种自然危机，因此组织应立即采取措施予以解决。

第二节 公共关系危机的预防

据调查，现代企业不可避免地要经历各种危机。不管一个组织采取什么措施，一旦危机发生，它就会蒙受很大的损失。因此，应该找出迹象，进行科学的分析和防范危机，即管理公共关系危机。

公共关系危机管理也被称为公共关系危机处理和危机公关，这意味着一个组织利用各种资源，采取各种切实可行的措施，防止、限制和消除危机或负面的公共关系危机管理的影响利用的知识，公共关系和管理技能根据不同学科的原理和方法科学解决潜在的或现有的一个组织的危机。

一、分析公共关系危机的原因

公关危机的原因可以分为两大类原因，即组织的外部原因和内部原因。

（一）组织内部原因

（1）决策失误。这意味着一个组织不能根据市场的现状和发展趋势制定正确的管理和公关策略。决策失误是管理危机的一个重要原因。

（2）管理不善。这意味着在产品和服务质量上存在着由基础工作管理不善，不科学的管理方法和手段以及不完整的法规等的造成的严重问题

（3）组织质量低下。它是除灾难危机之外其他所有危机的一个重要因素。它首先指的是组织领导和员工的低劣素质。人力资源对组织起决定性作用。

（4）在公共关系战略中的失误。这意味着一个组织不能根据客观事实根据公共关系政策制定公关战略，不能将真实的信息传递给公众，从而造成对组织的形象和声誉的损害。

（二）组织的外部原因

（1）不可抗拒的力量。也就是超出组织控制的外部力量或突发自然灾害超，这将影响到企业正常的生产经营，如地震或政变。

（2）政策或制度因素。一个国家的政策和政府制度对组织有很大的影响。

例如，193.11由于北京市政府出台禁止燃放烟花的法令，1994年在北京烟花经营企业损失惨重。

（3）社会因素。社会因素是指社会不正之风和不良倾向造成的阻碍，影响生产经营，扰乱正常的社会经济秩序。

二、公共关系危机的过程

危机是一种不稳定和异常情况，其过程可分为四期。

（1）潜伏期。它也被称为"危机前"时期，在此期间，导致危机的一些因素已经形成。如果这些因素没有被发现或消除，它们将导致危机。因此，组织的所有主管和公关从业者都应谨慎地找出危机信号，努力消除不利因素，防止危机发生在潜伏期。

（2）爆发期。潜伏期后，事故将是导火索并制造显而易见的危机，危机进入爆发阶段。如果人们能预见并做好准备，他们就能预见和控制危机的速度、幅度、方向和持续时间，将危及的伤害减少到最小。

（3）处理时期。这是工作人员集中注意危机解决危机事件的时期，工作人员应做出正确的决定，在紧急情况下采取果断行动应对危机。

（4）恢复期。危机过后，组织形象遭到严重破坏。该组织处于被动状态，接受政府有关部门的调查和审查，并接受媒体的采访和报道。组织要进行自我分析和自我批评，采取措施清理混乱局面，重建组织形象。

三、公共关系危机的防范

预防危机有两个环节：一是危机的预测，即危机的发现，另一是事前处理危机的对策。

（一）危机预警

企业更多的是在市场经济中遭遇危机。究其原因，一是企业面临的竞争更加激烈，充满了风险。第二，在宏观经济调控，政府的规章管理与监督下，企业有更多的管理自主权。第三，消费者和新闻媒体对企业存在的问题比较敏感，企业的任何危机事件都不会成为公众的秘密。

企业的环境虽然复杂，但要防范危机，利用危机，做好准备，可以从以下几个方面着手：

1. 做好心理应变准备。

无论是领导还是公关人员，都要意识到危机，做好心理应变准备。只有这样，组织才能进行危机预警，预见组织活动中可能出现的危机，并采取相应的对策。

2. 建立危机预警系统。

公关人员应协调相关部门建立危机预警系统，从以下几个方面捕捉危机征兆。

（1）加强对公共关系和企业经营信息的收集和分析，及时掌握公众对组织的反馈。

（2）密切关注我国的经济政策和经济、政治、教育体制改革，以便更好地运作与社会背景相协调。

（3）经常与VIP客户沟通，使他们成为本组织的坚定支持者。

（4）经常分析竞争对手的业务政策和市场需求趋势。

（5）定期进行自我诊断，分析经营情况和公共关系情况，对组织形象进行客观评价，找出不足，并采取必要的措施。

（6）开展各种调查、研究和预测潜在的危机事故，并试图在潜伏期消除危机因素。

3. 设置预警线。

公关从业人员或经理在每个子公司可以通知有关部门和人员通过预警线发现不寻常的东西，及时询问他们是否有遇到过这样的问题以及他们的经验，以采取适当的措施,避免类似的问题。

（二）危机应对计划

一旦事故发生，采取措施解决问题是至关重要的。危机应对计划必须在危机爆发前为紧急情况做好准备。

所谓的危机应对计划是一项提供一套解决紧急情况所需的人力资源、材料、方法和措施的应急计划。危机应对计划曾被比作"手电筒"，人们可以用它来有序应对危机。

一般来说，全面的危机应对计划包括以下内容：

1．建立危机应对小组。

制订危机应对计划的首要任务是建立一个危机应对小组，其中核心是组织领导，技术专家、公关专家、法律顾问等以及其他根据各种危机而设置的相关人员。一旦危机发生，团队成员将承担应对危机的责任，而他们应该在平时就做好准备应对危机。

2.研究危机应对计划

危机应对小组负责研究危机反应计划。这个计划应该包括任何可能的危机和对策，这些可以作为一个危机应对计划手册汇编。手册是处理各种危机的指南。尽管从企业到企业都有所不同，但所有的手册都应该有足够的细节来处理危机。

一般来说，在危机计划中应考虑以下的准备工作：

（1）制作危机应对手册。危机应对措施可以被编制成容易理解的小册子，分发给员工，以建立员工的危机感，让他们了解危机的可能性和采取好应对措施。

（2）研究危机应对的新闻方案。在危机发生后，如何应对新闻媒体对于一个组织来说显得非常重要，因为它事关公众的关注和意见。新闻媒体的报道将对组织形象产生巨大的影响。一个特别的主管比与新闻媒体接触更可取。

（3）事先确认发言者。应确认一名发言者代表本组织向公众介绍危机进程和解决危机所做的努力。发言者应及时公开危机事实，使公众了解事实，对危机进行理性分析。

（4）确认并联系救援组织。公关人员应该确认可能的救援组织，比如应急中心、警察局、消防处、邻近社区等，与他们建立友好的关系，并告知他们一旦危机发生，组织就会提出要求。

3.危机模拟演习

危机应对小组可以在特定的危机中进行实践和演练，以测试团队成员的反应能力决策能力、危机应对知识和心理耐力。

危机应对计划和演习只是应对危机的工具，有关部门和工作人员应相互配合，灵活运用应对危机的方案。

第三节　处理公共关系危机

一、公关危机管理的原则

公关危机的管理意味着公关人员采取措施处理突发事件所造成的公共关系危机的过程，以维护组织的良好形象。对一个组织来说在市场经济和信息时代中面临各种挑战。管理危机和处理突发事件是公共关系中的一个重要项目。在处理危机时，人们应遵循以下原则：

1. 快速反应

任何危机突然发生，就会迅速蔓延到媒体和社会公众的关注。陷入危机的组织要快速做出反应，并采取对策来应对危机，同时要公开真相，争取公众同情并减少危机带来的损失。

2. 诚实坦率

危机中的组织必须诚实坦率地揭露危机的真相，以争取公众和新闻媒体的信任。隐藏的事实越多，公众和新闻媒体就会越怀疑。

3. 人道主义

在大多数情况下，任何危机都会造成巨大的生命和财产损失，这将引起公众的高度关注。因此，在危机管理中应坚持人道主义原则。

4. 维护声誉

公共关系在危机中的作用是维护组织声誉，这是危机管理的目标。声誉是一个组织的生命，它在危机中一定会受到损害，公关人员应努力减少危机管理中声誉的损害，争取公众的理解和信任。遵循上述三项原则的宗旨是维护组织声誉。

二、公共关系危机管理程序

一旦发生危机，组织应迅速采取行动将损害减少到最低限度。科学程序是有效管理危机的关键。

（一）建立专门从事危机管理的组织

所有的社会组织都应该联合起来建立一个决策中心，以便管理危机和沟通，决策中心的领导人应该是一个组织的领导者。公关机构在其中负责协助领导者进行调查分析、与他人沟通、披露信息、制定策略等。

任何组织都会突然陷入危机，他们可以要求公共关系专家建立智囊团，帮助他们做出决策并管理危机。

（二）迅速掌握危机整体情况

相关人员应现场勘查，查明危机事件的真实情况：

（1）危机类型、时间、地点和来源。

（2）危机的影响范围、伤亡和财产损失、对组织和社会的负面影响。采取措施的效果和可能的社会影响。

（3）应对危机的危机趋势和机会。

（4）危机中的公众是谁？他们与组织如何沟通，以及组织该如何回应他们呢。

（三）迅速隔离危机

工作人员应采取以下措施来隔离调查中的危机。

（1）人员隔离。即危机发生后，将人员分成两个小组，一个负责危机管理，另一个负责日常工作。人们不应忽视其中任何一个。

（2）危机隔离。这意味着要抑制危机范围，防止危机蔓延，将危机地区从正常工作区隔离开来。危机预警期应采取行动，化解危机，减少危机。

（四）为应对危机采取的对策

建立危机管理中心，负责危机数据分析，制定对策计划。计划通常包括以下内容：

（1）深入分析危机的背景、来源、趋势，并说明其后果和对公众的影响。

（2）设定公关目标以应对危机。

（3）制定危机处理的基本对策，确定危机沟通的信息、原则和渠道，研究危机处置的后续处理，制定危机管理的时间表。

根据以往的经验和一些专家的看法，危机发生时，有针对性地针对不同的公众采取不同的对策。

1. 对内部的对策

（1）发布危机通知，呼吁全体工作人员共同努力，渡过危机，采取措施控制危机。

（2）事故原因如果是产品质量低劣，通知销售部门停止销售此类产品。召回不合格产品，送质量控制小组对不合格产品进行检测，找出原因，采取措施提高产品质量。

2. 对受害人对策

无论事故发生的受害者是组织内部还是外部，其家属或亲属都应尽早得到通知。组织应尽一切可能抢救受害者，解决由此产生的问题。

（1）如何对受害者及其家属进行抚慰是危机管理中一项敏感而重要的工作。工作人员要注意倾听对方的抱怨和不满，与他们沟通，根据实际情况承担责任，尽力满足他们的合理要求，提供必要的服务。在发生重大人员伤亡事故时，工作人员要注意家属的通知方式。

（2）重要的是告诉受害者和家人真相，并向他们表示同情和慰问。工作人员应与受害人和家属讨论赔偿损失。

3. 媒体应对策略

新闻媒体通常会关注危机事件和发展情况。危机事件后如何与新闻媒体联系，是公关工作者的重要任务之一。

（1）向媒体披露事故真相，明确组织的态度和应对措施。高级人员最好代表机构向新闻媒体介绍事故发生的过程和原因，以及采取的措施。

（2）应该有足够的沟通渠道来引领并统一陈述本组织相关的事故公告。

（3）如果有不清楚之处，应向记者解释，取得他们的理解。请不要说"无可奉告"拒绝回应。

（4）有必要设立一个临时接待中心来接待记者，并披露事故的发展情况及事后处理的措施。

（5）如果有信息披露错误必须及时纠正。公关从业人员应跟踪事故的覆盖范围，如有错误，应该改正并提供真实数据。

4. 对上级的对策

（1）真实地向上级汇报危机事件。

（2）定期汇报局势的进展情况并征求指导意见、支持和帮助。

（3）危机后向领导提交总体的危机管理报告，包括管理过程、解决方法和未来防范措施。

5. 对商业伙伴的对策

（1）尽可能快地传递危机信息。

（2）对所采取的措施进行书面通知。

（3）必要的时候派出代表面对面地解释情况。

（4）定期向合作伙伴展示处理过程的信息。

（5）解释合作的书面形式的危机管理程序。

6. 对消费者的策略

（1）通过零售商和其他渠道向消费者提供书面材料，解释事故的大致情况。

（2）通过新闻媒体解释危机的真相、处理过程和未来的预防措施。

（3）热情迎接并接待来访的代表。

（4）弥补消费者的损失。

（五）结论、检查和公布信息

这是最后时期危机管理的不可缺少的工作。危机管理工作小组应检查和评估整个危机管理，向董事会汇报结果，并让股东和公众知道。

三、危机管理应注意的战略问题

危机中有许多的不可控因素。因此,公关从业者应该冷静、果断、灵活应对危机管理。这里有一些危机管理策略的建议。

1. 在舆论中占主导地位

在危机发生后，要想在公众舆论中占据主导地位，组织应该尽早与公众沟通，以防因为媒体的不实报道而引发的猜测和而影响公众的判断。在事故真相被认定之前，组织应当是公布信息的唯一权威来源。组织应该介绍事故的一些背景资料，初步情况并采取措施，以取得公众舆论的支持,在公众舆论中占主导地位。

2. 与公众、社会和权威机构合作解决危机

与公众合作是一种有效的策略。社会和权威机构可以提高组织在公众中的信

誉，这是组织能在正常情况下与他们保持密切关系的战略的基础。因为如果他们代表组织行事，很容易得到公众的信任和同情。

3. 及时披露危机处理实际有效的行动

除了事故之外，公关人员应该关注组织采取的实际和有效的行动。特别是在造成人员伤亡和伤亡的事故中，他们应当突出宣传为拯救受害者所做的努力和采取的行动。

4. 组织领导者亲自面对事故

组织领导者应该亲自面对事故，将树立勇于承担责任、有能力的良好形象。果断、诚实地管理危机，组织领导者到事故现场管理危机。

5. 指定一名新闻发言人，并在危急时刻发言。

危机发生初期，由于形势不明，信息来源混乱，公众和新闻媒体容易对形势进行主观臆测，形成负面意见。组织应指定一名代表作为新闻发言人介绍危机的现实情况和采取的措施，团队成员的危机管理应该足够冷静，分析形势，做出正确的决定，用一个声音说话。

第八章
政府公共关系

越来越多的企业认识到公共关系在提高知名度、形象塑造与盈利方面的重要作用。政府作为国家上层建筑的核心应该要重视公共关系，这将有利于社会稳定，是对外开放和发展市场经济的必要条件。

第一节 政府公共关系的内涵和特征

一、政府公共关系的内涵

所谓政府公共关系，是指国家行政机关运用多种传播手段和沟通手段，与公众建立相互理解、信任、合作、持久的关系，以树立良好的政府形象的行政职能。定义至少有以下三个含义：

（1）政府公共关系是政府与公众之间的关系。政府是公共关系的主体，是公共关系活动的组织者和发起人，其作用取决于政府的影响。公众是公共关系和活动的对象。公众的作用是对政府形象和政府公共关系的效果进行评价。

（2）政府公共关系的目标是树立良好的形象，虽然政府公共关系的内容繁多，各种活动的直接目标不同，但最终的目标是树立良好的政府形象。

（3）传播是政府公共关系的方式和手段。不同的传播和沟通方法是政府与公众之间的联系，所以无论社会传播媒介，传播先进的渠道畅通将直接影响政府公共关系活动的影响。

二、政府公共关系的特征

政府公共关系具有一般公共关系的性质。它具有不同于其他类型公共关系的特点。

（一）公共关系目的特殊

不像其他社会组织那样营利，尤其是企业，政府公共关系的直接目的和根本目的是通过树立良好形象来提高行政效果。政府为公众服务，其权威必须建立在公众信任和支持的基础上，否则政府与公众之间的关系就会被破坏，从而降低政策效果。

（二）公共关系主体特殊

政府公共关系的主体是国家行政机关，其性质完全不同于各种经济、文化和政治组织。第一，政府有很大的权力。它可以制定政策，颁布法令，控制国家武装部队、警察、监狱和其他强武装机关。第二，政府在社会上是独一无二的。它超越任何社会组织，不受任何竞争规则的限制。最后，政府是一个庞大的体制和复杂的结构。它有一个从中央到地方的完整系统。从居民的生活必需品到经济发展，从国防外交到环境生态，政府都有着广泛的行政管辖权。

（三）公共关系对象特殊

政府公共关系的客体是广泛而无法比拟的。它的基本对象是公民，实际是整个社会公众。此外，国际公众也是其对象。另外，政府的公共利益是由不同利益集团组成的，政府在制定政策或颁布法令时，必须考虑到他们的不同意见。同时，不同的群体或组织在政府中有自己的公众，政府的公共性在结构上相当复杂。

（四）公共关系手段特殊

传播是公共关系活动的手段，与其他组织公共关系相比，政府公共关系传播在背景上具有以下无可比拟的优势：

1. 政府拥有巨大的信息资源

政府机关是汇集各种数据的地方。如果把社会比作机器，政府就是机器的操作者，有利于及时准确地掌握机器上不同部件的操作信息。此外，政府还担任社会协调员。一方面，它可以通过不同层次的组织收集各种数据，另一方面，不同的组织积极向政府提供数据，因此，政府拥有巨大的信息资源。

2. 政府直接或间接控制公共媒体

一方面，政府这一独特的社会组织具有巨大的大众传播媒介数量。以我国为例，我国政府对报纸、广播电台和电视台进行管理，利用其为政府开展公共关系活动。另一方面，政府可以间接支配大众媒体。以美国为例，政府可以通过对新闻调查的法律、政策、法规等进行间接管制，使政府能够掌握话语权，确保公共关系计划得到严格实施，公共关系目标得以顺利实现。

3.政府可以在内部严格、迅速的传播

政府规模庞大，结构复杂，组织严密。任何形式的组织都可以在组织内准确、快速地传递，不管是垂直还是横向。

4.政府公共关系可以把各种传播渠道、手段和载体综合与交叉运用

大多数政府政策最初是作为政府机构内的文件实施的，然后由公共媒体传播。有时，这些政策是以其他方式实施的。

5.政府信息传播中的有效性

在信息传播的四个环节，即从信息源的传播者、媒介、内容，还有公众。显然，政府在信息来源丰富、媒体数量大、传播手段多样等方面具有绝对优势，保证了政府信息传播的效果。

第二节　政府公共关系的意义和作用

一、政府公共关系的意义

政府公共关系是协调政府与公众关系的一系列行政行为，旨在发挥政府的作用。在管理中的意义可以概括为：

（一）有利于形象塑造

政府公共关系的首要任务是树立良好的形象，在公众中，政府将得到公众的信任和支持，政府的活动将得到公众的理解和合作。政府通过社会传播、网络化、舆论导向等手段，努力缩小理想形象与现实形象之间的差距。

（二）有利于决策制定

政府必须通过公共关系活动来了解人们的感受和需求，如制定政策时的民意调查，特别是一些重要的方针、政策和改革措施即将实施时。

（三）有利于政令实施

政府必须依靠公众的理解、信任和支持来有效地执行其政策，因此必须做大量的宣传工作，让公众接受和接受新的法令或政策。否则，一个新的法令或政策将很难被公众接受，这将成为政府公共关系的障碍。

（四）有利于内部关系的协调

政府公共关系的实质是通过传播来协调与公众的关系，因为行政效率的提高与外部的社会环境和内部的组织环境有着密切的关系。没有良好的内部组织环境，各部门、上下级和公务员之间就会产生摩擦，造成不必要的损失、互不信任和不负责任。因此，通过协调内部关系来沟通信息，是提高行政效率的重要环节，也是公共关系活动的目的。一个组织只有与全体员工保持和谐的内部关系，并与外界密切接触，才能有广泛的合作和良好的行政环境。

二、政府公共关系的功能

政府公共关系的目的在于塑造良好的政府形象，政府的一切实际活动和工作都是在政府职能范围内进行的。

（一）信息交换

信息，一种社会普遍联系的形式。在知识经济时代，生活的各个领域都得到了广泛的渗透，成为每个组织行动和发展的前提。政府能否获得信息，信息的数量和质量将成为政府制定政策的关键因素。

政府公共关系在信息交流中的作用表现在以下几个方面：

1. 组织内部的信息交流

在政府公共关系的相关人群里，组织是由领导和公务员组成的。领导者形象会影响整个政府的外在形象，影响着内部的凝聚力和团结。因此，领导者的组织能力、决策能力、协调与管理是组织信息交流的内容。

公务员是政府各部门的工作人员，他们之间的关系，以及和公众的关系会影响内外环境。

2. 政策信息交换

政府及时、全面、准确地理解政府的政策是否得到公众的理解非常重要的，对于一个国家或地区的政府管理，往往取决于他们所制定的政策。因此，政府必须交流政策是否正确的信息，政策制定水平是如何实施的，了解政策的公众评价。

3. 组织安装中的信息交换与工作效率

在与政府的接触中，公众自觉或不自觉地对政府的组织机构和工作效率有不同的看法。一些人认为，机构设置是合理的，能够有效地减少程序和机制灵活的工作；有人认为组织是人浮于事，他们程序复杂，工作效率低。不管公众的意见是什么，政府应该收集、整理和分析相关的信息。

（二）咨询和建议

这意味着政府公共关系从业人员向他们的领导人提供可靠的社会公共情况信息和值得信赖的意见。他们的磋商和建议包括以下几个方面：

1. 关于公众概况的咨询和建议

这是政府公共关系的日常工作，咨询能提供政府与公众之间的一般情况，如公务员的归属感、公众对政府形象的评估和媒体对政府的意见等。

2. 关于公众具体情况的咨询和建议

这意味着政府公共关系人员就政府将举办的一些特殊活动提供相关的情况说明和建议。

3. 公众心理变化与趋势的咨询与建议

它是指政府根据长期的观察和积累，结合中长期规划和提交给管理者的报告，就公众心理变化和趋势分析提出自己的看法。

（三）沟通和协调

政府与公众沟通是指政府作为公共关系主体，通过各种方式、多种方式与公众交流思想和信息，努力增进政府和公众之间的相互了解和信任，为政府工作创造更有利的环境和条件。政府与公众沟通的意义在于：

1. 民主政治要求

公众参与国家和社会事务的管理，是现代民主政治的本质。公众必须了解政治，以便参与和讨论政治事务，监督政府工作，这就要求政府及时、全面地向公众传递有关信息。只有这样，公众才能更多地了解政治事务。并且政府也能更多地了解公众的意见、建议、要求和声音，这些都可以被采纳，成为政策和决定的基础。

2. 提高政府透明度的要求

政府必须与公众紧密联系，以获得信任和支持。它是政府开展政治活动、提高工作透明度、疏通沟通渠道的有效途径。

3. 加强政府职能的要求

保证信息畅通、及时、准确，是政府提高工作效率的重要保证。

如果政府无法及时将决定、计划和安排及时传递给公众，将影响其执行。如果政府不能接受公众的反馈，他们的后续工作将受到影响。因此，政府必须利用现代传播手段和媒介与公众保持密切联系。

协调是指政府作为公共关系主体，通过协商、调整和沟通，调整和理顺政府与公众之间的关系，为政府开展一切工作创造适当的环境和条件。在与社会管理的关系中，整个社会是一个庞大的组织体系，存在着一套严肃的工作网和有序的程序。各行各业、团体、社会阶层和阶级都围绕着政府管理体制的核心工作，各子系统之间的关系错综复杂，与政府有利害关系。政府的协调职能在处理与他们的关系中显然是重要的。政府应协调下列各方之间的关系：（1）协调政府领导与公务员之间的关系；（2）协调政府各部门之间的关系；（3）协调政府与公众的关系。

（四）树立良好的形象

政府形象包括三个方面：一是政府价值。它是指政府在政府的目标、发展目标和行动中渗透的行为规范和动力。二是政府行为。它包括管理水平、服务水平、工作效率、敬业精神和执行公务的诚实等。三是社会发展目标。只有当政府设定一个有利的和现实的社会发展目标和传播，使其渗透到大众，才能得到社会公众的认同、支持和良好的评价。

公共关系是塑造形象的艺术，政府公共关系也是一种艺术。政府形象对其生存和发展具有重要意义。良好的形象是政府获得公众信任和支持的先决条件。

第三节　政府公共关系的原则

政府公共关系的原则意味着政府公共关系活动中遵循的准则和要求。

一、现实的原则

现实主义原则是指政府通过政府间的双向信息交流，在公共关系活动中传递信息，建立相互信任的关系，在政府内外建立良好的公众形象。

二、公开的原则

公众呼吁"公开"和"透明"的政府工作。政治权利应该是公共平等的民主社会。公众有权了解和参与政治事务，这是民主政治的基础。此外，政府工作的公开工作对预防和打击国家的腐败现象，具有重要的现实意义。

政府的工作应该是公开的，但这并不意味着公开得没有原则。公共关系人员应本着原则性和政策灵活性处理好公开与保密之间的关系。首先，要区分不同的公众，以不同的方式进行沟通，对不同的内容进行不同程度的公开。第二，区分不同的时间、条件和场合。最后，要区分法律和制度的不同界限。

三、利益原则

利益是建立和维持良好公共关系的基础，利益关系是公共关系的本质。这里的利益是指政府和公众之间的利益。如何处理好政府与公众在政府公共关系中的关系？

政府公共关系中的公众可以分为国内公众和国外公众，他们与政府有着不同的利益关系，这意味着政府公共关系活动应遵循不同的原则。

此外，国内公众也可以分为三类，即广大人民群众、一些群众团体和少数群众团体。

对于第一类公众，政府公共关系中任何时候都应遵循公共利益至上原则和公共利益原则。政府在制定政策、法律和实施任何项目之前，应该考虑公众对他们的评价，以及他们是否符合公众的利益。只有政府把公众放在心中，切实为人民解决问题，全心全意为人民服务，才能在公共关系活动中得到公众的理解和支持。

对于第二和第三类公众，如果广大人民群众的利益与广大人民群众的利益相矛盾，政府将毫不犹豫地把广大人民群众的利益放在第一位。如果与政府的利益不相抵触，政府将考虑他们所有的利益。

对于国外公众，我们政府采取互利的原则进行中国和外国的外交活动，而不是考虑很多国家采用的国家利益至上的原则，我们国家的原则也被证明是非常成功的。

总而言之，政府在处理与公众的利益关系时，不应因其复杂性而一概而论。

四、整体原则

这意味着政府公共关系组织或实践者应该从整体上对政府公共关系进行研究和评价，即从整体出发，努力为政府的整体效果进行合作。

整体原则涉及面广，但主要涉及以下几个方面：

首先，政府应该从整体的角度来处理外部公共关系。在任何具体的公共关系活动中，政府都要面对公众，工作人员不应仅仅局限于事实本身。他们应该把一些利益和整体利益、局部利益和地方利益结合起来。

其次，政府应该从整体的角度来处理内部公共关系。虽然政府的机关各不相同，有不同的职能和工作范围，但他们都是为了公众的最高利益工作。因此，各政府机关和公务员要相互配合，尽力去有效发挥整个政府系统的功能。

这里有一些关于在政府公共关系中执行整体原则的建议：

（1）要意识到心中的整体形象，加强整体意识并充分发挥成员的能力。

（2）制定统一的公共关系政策，统一所有行动和步调，密切合作。

（3）正确处理个人与组织、下级和上级、部分和整体之间的关系，并强调整体情况和整个目标。

第四节 政府公共关系的模式

由于不同的对象和特定的目标，政府要以不同的模式来实行公共关系活动，主要如下：

一、宣传模式的公共关系

宣传模式是指政府利用公共媒体或其他传播渠道，将其工作或活动的信息主动传递给国内外公众，政府在其服务宗旨、服务项目、工作目标及各项政策等方面，及时公开并能宣传政府。目前，政府主要通过以下渠道进行自我宣传：

（一）举行新闻发布会

它也被称为新闻会议，一个组织将邀请一些记者参加，会议上指定一个发言人宣布一些重要的信息，并接受记者的采访。以下是新闻发布会的一些特点：（1）正式、隆重、可信；（2）全面客观地发布信息对组织是有好处的；（3）新闻发布会的传播效果与它的支持者和播音员的水平有关。

目前，新闻发布会已成为许多国家政府发布信息的一种普遍形式。自从党的十三大以来，我们的中央政府举行新闻发布会已经成为一种体系。人们发现，这对于开放政府工作，通知公众大事件，提升政府和公众之间的关系，塑造政府良好形象是有益的。

（二）利用新闻媒体进行大众传播

在大众传播方面，广播、电视、报纸、网络等媒体是传播信息的最有效手段。

此外，政府有自己的优势使用新闻媒体，因为政府是信息来源的聚集地，这意味着新闻媒体会主动联系政府以获得信息。更重要的是，政府是权威的，具有新闻媒体的话语权，这使得新闻媒体很容易根据政府的意图进行传播。

（三）利用政府公共关系广告

政府公共关系广告是指政府机关购买印刷媒体的空间或电子媒体的时间，以语言或其他方式进行宣传，不受编辑的干扰。与其他广告相比，政府公共关系广告有两个独特的特点：（1）不同的目标：消费者是一般广告的目标，而政府公共关系广告的目标则是各个领域的国内外公众，前者的范围更广。（2）不同目的：一般广告的目的是促进某些产品或服务的销售，而政府的目标是在政府的政策、法律、法令和一些社会议题上与公众沟通，包括经济、教育或公共福利等方面的话题，以交流感情，加深了解，赢得公众的赞扬；前者以利益为导向，而后者更多地以公益为导向。

（四）举办博览会

这意味着政府要综合运用词汇、图片、实物、插图、幻灯、视频、音响、现场演示等，宣传政府的政策、法律和法令。这种形式是直接的、视听的、有趣的和实用的，很容易吸引公众，为政府提供机会以了解公众并与他们交换意见。

二、咨询模式的公共关系

这类公共关系是指政府试图通过征求内部和外部公众的意见来收集社会信息。

这类公共关系的职能是"政府智囊团"，目的是为政府管理提供科学依据、设计合理或优化的理论、政策和方法，并预测某些情况。

它的工作方法如下：

（一）民意测验

民意测验是指通过现代科学方法和数学计算方法，及时、准确地收集、整理、汇总、报告公众意见，确定社会舆论的变化。它的作用是反映不同社会阶层对某个人、某一政策或任何社会问题的不同意见、态度、看法和估计，给各级政府做出决策和改善政府提供依据。

（二）信访

信访是指社会公众访问政府部门，或给他们写信，包括意见、建议或提出要求、请愿和投诉。请愿书方便政府收集信息、接受公众反馈和监督。

（三）访谈

访谈作为政府公共关系中常用的一种方法，是通过与被采访者交谈来收集数据。

访谈通常是面对面进行的，调查人员向受访者提出问题，而调查员对受访者的回答、反应以及留下的印象进行记录。访谈既可以以集体方式来进行，即研讨会，也可以以个人方式来进行，有利于保密。

三、沟通模式的公共关系

这种公共关系的模式是指政府通过和公众联系来进行公共关系。政府在正式场合看上去很严肃，可以直接与公众接触传递信息和收集数据，或者在非正式场合，比如茶话会，鸡尾酒会等，他们看上去很和蔼可亲，比较容易接触公众并与其交流，塑造以人为本，心怀人民的形象。

四、防御模式的公共关系

它也被称为危机管理，是指政府通过对即将到来的危机的分析，得出相关的对策，在这种情况下，政府可以很好的解决这场危机，一旦危机发生能够恢复其良好形象和信誉。这种公共关系模式作为警示和防范，消除了萌芽中的消极趋势，将危机的不良影响降到最低。

五、矫正模式的公共关系

它也被称为修正式公共关系或危机管理的救济方式，是指政府采取正确的措施来处理或纠正危机给政府公共关系或利益带来的负面影响。

在这个过程中有三个步骤：

（一）亲自管理，了解情况

这是整顿公共关系的第一步，也是国内外政府成功处理问题的共识。

（二）分析形势，寻找对策

第二步是分析形势，找出问题的原因，并与相关部门和工作人员制定补救措施。

（三）采取措施化解危机

这是程序中一个非常重要的阶段，采取行动将应对措施付诸实施，化解危机。没有这一步，前面的步骤就不会成功。

除了上述五种模式，政府公共关系还有许多其他模式。政府公共关系实践者最重要的是要培养强烈的公共关系意识，并掌握这些方法和技术。

参考书目

1. Dennis l. Wilcox , Glen T. Cameron . Public relations -- strategies and tactics ninth edition Printed in the United States of America. 2007,5

2. James E. Gruning. Excellence in Public Relations and Communication Management. Lawrence Erlbaum Associates, Publishers Hillsdale, New Jersey Hove and London. 1992

3. Richard Campbell . Christopher R. Martin . Bettina Fabos. An Introduction to Mass Communication seventh edition. Bedford/ST. Martin's Boston. New York

4. 于朝晖，邵喜武. 公共关系学. 北京：北京大学出版社，2008.03

5．蔡炜主编. 公共关系学. 上海：华东理工大学出版社，2014．01
《公共关系学》编写组编. 公共关系学. 珠海：珠海出版社，2011

6. 林祖华主编. 公共关系学. 北京：中国时代经济出版社，2005.01

7. 于中涛，景庆虹主编. 公共关系学. 北京：中国农业大学出版社，2004.02

8. 龙志鹤，张岩松编著. 现代公共关系学. 北京：经济管理出版社，2006.06

9. 李树青等著.《大学生公共关系礼仪》. 北京：中国物价出版社，2001

10. 夏赞君，谢伯端主编. 公共关系学. 长沙：国防科技大学出版社，2004,02

11. 黄正泉主编. 公共关系学. 北京：中国农业出版社，2004.08

12. 金实青，来惠民编著. 公共关系学. 北京：北京工业出版社，2004.08

13. 刘用卿，段开军主编. 公共关系学. 重庆：重庆大学出版社，2003.01

14. 段淳林编著. 公共关系学. 广州：华南理工大学出版社，2001.10

15. 吴勤堂著. 公共关系学. 武汉：武汉大学出版社，2004.02

16. 袁凯锋，刘敏编著. 公共关系学. 沈阳：东北大学出版社，2004,8

17. 居延安等编著. 公共关系学. 上海：复旦大学出版社，1989.10

18. 王新华等编著. 公共关系学. 北京：机械工业出版社，1996,10

19. 周德绪主编. 公共关系学. 广州：科学普及出版社广州分社，1989.05

20. 许春珍主编. 公共关系学. 海口：海南出版公司，2002,7

21. 张延军编著. 公共关系学. 北京：学术书刊出版社，1989,06

22. 黄荣生主编. 公共关系学. 大连：东北财经出版社，2005.08

23. 吴翠珍等编著. 公共关系学. 西安：西北大学出版社，2001.08

24. 华烨主编. 公共关系学. 贵阳：贵州教育出版社，2003,2

25. 卢忠萍，严由铭，曾冰等主编. 公共关系学. 南昌：江西高校出版社，2007,3

26. 张笃行主编. 公共关系学. 成都：四川大学出版社，2002,8

27. 谢俊贵主编. 公共关系学. 北京：工商出版社，2002.09

28. 乜瑛主编. 公共关系学. 杭州：浙江大学出版社，2010.09

29. 刘晓昆，梁诗智主编. 公共关系学. 贵阳：贵州人民出版社，2002.03

30. 徐维琳，刘兴武主编. 公共关系学. 南京：江苏科技出版社，2005.09

31. 沈永祥，洪霄主编. 公共关系学. 北京：化学工业出版社，2003.07

32. 黄忠怀，邓宏武，张垄编著. 公共关系学. 上海：华东理工大学出版社，2010.03

33. 邱锐主编. 公共关系学. 北京：中国经济出版社，2003.01

34. 杨明娜，陈敏，王凤主编. 公共关系学. 成都：电子科技大学出版社，2008.01

35. 汪秀英. 当代公共关系学，北京：首都经济贸易出版社，2008.8

36. 柳宝珠主编. 公共关系学. 上海：立信会计出版社，2008.08

37. 李秀忠，刘桂莉主编. 公共关系学. 武汉：武汉大学出版社，2009.05

38. 刘建伟，于立宏主编. 公共关系学. 徐州：中国矿业大学出版社，2001.08

39. 冉戎主编. 公共关系学. 重庆：重庆大学出版社，2012.08

40. 陈丽清，李志平主编. 公共关系学. 北京：经济科学出版社， 2010.07

41. 袁凯锋，刘敏编著. 公共关系学. 沈阳：东北大学出版社，2009.01

42. 鲍日新主编. 社交礼仪，让你的形象更美好 ——献给大学生朋友. 上海：上海教育出版社，2005.03

43. 李宁等编著. 公共关系学. 北京：北京出版社，2005.06